More Food That Really Schmecks

Edna Staebler

More Food That Really Schmecks

M&S

Copyright © 1979 by Edna Staebler

Cloth edition published 1979, reprinted 1985, 1988
Trade paperback edition published 1998

All rights reserved. The use of any part of this publication reproduced, transmitted in any form or by any means, electronic, mechanical, photocopying, recording, or otherwise, or stored in a retrieval system, without the prior written consent of the publisher – or, in case of photocopying or other reprographic copying, a licence from the Canadian Copyright Licensing Agency – is an infringement of the copyright law.

Canadian Cataloguing in Publication Data

Staebler, Edna, 1906-
More food that really schmecks

Includes index.
ISBN 0-7710-8295-9 (bound)   ISBN 0-7710-8258-4 (pbk.)

1. Cookery, Mennonite.   2. Cookery, Canadian –
Ontario – Waterloo (County).   I. Title.

TX715.S74   641.59'713'44   C79-094644-0

Illustrations by Carol Noel

Printed and bound in Canada

McClelland & Stewart Inc.
The Canadian Publishers
481 University Avenue
Toronto, Ontario
M5G 2E9

1 2 3 4 5   02 01 00 99 98

Contents

Introduction

Right after *Food That Really Schmecks* was published people started asking me when was I going to write another cookbook!

"Never," I told them. "I've put everything I know about cooking into *Schmecks*, I couldn't possibly write any more."

But as I kept finding easier or better ways to make some of the recipes, I felt a niggling compulsion to pass on the improvements. Besides, I had some good recipes that didn't get into *Food That Really Schmecks* because I'd forgotten them or thought they were too fancy for a book on Mennonite country cooking. Also I'd found or invented some new ones that I was really excited about.

During the years since *Food That Really Schmecks* appeared, thousands of people, it seems, told me that they love reading and using the book and hope I will write another one; many have sent me their favourite recipes to put in it.

Meantime also, I've done a lot of good eating with friends and relations who have given me their cherished recipes. "For the next cookbook," they say. I've spent much time enjoying great food and exchanging recipes with my Old Order Mennonite friends on their farms. I've learned a few things from a healthy young vegetarian niece. As well, I've inherited my mother's old cookbooks with the tried and true standbys that brought joy to my childhood and gave Mother the reputation of being a wonderful cook.

And I've made some discoveries: the uncollected recipes in Waterloo County are boundless. Strangers often phoned me to say, "You haven't a recipe for prune moos in your cookbook." Or wunderschnitten, beer cake, yogurt, or whatever; and they'd give me one. Or I'd be told of a different way to make some local specialty.

As a perennial judge of the Kitchener-Waterloo Kinder-kochfest Competition I've acquired prize-winning *German* recipes. Local *Russian* Mennonites have told me how to make some of their unusual dishes. *English* friends have been generous with traditional favourites. At Rundles Restaurant in Stratford I watched the *chef de cuisine* prepare superb French party meals during a Stylish Entertainment course. Harold Horwood, the Newfoundland writer, showed me how to make a *Chinese* supper. And whenever I've travelled I've come home with recipes.

Of course I've kept trying and typing out recipes. For years. The yellow copy pages have been piling up on my desk, on my kitchen counter, on the long windowseat in my living room, and in a carton under my bed. There are so many now that I've got to do something with them. I can't let all those possibilities for good eating go to waste, can I?

I've thrown out or rejected all the recipes that use mixes or prepared foods loaded with additives. I've kept to the fruits, vegetables, and meats that are produced in my county and sold at the Kitchener and Waterloo Farmers' Markets: no mangos, she-crabs, kiwis, or other exotic, hard-to-get and pay-for things that would be a treat when you travel or go to an expensive restaurant.

As before, I've stuck to the good old Mennonite tradition of economy, with no waste, only quick, easy and inventive ways to make things that really taste good, and use ingredients that are usually in one's cupboard, freezer, or fridge. Some are perfect for a loner, others for a family, or for company one can relax with. And some are dishes one can show off with.

I included dozens of recipes to make gorgeous plump muffins in half an hour. I've collected a whole chapter of biscuits and bannocks, found things to do with those backyard plums. Drinks, soups, salads, casseroles, main dishes, and accompaniments are innumerable. Bread, cake, cookie, pie and dessert recipes are infinite and irresistible.

So you see I am hooked: I must write this cookbook because I have all these recipes. For those brides who say *Food That Really Schmecks* is their bible, for all those kind people who asked me to please give them more: here it is!

May you have as much fun experimenting and eating as I have.

CONFESSION

I approach the writing of this book with some trepidation. Though I think I have learned a few things since *Food That Really Schmecks* was published, I am often embarrassed when people ask me questions about food that I can't answer, or when they say, "You are an authority on Mennonite cooking," and I have to tell them I'm not an authority on anything, just an amateur with a preference for schmecksy food that is easy to prepare.

I don't spend my life testing recipes. I cook because I love to eat. When I come across what sounds like a great-tasting dish I can hardly wait to get at it – often with blissful abandon and disastrous results. I take short-cuts; sometimes I change the amounts in a recipe or the method of putting things together.

Though I appreciate so-called gourmet cookery when someone else does it, I haven't the patience to spend hours in the kitchen fiddling with complicated directions. Nor can I be constantly producing great feasts – not when I have to eat alone whatever I make. I splurge only when I have company. And that's when the bannocks burn and the custard curdles.

One Saturday I had a dinner party for a distinguished weekend visitor. When I was serving a second round of drinks I realized that my guests were chatting in a haze as smoke billowed from the oven. The casseroles were boiling over. I had to fuss to control them.

My guests were delighted. They said, "After tonight we won't be afraid to invite you for dinner." I had proved I was not the great cook that *Schmecks* made them think I was.

And I wasn't sorry; I love being invited out for dinner.

I hope this recitation of my limitations hasn't shattered your faith in me as a collector of good-tasting recipes. I've tried most of those I'm giving you here and I think you'll find them pretty good. And some are fantastic.

Good luck and have fun.

WHO IS THIS FOR?

What is schnitz?
What does schmecks mean?
What are drepsly?

People ask me these questions. As I sit at my typewriter putting down recipes, I wonder who is going to be using them.

1. People who must have precise directions and won't make a move unless it's been carefully described? (Heaven help them and me if I blunder. And I might.)
2. Experienced cooks who have tried everything, but are still looking for something new? (Some of these recipes have just been invented.)
3. The experimenters, like me, who seldom follow a recipe exactly, then wonder why it's a flop? (They have fun, occasionally produce something not short of genius – they think.)
4. The inexperienced: brides, grooms, children, students, retired gentlemen who are anxious to learn? (They're my best friends. One young woman told me how thrilled she was when she realized that "eggs, beaten separately," meant the whites were to be beaten separately from the yolks. She had thought it meant one egg beaten, then the other egg beaten.)
5. The sophisticates who eat in flossy restaurants around the world but are not averse to finding something unusual they can try at home without too much effort? (Have they ever tried Easter Cheese, Piroschky, or Raisin Mumbles?)
6. The loners, looking for something easy but nutritious and tasty? (I'm a loner, too. I keep healthy on a minimum of effort with occasional splurges.)

7. The vegetarians, wanting something nourishing and inoffensive? (They can strike out the meat recipes: there are plenty of others for them.)

8. The curious, also like me, who can hardly wait to see what a recipe tastes like? (They're also always trying to lose weight.)

9. Those who like to read a cookbook in bed when they can fantasize freely and happily without yielding to the temptation of actually eating a Wiener Schnitzel or Rum Chocolate Pie? (Sweet dreams. There was a doctor in Toronto who told his patients to read *Food That Really Schmecks* in bed at night, pick out something to try the next day and invite someone in to share it; he said the book was better for them than any medication he could prescribe.)

10. For the strangers who say to me, "The food you describe sounds fabulous but where can we buy it when we come to your area? (Read further, I think you'll find out.)

11. For all those people I meet at the Kitchener and Waterloo Farmers' Markets who ask, "What do you do with all this wonderful food that you get here? How do you cook it?" (I'll tell them, I hope, in about 600 recipes.)

Market Days in Kitchener and Waterloo

Almost every Saturday morning of my life I have gone to the bountiful farmers' markets in Kitchener or Waterloo, where plump, placid women, wearing the plain clothes and bonnets of various Amish and Mennonite sects, come – as they have come since 1839 – to sell tiny cobs of pickled corn, apple butter, shoo-fly pie, kochkäse und kümmel, schwadamahga sausage, crocheted doilies, and goose wings that are "extra goot for cleaning out the corners."

Every Saturday, and Wednesday in the summer and fall, I go to feast my eyes and prepare to feast my stomach on cheeses, meat, fowl, fresh-picked vegetables, fruits, and flowers that to me seem more lavish and beautiful than any I have seen in the famous markets I have visited in faraway places of the world: Paris and Colmar in France, Berne and Fribourg in

Switzerland, Seville and Valencia, Caernarvon in Wales, Haarlem and Amsterdam, Cuernavaca and Mexico City, Nassau, Honolulu, New Orleans, and Lancaster in Pennsylvania.

Part of my preference for the produce of our local markets may be that when I visited markets abroad I was not able to buy and take back to my hotel room a nice smelly piece of cheese, a bunch of crisp asparagus, a garlic-flavoured raw sausage, or a tall, blooming lilac bush to be planted. When I go to the markets in Kitchener and Waterloo I buy until I fill up the trunk of my car; then I go home and prepare dandelion salad, schnitz and knepp (apples and dumplings), schmierkäse, and Dutch apple pie, with recipes brought to Waterloo County by the Mennonite settlers 180 years ago.

Another joy of the local markets is meeting friends and watching the crowd of shoppers: pert housewives in slacks, shuffling old men, couples haggling in German or Greek, old-country women wearing babushkas and broad, flat, black shoes, goggle-eyed tourists with cameras or sketch pads. In summer I greet acquaintances on their way to the Shakespearean Festival at Stratford, and show them where to buy gingerbread men or smoked pork chops.

The markets open at five in the morning and close at two in the afternoon. I've never been there so early and I know better than to go there so late since by noon many of the farmers have sold out and gone home. If I get there before eight I'll meet people who want a choice of the best, or chefs selecting delicacies for their dining rooms: kohlrabi, watercress, gooseberries to stuff geese, Heidelfingen cherries and duckling. If I arrive after nine and want kochkäse, I'm sure to be told by the Mennonite woman whose cheese I prefer, "If I hat some I'd gif you any but what I got iss all."

At the height of the Saturday-morning trade it is impossible to hurry (but who would want to?) through the aisles made by the long rows of tables inside the buildings, or to buck the crowds around the vendors' trucks lined up outside. For blocks around the streets are jammed with cars; parking lots and garages are packed solid, and traffic police try almost in vain to keep people moving.

Hundreds of local shoppers are regular customers at certain tables and stalls. Year after year, from childhood until old age, they go faithfully to the same farmers every week carrying bottles for cream, boxes for eggs, and bowls for kochkäse in their large wicker baskets. Though I buy regularly from certain farmers I don't know their names and I don't think they know mine – except such old-timers as Menno Brubacher, who only last week said to me, "I remember you from way back yet when you used to come with your ma."

In those days, drawing my little red-wheeled express wagon, I waited for my mother at the end of the long cement platform with all the kids who, by delivering customers' baskets to their homes, earned enough five-cent pieces to admit them to the Roma theatre to see *The Phantom Rider* on Saturday afternoon. I always waited impatiently while Mother shopped and visited, eventually filled her baskets, and was ready to have me pull them home as she walked alongside to steady the load and retrieve a peach or a cabbage that might bump off when the wagon went over a curb.

When Mother learned to run the family Nash, she drove the two blocks from our house to the market, but I still had to go with her to help carry her baskets to the car. The only things that interested me in those days were the kittens and puppies sold by farm children just outside the back door, and the fluffy chicks and baby bunnies they brought for sale at Easter.

Now I go eagerly to the market because I thoroughly enjoy every bit of it. Variety ranges from sauerkraut to shell jewellery; home baking, sewing, and handicrafts are sold along with comb honey, wool socks, homemade soap, and everything else that the vendors have grown or made themselves. Farm women with butternuts or sticky buns often bring quilts, gaily-coloured hooked mats, or hand-woven runners. A blond young man has bundles of freshly dried herbs; a Mennonite woman, wearing a white organdie prayer cap, offers crisp, deep-fried rosettes. She tells me, "With ice cream on top and crushed berries over, they gif a dessert good enough for a funeral."

Buyers are always three deep in front of the glass-covered stalls of the butchers: they jostle one another to buy pigs' tails,

Black Forest-style hams, and an incredible assortment of sausages. One German butcher has seventy-five varieties of processed meats; many farmers sell fresh fowl, squabs, and rabbits; one country butcher sells half a ton of smoked or fresh pork sausage every week. In great demand are braunschweiger, blood-and-tongue sausage, gefuellte kalbs-brust (veal stuffed with pork and pistachios), galrich (jellied pigs' hocks), and summer sausage. Occasionally, for an old-fashioned treat, I buy a small piece of head cheese to melt and spread over boiled potatoes.

All the cheeses at the markets are sold inside the buildings. Several vendors have limburger, Tilsit, Essrum, and other varieties made in Waterloo County cheese factories. Many of the farm women, along with their eggs or tatted fancies, bring a crock of kochkäse und kümmel that they make every week by boiling ripened sour milk curd until it looks like congealed glue; flecked with caraway seed, it has a delicate flavour. If you don't come early to get it you'll be told, "Ach it's all already, you should haf come sooner yet."

At one table a plump, black-bonneted woman offers little pats of schmierkäse to take home and prepare as she tells me: "You chust mix it with a little salt and plenty sweet cream till it's real extra smooth, then you put some in a nappie, pour lots of maple syrup over," she winks and smiles broadly, "and that really schmecks."

A few farmers' wives sell pasteurized sour cream. The supply seldom meets the demand. The women will tell you how to make cold and warm sour cream dressings for salads that are an essential of all good local dinners.

Schnitz and shoo-fly pies can be bought from any number of well-rounded farm women who sell home baking that is hard to resist; they'll gladly tell you how to make them. Rich warm flavour and experience are the keynotes of recipes which have passed from generation to generation of market vendors to market customers.

The peace-loving Mennonites, fleeing religious persecution in Switzerland, probably brought the recipes with them to Pennsylvania in the seventeenth century and from there to Waterloo County in the early 1800s. When these hard-working pioneers had cleared the forest and were able to grow more than they needed for themselves, they traded what they could in the stores and in 1839 started selling the rest of their surplus in an open area near the main street of the village of Berlin (now Kitchener) as farmers still do on market day in Switzerland's cities. In 1869 Jacob Y. Shantz, an enterprising Mennonite, established a year-round market in the basement of the building that housed the village council chamber and the post office.

The market quickly outgrew its quarters and spread out round the building till a separate structure was erected in 1907. Most of the vendors in the early days were Mennonites and bearded Amish farmers who, in winter, came in cutters with sleighbells ringing, their wives and children bundled to their eyes in shawls and cowhide robes. In summer they came in topless buggies or wagons, their wives wearing stiff black bonnets over white prayer caps, and clean print aprons over their modestly long cotton dresses – exactly as they do now.

Through the years the market kept changing. Butchers and farmers who emigrated from Europe rented tables beside the Mennonites and Amish. In the later 1920's a long cement platform took the place of some of the horse stalls that were no longer needed because many of the vendors were driving to the market in automobiles. Truckers came in the night from the Niagara Peninsula and waited till the five o'clock opening bell rang to unload their fruit – sometimes resorting to fist fights to determine who got the best places. As the cities kept growing and traffic became hazardous, most of the Old Mennonites who had come to the market in buggies stopped coming except to sell maple syrup in early spring.

In 1973, despite vigorous protest, the beloved sixty-six-year-old red market building and Kitchener's neo-classic City Hall were demolished to make space for a solid brown brick shopping mall which incorporated a parking garage whose two lower floors now house facilities for a modern market. Vendors who used to stand in the sun and the rain along the old market's outside platforms now line up their trucks in the parking garage and enjoy the shelter it gives them. The new market is more functional, more sanitary, and more crowded than ever with shoppers; vendors are more numerous, their produce more varied and abundant.

During the bitter controversy about the new development, a number of farmers bought Amsey Martin's field on the north-west edge of the City of Waterloo where they built a low flat utilitarian market building. Here the Old Order Mennonites come with their horses and buggies to sell things they grow in their gardens and orchards or bake in their kitchens. Other farmers, craftsmen, and butchers display their wares on the plain pine tables inside. Vendors from the fruitland line up their trucks along the outside. The great gravelled parking area surrounding the building is always filled with shoppers carrying loaded baskets to their cars.

The markets change with the changing seasons. In January and February only a few trucks use the outer areas; everyone else crowds into the buildings. Old Mrs. Kieswetter, walking like a queen, comes every week with her bowl to buy kochkäse; Mrs. Czezuliki, wearing mink and plaid slacks, comes for root vegetables and house plants. One farm woman wouldn't miss coming to market though she has only four quarts of onions and half a dozen bottles of horseradish to sell. Other farm women who have no grown things for sale in winter, bring homemade bread, fastnachts (raised doughnuts), and dried schnitz.

The sight of schnitz at the market on a cold winter day suggests a warm steamy Mennonite kitchen with a couch in a corner, a table set with ironstone china, and a big, black wood-burning cook-stove with a ham bubbling slowly.

From the middle of blustery March I start looking at the market for pussy willows and the first maple syrup. That's when my mother used to make her own version of shoo-fly pie, so chewy and sweet we called it candy pie.

The market looks like a garden when spring comes. Smiling farm women dig sprouting perennials from their gardens and sell them with plenty of earth round the roots. Almost every table has bunches of rhubarb and pailfuls of flowers: violets, bleeding hearts, daffodils, apple blossoms, lily-of-the-valley. In the outside areas hopeful gardeners flit from flats of seedlings to baskets of pansies and petunias, to rose bushes, shrubs, trees, raspberry canes, and almost anything you can think of that will grow in this part of the world.

Early summer gets me out of bed with the sunrise to be at the market in time to buy fruit and vegetables while the dew is still on them – I like to think. Because they're so perfect and fresh I always buy too many berries and cherries – but never quite enough tender garden peas, since I always manage to shell and eat half of my basketful before I reach home.

From the time the strawberries ripen, and until the last grapes disappear in the fall, the markets are open on Wednesday as well as on Saturday. They are not so well stocked or attended on Wednesdays, but there is less traffic congestion and the usual thrilling abundance.

As summer progresses the colours of the markets change from delicate shades to the bold hues of marigolds and delphinium. The tables are loaded with bushels of cucumbers, melons, and corn. Families come to carry fruits and pickles for Mamma to can and make into relishes and jam. I run back and forth many times to my car with baskets of tomatoes, peaches, and yellow transparents that make the best applesauce.

There is a mellow air of thanksgiving as fall comes to the markets with sweet cider, grapes for making wine, pumpkins, wild mushrooms, and wierdly shaped gourds, everlasting straw flowers, purple plums, and big winter pears.

From the end of November the markets begin to look like Christmas bazaars as the farmers' wives display the work of their ever-busy hands; crocheted baskets stiffened with sugar, knitted mitts, scarves, and tuques, cushion tops, dolls' clothes, aprons, smocked dresses for little girls; there are innumerable (and awful) novelties made of styrofoam, ribbons and lace, driftwood centrepieces and decorations for mantels, Indian baskets, carved wood and leather goods, ceramics. The Christmas baking is irresistible: hard round pfeffernusse, anise-flavoured lebkuchen, springerle with bas relief pictures, and thousands of cookies shaped like stars, trees, bells, Santa Claus, and Kriss Kringle.

People often say to me, "Why do you go to the market every week? You can buy just as well at the stores."

I tell them the market is much more exciting, more sociable, and more fun. The market is marvellous, nowhere else in the world that I've seen is there such fresh, clean, lush profusion. It gives me a feeling of security, abundance, and anticipation of joy. It gives me deep satisfaction.

When I get home from my market shopping I unload the baskets from the trunk of my car and try to find place to stow things away in my fridge, my freezer, my kitchen, guest bedroom, and back porch. Then I get out my cookbooks, choose recipes that will use the most perishable foods first, then the next – and I hope friends will call to say they'll be coming to help me eat up.

Friends and Relations, Thank You

MY SISTERS: Both my sisters are sociable; they belong to bridge clubs and constantly have friends in for meals – Norma in Waterloo, Ruby in Peterborough. I've had few letters from Ruby in the last five years that didn't enclose recipes she especially liked. Whenever I talk to Norm on the phone I have my notebook ready for her dictation of ways to make fabulous dishes she has eaten at one of her clubs, at somebody's luncheon, or in Majorca, Hawaii, Acapulco, Morocco, Greece, wherever she's travelled. Without the generosity of my sisters this book would be a lot thinner and so would we.

LORNA AND ROSS: Almost every week my friends Lorna and Ross Carruthers come to my house for tea and a sample of the muffins or cakes I have tried for this book. Lorna loves cooking and eating, is always experimenting, looking for new recipes and reading cookbooks. She was a nurse, knows what is good for you, and everything she makes seems to turn out as it should. Lorna has given me many good ideas and her favourite recipes which you'll find scattered throughout every chapter from Drinks to Uncategoricals. She kindly offered to check for mistakes all the recipes I've typed; she's tried and improved some of them, too. I can't tell you how grateful I am – and you will be when you encounter Lorna's contributions to *More Schmecks*.

JEAN and DON SALTER came to Canada from England, lived in a house at the other end of Sunfish Lake. Don taught geology at the University of Waterloo but dreamed of crossing the Atlantic in a sailboat. Jean painted landscapes and often invited me for a cuppa tea. Always she served such professional-looking goodies that I asked her where she had bought them. "I'd never buy baking," she told me, "I love making my own."

After a few years the Salters sold their house, flew to England, bought a sailboat, and crossed the Atlantic. On the twenty-six-day sail from the Canaries to Barbados and throughout their winter cruising among the Caribbean Islands, Jean strapped herself into the neat little galley of the yacht with a seatbelt and made bread, muffins, seed cake, and other well-planned foods that kept them healthy while they were afloat.

When they returned to Canada after their year of adventuring – besides giving me a white-footed kitten named Wilmot – Jean typed her favourite old English recipes for my new cookbook.

BEVVY MARTIN: With as much joy, and as often as ever, I visit my Old Order Mennonite friend Bevvy Martin, who so generously loaned me her little hand-written recipe book when I wrote *Food That Really Schmecks*. Bevvy no longer prepares three feasts a day for her growing family. She and her husband David live alone now in a small house in the country beside the big home of their son Amsey; their daughters Salome and Lyddy Ann are married and have farms of their own. The Martin's sprawling ancestral stone farmhouse has fallen a victim of the city's voracity; soon David's well-tilled fields will become a housing development.

Not only is the city gobbling up the farms of the Old Order Mennonites, forcing them to give up the lands they love and move farther away, it is also presenting the temptation of the supermarkets that have replaced the old-fashioned general stores where they used to buy sugar, spices, and salt. One time when I had supper with Bevvy and David she shyly produced a store-bought package of chocolate wafers.

And Christmas before last when they were planning their gathering of married children and eighteen grandchildren, David said to Bevvy, "You're too old now to work so hard preparing a great big turkey, we'll make it real easy by getting some buckets of Kentucky fried chicken."

That's what they did. David drove his dachwaegle (top buggy) to Col. Sanders' nearest outlet and they had Kentucky fried chicken for Christmas dinner in their Old Order Mennonite doddy house!

"And it went down real good, too," David told me. "Some of the grandchildren had never tasted it before and they really enjoyed it. And with what we had left we invited Bevvy's sister and her husband for supper the next day and that went good, too."

1

Drinks, Shakes, Wines and Punches

For children, for adults, for health, and for fun.

My friend Kath Reeves lives in a Devon cottage overlooking a meadow with grazing sheep and wild rabbits. She works in a boys' boarding school that is nutrition-conscious and won't allow pupils to get fat. Every summer vacation Kath leaves her garden, her little dog, and two cats to visit Sunfish Lake where she is a victim of my culinary experiments. Kath is an interesting and inventive cook and has given me a number of old Devon recipes including: Damson Gin, Apple Ale, Rose Petal Wine, and Cherry Bounce.

A BLENDER – YOU MUST HAVE A BLENDER: If you don't have a blender – or the wherewithal – use the time you'd spend pushing things through a sieve to go out and sell greeting cards, or babysit, or cut grass till you've earned enough to pay for this glorious device. Keep it on your kitchen counter where you will use it everyday.

You can do so many interesting things with a blender; rescue so many leftovers, chop vegetables, make smooth soups and sauces, salad dressings, drinks that will thrill and nourish you. If you kept account of the pennies you'd save here and there, you'd soon have the cost of a blender which for years will keep giving you pleasure.

PINK POODLE

I don't like the texture of watermelon – but a drink of watermelon juice with crushed ice is divine, naturally sweet, has a beautiful colour, and is cool and refreshing. Remove the seeds, liquify the pulp and juice in your blender, and you'll wish summer would last forever.

FRESH APPLE COCKTAIL

Good for all seasons.

¹/₂ cup cold water
1 tablespoon lemon juice
1 tablespoon sugar

1 apple, cored and chopped
  but not peeled

Put everything into the blender and whirl till the apple is liquified. Drop in some crushed ice and serve at once. If you drop ice cream into it instead of ice you could use it as a dessert.

VEGETABLE COCKTAIL

I keep this in my fridge all the time: after I walk the half mile to my mailbox I drink a mug or a glassful – hot or cold – and I don't worry if I'm too lazy to cook a variety of vegetables for my dinner.

3 cups or more tomato juice
1 stalk celery, with leaves
1 slice green pepper
  (optional)
1 carrot
¹/₂ teaspoon Worcestershire
  sauce (optional)

¹/₂ cup parsley
¹/₄ cup onion (optional)
¹/₄ cup lemon juice (optional)
Seasoning to taste
Any leftover vegetables in
  your fridge

Blend all the ingredients, including as many vegetables as you like, until they are completely liquified. Chill.

COFFEE MILK

I know I should drink one or two glasses of milk every day but I don't like the sweet cowy taste. Adding chocolate syrup would make it a treat but fattening. So: I blend 1 rounded teaspoon instant coffee powder with 1 glass milk and drink it through a straw with enjoyment. (A blob of ice cream dropped in the glass would make it super – but heaven forbids.)

SINGLE EGGNOG

Double, triple, quadruple it. Call it an instant meal.

1 fresh egg
Sugar and salt to taste
1 cup whole milk
1 teaspoon vanilla
Nutmeg

¹/₂ teaspoon rum flavouring
or 1 ounce of the real
thing,whiskey, sherry or
brandy

Drop everything into your blender and give it a whirl; pour it into a tall glass over ice cubes with a sprinkle of nutmeg on top. You might like more rum – occasionally.

COCOA PASTE
about 1 pint

Lorna told me that every morning all the children in Toronto's Hospital for Sick Children used to be given a drink of cocoa made with this nutritious paste. They loved it.

1 cup sugar
1 cup cocoa
Water

1 large tablespoon butter
1 teaspoon vanilla
Yolk and white of 1 egg

Blend the sugar and cocoa with enough water to make a fairly thick paste. Cook gently, adding the butter until it is melted. Remove from heat, add vanilla. Beat the yolk and white of the egg separately, mix and fold into the cocoa paste. Keep it in the fridge and stir a good tablespoonful into a glass of milk, making sure it is well blended.

AN ENGLISH HEALTH DRINK

Kath says this one is for the book.

¹/₂ cup walnuts	**¹/₂ a cored apple with skin left**
1 slice brown bread	**on**
1 pat butter	**1 leaf of lettuce**
1 pint milk (gradually add	**1 carrot**
more)	**1 peeled banana**
2 egg yolks	**1¹/₂ cups raisins**
Juice of ¹/₂ a lemon with some	
grated peel	

Place in a blender in the above order and test the flavour as you mix it. If too sour, add more raisins, if too sweet, add more lemon. The finished mixture should have the consistency of very soft ice cream. Kids love it – so do adults.

PEACH SHAKE
enough for two glasses

If you really want to indulge yourself try this! I do it more often than I care to admit – but the peach season is short, and if they keep selling off all the Niagara Peninsula's land to developers we soon won't have any peaches.

2 big fresh peaches – or	**1 cup milk**
enough canned ones to	**1 cup vanilla ice cream**
make 1 solid cupful	**1 ounce rum or almond**
¹/₄ cup white sugar	**liqueur (optional)**

Cut the unpeeled peaches into the blender, add the rest of the ingredients except the liquor and blend till it's frothy. Pour into tall, chilled glasses. Drizzle the liquor on top. Try drinking it through a straw, or with a sherbet spoon. It is ambrosia. I serve it as a dessert. You might try it with other fruit.

PEACH SODA

Instead of milk in the above recipe use soda water, but don't put it in the blender – you'll lose the bubbles.

ICED CHOCOLATE MINT
3 or 4 glasses

Your skinny friends will love this – and so will your fat ones.

5 tablespoons cocoa
1/2 cup sugar
1/2 cup hot water
Pinch of salt
3 cups whole milk
1/2 teaspoon vanilla
Several leaves of fresh mint

Ice cubes
Chocolate or vanilla ice
** cream**
Chocolate or coffee or crème
** de menthe liqueur**
** (optional)**

Put the cocoa, sugar, hot water, and salt into your blender and whirl till the cocoa is dissolved; add the milk, vanilla, and mint leaves; give it another whirl then add 6 crushed ice cubes. Pour into 3 or 4 glasses and drop into each a scoop of ice cream. Drizzle the liqueur on top.

BANANA COW
2 drinks

I met my first Banana Cow in Hawaii where the bartender in the hotel gave us his recipe. Serve it as a dessert or mid-afternoon when dinner is going to be late.

2 teaspoons sugar
1/2 cup milk
2 ounces rum

1 small banana
Crushed ice
Nutmeg to sprinkle on top

Mix sugar, milk, rum, and banana in a blender till the banana is liquified. Add crushed ice, give it another whirl and pour into tall glasses. Sprinkle nutmeg on top, balance an orchid on the rim of the glass and sip the drink through a straw.

MULLED WINE
about 12 servings

For a frosty evening. Sip it from those comfortable little pottery wine cups that someone gave you for Christmas.

1 quart wine (burgundy or claret)	**6 whole cloves**
Zest of 1 orange and 1 lemon	**1 tablespoon sugar**
2 or 3 inches of cinnamon stick	**Sprinkle of nutmeg**

Simmer all the ingredients in a saucepan gently for 5 minutes. Strain into the pottery carafe that came with the wine cups, serve hot and keep sipping.

SPICED CIDER

Made the same way as Mulled Wine but with 2 quarts of cider instead of wine. Keep what might be left over in your fridge and have another pleasant evening.

JOHNNIE'S GRAPE JUICE WINE

The last time I called on Johnnie at Neil's Harbour, he was enjoying a glass of wine he'd made himself. "It's roight easy," he told me. "All ye need is a big bottle of grape juice ye can buy in the store, 5 or 6 cups of sugar, boil it to a syrup – but not thick. Put it in a gallon bottle, drop in a handful of raisins and one o' them yeast packets, fill the bottle with water and let it sit for a week with the cork not in tight. That's all ye need to do. You git about 5 quarts out of that. Cool it before ye drink it and it's roight good."

TEA WINE

In Devon they say it's rather like sherry.

4 pints cold tea	**1 orange, sliced**
4 cups sugar	**1 lemon, sliced**
¹/₂ pound large raisins, chopped	

Put the cold tea into a jar, add the sugar, raisins, finely sliced orange and lemon. Stir well and let stand for 1 month. Strain and bottle. It should be drinkable in another 6 weeks.

ROSE PETAL WINE

Imagine drinking rose petals from an English garden!

1 quart dried rose petals   **1¹/₂ cups sugar to 1 quart**
1 quart water   **liquid**

Cover the rose petals with water and let them stand in a jug for 10 days, stirring each day. Strain through muslin, then add sugar and leave several days until the sugar dissolves and it begins to work. Strain carefully, bottle and cork lightly at first.

DAMSON GIN

An old Devon recipe that will give you some exercise.

1 gallon unsweetened dry gin   **4 cups sugar**
4 quarts damson plums

Put all the ingredients together in a 2-gallon jar, lightly corked. Shake well twice a day for 6 weeks. Strain and rebottle, tightly corked. Good luck.

CHERRY BOUNCE

You never know what goes on behind those high Devon hedges!

1 quart sour cherries   **1 quart whiskey**
1 cup sugar

Wash the cherries, put them in a large-mouthed jar with the sugar. Let stand until the juice draws then add the whiskey. Cover lightly and steep about ten days. Drain off the liquor and bottle it to keep as long as your curiosity will let you.

KATH'S FRUIT PUNCH

Innocent and delicious.

1 cup berries in season	**1 cup honey**
1 cup orange juice	**2 cups strong cold tea**
¹/₂ cup lemon juice	**1 pint ginger ale or cider**

Crush the berries. Mix all the ingredients. Chill and serve over ice.

RHUBARB PUNCH

Eva says this refreshes the men when they come in hot from haying.

16 cups rhubarb (or thereabouts – Eva doesn't count)	**3 cups sugar**
	³/₄ cup lemon juice
3 quarts water, approximately	**1 large tin frozen orange juice**
	4 quarts chilled ginger ale

Cut the rhubarb and cook in the water until tender, adding the sugar at the last and stirring it in. Strain, chill, and add the other juices. Just before serving pour in the ginger ale and lots of ice cubes. A few sprigs of fresh mint make it look pretty.

LORNA'S CRANBERRY PUNCH
5 quarts – non-alcoholic

A lovely colour and very popular at a party.

2¹/₂ cups cranberry juice	**2 cups grape juice**
2 cups strong cold tea	**1 quart ginger ale**
3 cups orange juice	**Soda water (optional)**
1¹/₂ cups lemon juice	

Chill all the ingredients until serving time. Pour into a chilled punch bowl with ice cubes or a block of ice. Add some soda water if you want to thin it. Pour the ginger ale and soda water carefully down the inside of the bowl to prevent bubbles from escaping.

GOLDEN MINT RECEPTION PUNCH
50 punch cups – non-alcoholic

From a patch of mint in her garden, Lorna made this refreshing drink when she had summer parties or a wedding reception in the family.

30 to 35 mint sprigs
2 cups white sugar
2 quarts boiling water
2 quarts orange juice
2¹/₃ cups fresh lemon juice

1 large can (No. 2) pineapple juice
1 quart ginger ale
1 quart soda water
Lemon slices

Simmer the mint sprigs (reserving a few for garnish) and sugar in the boiling water, uncovered, for 10 minutes. Chill this and all the other ingredients. Just before serving strain the mint syrup into a chilled punch bowl with a block of ice. Stir in the fruit juices, pour the ginger ale and soda water down the side of the bowl and don't stir it. Top with the tips of mint sprigs and thin lemon slices.

CELEBRATION EGG NOG
2 rum bottles full

Lorna's egg nogs really do bring Christmas cheer.

1 bottle (26 oz.) amber rum
12 eggs, well beaten
2 cans sweetened condensed milk

2% milk to thin (2 cups or more)

Blend all ingredients well and chill. Serve dusted with nutmeg in the cup. Store it in your fridge in rum bottles.

2

Soups

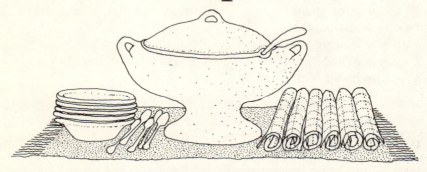

For loners and large families, couples and company, for the
very young, very old, ill or toothless, for anybody, soup is the
most effective and effortless way to load up with vitamins.

It's so easy to make nourishing soup simply by cooking a
number of vegetables: asparagus, beans, cabbage, carrots,
corn, tomatoes – whatever you happen to have – fresh, frozen,
or leftover. Throw in some bones, cut up an onion, cube a
potato, slice a celery stalk, shred a few leaves of lettuce,
spinach, or cress. Add broth or salted water; season to taste
with a bouquet garni, a bouillon cube, or a bay leaf. Let it
simmer till you can't wait any longer. Whirl it in a blender till
the mixture is smooth and anonymous. Keep tasting. Add a
dollop of butter, sour cream, or wine, if you think it needs help.

Tired old casseroles smoothed in a blender with water or
broth make delicious soup; so do yesterday's vegetables with
giblets, poultry stuffing, and gravy. I regret not having re-
corded all the marvellous soups I've made out of leftovers.

You can make soup out of almost anything edible. Who's to
know what's in it after it's been whirled around in a blender or
pushed through a sieve? I've read recipes for an odd variety
(although you won't find them here): peanut, she-crab, ter-
rapin, eel ("nail eel up by the tail and peel the skin off over the
head"), catfish, elderberry, calf's head ("remove the brain

32

first"), grape, black walnut and cooter ("kill cooter by chopping off head"). If you want to add angostura bitters, puréed apricots and anchovies to soup, that is your privilege; I prefer a broth with drepsly (page 38) and plenty of parsley.

You have to be daring: and by guess and good luck you'll achieve some great soups – and the odd one that even your dog wouldn't eat. I'll give you some recipes that have been approved by humans.

BOUQUET GARNI

During the Stylish Entertainment course at Rundles Restaurant in Stratford, John Walker, the *chef de cuisine*, would often say, "Drop in a bouquet garni." He told us to keep a small supply on hand to use often to pep up soup, stock, or a sauce.

Cut cheese cloth or muslin into 3- or 4-inch squares and in each one put whatever herbs you like; tie up the cloth with string so the herbs can't escape and store them in a tight jar. Don't make too many at a time, the fresher they are the better. You can vary the flavours: parsley, thyme, celery leaves, bay leaf; or parsley, chives, tarragon, chervil; or celery leaves, garlic, fennel; you might include marjoram, basil, sage, a bit of rosemary, etcetera.

MOTHER'S VEGETABLE SOUP

One of the favourite dinners of my childhood. Mother made it with a large meaty beef bone.

At least 2 quarts of stock from a large meaty beef bone
1/2 cup raw rice
2 or 3 carrots, sliced
2 potatoes, sliced
1 cup celery, cut up
1 small onion, chopped (optional)
1 cup cut-up string beans
1/2 cup green peas
1/2 cup coarsely sliced cabbage
Salt and pepper to taste
Lots of parsley

Boil the beef till almost tender; add the rice and boil for 15 minutes; add the vegetables and seasonings, and cook till they are soft but not mushy – about 15 minutes. Add the cut-up parsley and serve with the meat cut into bite-sized pieces – 2 or 3 helpings for each hungry child or adult.

Ruby wrote me in a letter: "I'm having vegetable soup for dinner and it takes so long to peel the stuff. I'll put it through the grinder – saves time and tastes just as good – but wouldn't Mother think that was terrible? Not how she taught us."

I agree with Mother: I like to see the carrot slices and pieces of celery and potato. But I do agree about the peeling; they say it's nutritious, and scrubbing vegetables is a lot easier than taking off the skins.

Beef being a rarity, you can make this soup with stock from chicken or spare-rib bones. It's not as good but not bad.

GLORIA DIRK'S BORSCHT

There seem to be as many ways of making borscht as there are Russian Mennonites and Ukrainians in our community who make it. Rich and flavourful, it is a complete meal.

A nice piece of beef with a
  bone
Salted water to cover
Several potatoes, diced
2 or 3 carrots, sliced
1 large onion, sliced
  (optional)
Stem or 2 of celery
1 quart tomatoes
1 bay leaf
Several peppercorns
Lots of dill (optional)
Several cupfuls of shredded
  cabbage
3 beets, cooked and chopped
  (optional)
Lots of parsley, cut up
Sour cream

Boil the beef in salted water until it is almost tender. Except the beets, parsley, and sour cream, put in all the rest and simmer until cooked. (Tie the dill and bay leaf together so you can fish them out.) Drop in the beets and parsley at the last minute. Put a tablespoon of sour cream on each serving and pass a bowl of cream at the table for those who want more.

Many recipes are invented because you happen to have something in your fridge or your storage bin and if you don't use it soon it will be too late; to save it – and your conscience – you get out a cookbook, look in the index for lemon, or cabbage, or whatever it is, and if it's not too much bother, you make it.

Of course, sometimes the recipes you find require ingredients you don't have. Then what? You make whatever it is without them, or you substitute, or you improvise, and if you do that you'll have something new and different, maybe wonderful, maybe yucky. Give it a French name and your eaters will be impressed – one way or another.

If you wait till you get all the ingredients to make a new recipe – as you should do to be fair and successful – you might never achieve it. Kath told me she had read a good-sounding recipe that used cardamom seeds, of which she had none. By the time she had finally bought some a year later, she had forgotten where she saw the recipe that needed them.

CANNED VEGETABLE SOUP
about 20 quarts

Eva makes this when the tomatoes are ripe in her garden. It's a lot of work. "It takes a whole day," Eva says, "and when you're done you're thankful. But it's so nice to have in the winter when you just have to heat it for soup or a sauce for macaroni, or with noodles and meat in a casserole. You can vary it as much as you like – put in whatever you have, leave out what you don't like."

4 gallons of tomato juice
1 quart carrots, cut up
1 quart peas
1 quart yellow string beans,
  cut in pieces
5 onions, finely chopped
3 to 5 green peppers
1 quart corn, cut from cob
1 quart cabbage, cut fine
¼ cup salt (but taste as you
  add)

¼ cup sugar
1 cup barley, soaked several
  hours, then boiled a long
  time before adding
1 cup navy beans, soaked
  overnight and boiled till
  soft before adding
1 to 2 cups chopped parsley

Cook each vegetable separately in boiling water for about 10 minutes – the beans and barley longer. Combine all the cooked vegetables and tomato juice in a huge kettle, adding more tomato juice if you think the mixture is too thick. Boil 10 minutes longer. Seal in sterilized jars and steam the small jars for 10 minutes. Eva says she steams hers 20 to be sure and 30 minutes for the quart jars. She adds more tomato juice when she heats it for serving as soup.

HOT OR COLD TOMATO SOUP
3 or 4 servings

Whirled in a blender this is quick, easy, and tasty.

3 or 4 cups unpeeled tomatoes (fresh, frozen or canned)
1/4 cup chopped green onions or 1 regular
2 teaspoons cornstarch
1 tablespoon lemon juice
Pinch of powdered thyme
1 teaspoon salt
1 1/2 teaspoons sugar
Pepper to taste
1/2 to 1 cup sour cream
Chopped parsley

Drop all ingredients but sour cream and parsley into the blender and whirl till perfectly smooth. Put through a sieve to remove tomato seeds. Bring to a slow boil until thickened. Before serving, hot or chilled, stir in sour cream and sprinkle parsley on top.

PEA POD SOUP

To save juicy fresh pea pods from the compost heap, Kath devised this delicious, delicate soup that is bothersome to prepare but really special. Whenever she comes from Devon to visit I get her to make it.

2 or 3 quarts strictly fresh pea pods (if they're limp, throw them out)
1 small onion, or 1 leek, chopped
3 tablespoons butter
2 cups cream sauce
Salt to taste
1 tablespoon butter
1/2 cup cream
2 fresh mint leaves

As soon as the peas are podded, Kath sweats the pods in butter in a heavy pan with the chopped onion. She keeps stirring them over medium heat until they are soft, then she rubs them through a sieve. (I thought I'd save a lot of trouble by putting them into my blender but the fibre of the pods was so tough it almost ruined the machine by wrapping around the blades. It has to be done the hard way.)

Kath makes a cream sauce of 2 tablespoons butter, 2 tablespoons flour, 2 cups milk; she stirs in the pea pod purée, melts in butter, and adds cream to make it superb. She serves it hot with a bit of chopped mint leaf on top. "But don't overdo it," she warns. "The flavour of the pods is delicate and could be overpowered."

SMOKED SAUSAGE SOUP

A good, gutsy, masculine Mennonite soup with that old-fashioned smoky flavour.

At least ¹/₂ pound of smoked pork sausage	**2 carrots**
2 quarts water	**1 stalk celery**
2 or 3 cups of cabbage	**1 onion**
¹/₂ small turnip or 4 large potatoes	**Salt to taste**
	Milk or cream

Slice all the vegetables while the pork sausage is boiling gently in water. Add vegetables and seasonings to the sausage, stir occasionally. Cook about 20 minutes until the vegetables are soft and the bree is very thick. Remove the pork sausage and slice to ¹/₄-inch pieces. Return sausage to soup, pour in some milk or cream to thin the soup if you like, cover and heat. Don't bother making anything else when you serve this; it's a meal.

If you double or halve a recipe always write the half or double amounts beside the printed figures and be sure to stick to the right column. I've ruined so many things by putting in a full amount of something when all the rest was halved.

NOODLE SOUP – THE HUTTERITE WAY

A long time ago, while writing a story for *Maclean's* magazine, I stayed on a Hutterite Colony in Alberta. Every morning a bell would ring to summon a group of the women to the kitchen to prepare dinner for the two hundred people living in the commune. Wearing traditional kerchiefs over their prayer caps, and plaid aprons over their identically styled long dresses, the women would come with their rolling pins to make noodles several times a week.

Into 2 beaten eggs each woman would stir as much flour as was needed to make a smooth pastry-like dough. Dividing the dough into portions the size of an apple, she would then roll out each piece thin as parchment. She'd drape a clean dish-towel over her arm, carefully put several sheets of noodle dough over it and take them home to spread out on her bed. She'd turn them occasionally till they were dry but not stiff, roll them like a jelly roll, then return them to the kitchen to be cut in narrow slices that unrolled into noodles to be boiled in beef or chicken broth with plenty of parsley.

I visited the Hutterites again recently: the women were still being summoned by a bell to the kitchen, still wearing the traditional garb of their Bavarian ancestors. But the first thing they showed me – with great pride – was how they are now making their noodles with a noodle machine.

DREPSLY SUPP

Whenever I have a good strong meat broth I like to drop good old Mennonite drepsly into it.

¼ cup milk   **½ cup flour**
1 egg

Beat the egg, blend in the milk, then the flour. Pour the runny batter into boiling broth through a colander, stirring to quicken the dribbling. Put on the lid, turn down the heat, and cook slowly for 4 minutes. Add plenty of parsley and serve before the drepsly – like tiny dumplings – absorb too much of the broth.

STOCK FOR SOUP

Our family always disdained boiling the bones of chickens or turkeys for soup stock; the idea of taking bones off people's dinner plates and putting them together into a pot somehow just didn't appeal to us. "It must be unsanitary," Mother said.

But whenever I visited the Bertons at Kleinberg, Janet, who is one of the best cooks in the world, served delicious, stylish soups made with stock she had ladled from a huge kettle that was constantly simmering on the back of the stove. All the bones, vegetables, salad bits, and meat scraps of her household went into the pot. "The kids call it garbage soup," Janet told me, "but it's all sterilized in the cooking."

Having tried Janet's method and become a convert, I regret the mountains of bones I've wasted over the years. So many great soup recipes nonchalantly list cupfuls of stock among their ingredients: cooking bones is such an easy, economical way to keep it on hand.

When the plates come back to the kitchen simply collect all the bones and pieces of skin that have been discarded: remove and refrigerate all the meat from the carcass, put those bones with the rest into a good-sized pot with enough boiling, salted water to cover them, then let them simmer for hours and hours, humidifying your house in the process.

Eventually pour the whole thing through a colander to strain out the bones and bits–but keep them. Cool the stock and when the fat has congealed on top, remove it for cooking and baking. Store the jelled broth in your fridge for a while, or freeze it.

More. After the first simmering of the bones you can put them back in the kettle with water to cover and simmer them again. By this time you might have more leftovers to add, if not put in a couple of carrots, a cut-up onion, herbs or a bay leaf, some celery leaves and coarse stalks, lettuce leaves and anything else you have that might add flavour and nourishment–except starchy vegetables that disintegrate. Again let it simmer for ages. Drain it and you'll have more stock to make super soups.

KARTOFFEL SUPPE (Potato Soup)
4 servings

Minnie Vogel can't eat onions: she makes her potato soup this way. "Smoos as welvet," she told me.

2 cups potatoes, sliced
(Minnie sometimes uses
leftover potatoes)
1 big carrot, thinly sliced
1 stalk of celery, cut finely
6 cups chicken or beef broth

$1/8$ teaspoon marjoram
Salt and pepper to taste
2 tablespoons butter
3 tablespoons flour
2 or 3 tablespoons chopped
parsley

Put the potatoes, carrot, and celery into a pot with boiling stock and seasonings; boil gently until the vegetables are very tender. Put them through a colander or purée them in a blender, return to the heat and let simmer. Melt the butter, add the flour and stir until it is golden. Gradually stir in some of the soup stock then blend with the rest of the soup. Stir and let it simmer 10 minutes longer, till it is bound together. When you serve it add the parsley, sprinkling some on top.

MARROW BALL SOUP
4 servings

Hilda Gremmelmaier comes to my house every Monday. Last time she brought with her two pieces of leg bone and showed me how to make her favourite soup.

2 pieces of beef leg bone
2 quarts salted water
1 carrot, sliced
Stem of celery with leaves
$1/2$ onion, chopped fine
1 bay leaf
4 peppercorns
Herbs to taste

Marrow balls
Marrow from the bones
$1/2$ onion, chopped very fine
$1/2$ tablespoon margarine
3 sprigs parsley, finely
chopped
1 small egg
Salt and pepper
Sprinkle of nutmeg
1 to $1^1/4$ cups fine dry bread
crumbs

Hilda scraped all the marrow from the bones and in 2 dishes soaked bones and marrow in cold water to get rid of the redness. She kept changing the water in both until clear, breaking up the marrow with a fork and straining off the water with a sieve. She put the bones in 2 quarts of water in a pot, dropped in the vegetable pieces and seasonings, and simmered them for several hours.

Meanwhile Hilda sautéed the chopped onion in the margarine till it was soft then, with a fork, worked it into the marrow, adding the parsley, egg, seasonings, and the bread crumbs until the mixture was firm enough to form into balls the size of a marble. (She tested a couple in the broth: when they came to the surface and started to disintegrate she knew she needed more crumbs.) She placed all the little balls on a plate, covered them and put them in the fridge until eating time. She strained the broth, returned it to the pot to simmer, gently dropped all the balls into it, and turned off the heat. The moment the balls came to the surface she scooped them out and served them with the broth. If the balls were left in the pot they'd break up – but still taste good.

GOOD AS GOLD SOUP
about 7 servings

Don't tell anyone this soup is made with leftover cooked turnips; it is slithery-smooth, delicate, and delicious.

2 cups cooked turnip	2 tablespoons butter
4 cups broth (or bouillon)	1 cup sweet or sour cream
Salt and pepper to taste	1 beaten egg or 2 yolks
1 tablespoon brown sugar	Parsley or paprika to garnish

Simmer the cooked turnip in the broth for 10 minutes then rub it through a sieve or purée it in your blender till it is smooth, smooth. Heat it again, as you add the other ingredients, except the egg. Stir a few tablespoons of soup into the beaten egg or yolks, remove the soup from the heat, stir the egg mixture into it till it is smooth as satin. Serve very hot with a sprinkle of parsley or paprika on top and cubed, buttered toast strips or homemade croutons alongside.

LETTUCE PEA SOUP
6 servings

Don't throw out those rather coarse or slightly wilted lettuce leaves to the rabbits; they can be made into the kind of smooth green soup that would delight you in a ritzy restaurant.

2 cups (6 to 8 leaves) lettuce cut in shreds across the stem
1 small onion, minced
¹/₂ cup celery leaves (optional)
1 to 2 cups green peas (fresh, frozen, leftover, or canned)

2 cups chicken stock
Salt and pepper to taste
1 egg or 2 egg yolks
¹/₂ cup milk
3 tablespoons butter
1 cup cream (sweet or sour)
¹/₂ cup finely chopped parsley

Simmer the lettuce, onion, celery, and peas in the chicken stock seasoned with salt and pepper, for about 15 minutes. Pour it into your blender and turn it to purée or force it through a sieve. Beat up 2 egg yolks or a whole egg, stir in the milk, blend with the hot puréed vegetables and return to low heat, stirring till it is thickened. Just before serving, stir in the butter, cream, and half the parsley; heat it but don't let it boil. Serve with parsley sprinkled on top and croutons or buttered toast squares alongside.

GREEN SOUP
6 servings

Even non-spinach eaters will ask for a second helping of this mild cream soup. Be sure you have enough.

2 slices of bacon (optional)
2 tablespoons bacon fat (or butter)
1 medium onion, sliced thin
1 garlic clove, minced (optional)
2 cups potatoes, sliced (raw or cooked)
1¹/₂ cups boiling broth or bouillon

1 cup cooked or frozen spinach – or 2 big handfuls of fresh spinach, shredded
2 tablespoons butter
2 tablespoons flour
2 cups hot milk, or 1 cup each milk and cream
Salt, pepper to taste

Fry the bacon till crisp, remove and drain. Leave 2 tablespoons of fat in the pan, add the onion and garlic, let sizzle gently, but not brown. Add the potatoes and the boiling broth. Cover and let simmer till the vegetables are soft. Add the spinach and simmer 5 minutes longer. Purée in your blender, or press through a colander, and simmer again. In another saucepan melt 2 tablespoons butter, blend in the flour, stir it till golden, add the hot milk, stir till it thickens then mix it with the vegetable purée. Serve hot with crumbled bacon on top.

CREAM OF BROCCOLI SOUP

Use 2 cups coarsely chopped cooked or raw broccoli instead of spinach in the recipe for Green Soup. Cook the raw broccoli along with only one cup potato.

GREEN PEA SOUP

Another Green Soup – use 2 cups peas instead of spinach and a touch of mint or curry. Omit the potatoes entirely, if you like.

CREAM OF CARROT SOUP

The same as Pea Soup, using 2 cups sliced carrots and a stalk of finely sliced celery instead of spinach and 1 cup potatoes.

PUMPKIN SOUP

Use 2 cups cooked pumpkin instead of spinach and 1 cup potato. Drop a Bouquet Garni into the broth.

WATERCRESS SOUP
6 servings

A charming little French restaurant would no doubt call this delicate delicious soup Velouté Cressonière. Some people think things taste better if they have a fancy name.

A large bunch of watercress
(2 or 3 cupfuls), coarsely
chopped, reserving a few
perfect leaves for
garnishing
2 tablespoons butter
6 cups boiling chicken stock

2 or 3 potatoes, peeled and
sliced
Salt and pepper to taste
2 egg yolks or 1 egg
$^1/_4$ cup thick or sour cream
Lump of butter

Melt 2 tablespoons butter in a soup kettle over medium heat.
Drop in the cress and stir it around till it is somewhat limp.
Add the boiling stock and the sliced potatoes. Simmer all
together for about 20 minutes until the potatoes are soft. Pour
the soup through a sieve and force as much as possible
through it – or whirl till smooth in your blender. Bring the
purée back to simmer for 2 or 3 minutes while you beat the egg
yolks or egg slightly in a small bowl. Stir the cream into the
egg, blending it well; stir a few spoonfuls of the hot soup into
the egg mixture, take the soup off the stove and gradually stir
in the egg combination. Add a lump of butter and more seasoning if you think it needs it. Heat again, but *not* to boiling point.
Serve with a sprinkling of paprika on top and a few floating
cress leaves.

You might substitute spinach or lettuce if watercress is
hard to come by.

COLD CUCUMBER SOUP
4 servings – it can be easily doubled

A refreshing, first cousin of Vichyssoise: nourishing cold soup
to serve on a hot summer day. It can be made a day or two
ahead and kept in your fridge.

2 tablespoons butter
1 medium onion, or 1 leek, or
green onions with leaves,
sliced
1 unpeeled cucumber, diced
1 large potato, sliced (or 1
cup leftover or mashed
potato)

2 cups chicken broth or
bouillon
Salt and pepper to taste
Several sprigs of parsley
$^1/_2$ teaspoon thyme
1 cup thick or sour cream
Chopped chives for garnishing

Melt the butter and cook the onion in it until it is transparent but not brown. Add the remaining ingredients, except the cream and chives; bring to a boil. Lower the heat and simmer until the potatoes are tender, about 25 minutes. Purée in your blender or put the mixture through a colander. (I blend mine then put it through a sieve to remove the cucumber seeds.) Taste for seasonings. There's nothing to prevent you from eating this soup hot, but it's best when chilled thoroughly. Before serving, stir in the cream, sprinkle the chives on top. I serve it with hot cheese biscuits or cheese onion squares.

CHILLED BEET SOUP

Instead of a cucumber use 1 cup of sliced, cooked beets, but don't put them into the soup till you are ready to put the mixture into your blender.

PRUNE MOOS

A popular European soup that can be eaten hot or chilled "at the front or back part of a meal," a Mennonite friend told me.

2 cups prunes
1 cup raisins
Water
1/2 cup sugar
1 teaspoon cinnamon
  (optional)

3 tablespoons flour or 2
  tablespoons cornstarch
1/2 teaspoon salt
1 cup sweet cream

Cover the prunes and raisins with water and cook until tender; remove the fruit. Combine the sugar, cinnamon, flour and salt; blend together with enough water to make a thick pouring consistency and stir into the water in which the fruit was cooked; stir over low heat until thick as white sauce. Add the fruit. Stir in the cream and heat but don't boil.

Moos or Mus is sometimes made with buttermilk instead of water. It is also made with a variety of fruits, dried, raw, or canned: cherries, plums, rhubarb, apples, gooseberries, apricots. It can be made in advance and reheated, or chilled and used as a dessert.

3

Sweets and Sours

When Eva married Melvin they went to live in a seven-bedroom, white brick house with an addition which was a self-contained living unit. "Such a big house for a young couple," I said, as Eva showed me around. "Why did you add more?"

"Well, you see, Melvin and I are taking over the farm from Eli and Lovina; they have no children so when they're old we'll look after them as if we were their children." She smiled happily. "The new part where they live is like a doddy house." (A doddy house is a grandfather house where parents retire when a younger son takes over; the ideal way in which the Old Order Mennonites look after their aged.)

Whenever I stop my car at Eva's gate she runs out to greet me with her welcoming smile. Three of the previously empty bedrooms are occupied now by Joanna, Julia, and little Florence. The hired man and hired girl have two others, and Eva and Melvin sleep in the bedroom downstairs. There is a new bathroom and another large addition for laundry, soap-making, and storage.

"Will you have a cup of coffee?" Eva always asks me. She plugs in the kettle and puts on the table a dish of jamjams, cake, or a piece of pie she's just made. She rarely sits down to enjoy them with me: there's always something she must stir or take out of the oven – though she never makes me feel that her attention is divided.

Eva's kitchen has been modernized: pass-through cupboards divide the working area from the long table where meals are served. There is a dry sink at one end, a brown refrigerator and electric stove on one side, a big, shiny black cookstove on the other side, and under a window with plants blooming on the sill is a dough trough that Eva's pioneering forebears brought with them to Canada from Pennsylvania in 1801. "I've got bread rising," she shows me with her usual eagerness.

I don't know how Eva does it. Her big house is spotless and tidy; she always looks radiant. She makes all her own clothes and those of the children, and is ready to give Melvin a hand in the barn or the sugarbush if he needs her. Morning and evening she milks twenty-one cows. Every day she cooks for at least seven people; very often sixteen. In the summer she picks fruit from the trees in her yard, hoes, weeds, and harvests the bountiful garden that runs along the lane bordered by well-tended roses, hollyhocks, marigolds. She processes all the food that fills two large freezers, cans and preserves all the fruits, meats, and vegetables in hundreds of jars that stand, shining and colourful, on shelves from floor to ceiling along two basement walls.

Yet Eva always has time to be friendly, to read to the children, help her brother George at his stand at the Farmers' Market, help her sister Hannah with picking and canning. She has time to make quilts, to read books, go to church and family gatherings, and to copy her favourite recipes for me to scatter throughout this book.

Of course, Eva, blissfully accepting the disciplines of the Old Order Mennonite sect, doesn't have the distraction of television, radio, telephone, or a car; with a black bonnet over her organdie prayer cap she rides briskly – but not many miles – in a shiny black buggy behind one of Melvin's smartly groomed horses, come wind, come rain, sunshine, or snow.

All the recipes in this chapter come well recommended. I haven't tried them. I make only marmalade and one kind of relish that lasts about five years. I used to think I would starve to death in a famine if I didn't can everything canable; I now don't can anything – though I feel a twinge of guilt when I see the beautiful array of jars in Eva's basement.

EVA'S RIPE TOMATO KETCHUP
about 5 quarts

Eva doesn't like ketchup splashed all over other foods on her plate. "You can't taste anything but ketchup," she told me. But she makes it to please those who can't enjoy a meal without it.

2 crocks (about 8 quarts) tomatoes, cut up
3 quarts quartered apples

5 or 6 large onions, cut up finely

Boil together till soft then put through a ricer or sieve.

Add:
4 cups sugar
3¹/₂ cups white vinegar

²/₃ cup mixed pickling spice tied in a bag
3 or 4 tablespoons salt

Eva puts all this in her roasting pan and boils it for several hours, stirring fairly often as it thickens. She pours it into sterilized bottles and carries it to the cellar.

MOTHER'S PICKLED BEANS

For bean salad in winter Mother schnippeled (frenched) the beans, cooked them in salted water till they were barely tender, drained off the water, and while hot put the beans into sterilized jars. Meanwhile she had prepared a syrup by bringing to a rolling boil 4 cups water, 1 cup vinegar and 2 tablespoons sugar. She poured the syrup over the beans to fill the jars; she slid a knife into the jar to be sure no bubbles formed there, covered the jars tightly and stored them away in the cellar.

To make Bean Salad she drained the beans and stirred into them a blend of salt and pepper to taste, a teaspoon of sugar, and enough sour cream to give the beans a thin coating.

EVA'S LITTLE PICKLED CORN

These are the most special treat of all the pickled things in a Waterloo County housewife's storage room. The immature cobs are picked when they are about three to five inches long.

Boil as much corn as you are able to find in salt water for 15 to 20 minutes; drain and put it in sterilized jars and cover with hot syrup.

2 cups white wine vinegar
1 cup water
2 teaspoons salt

2 cups sugar
1 tablespoon celery seed and
mixed spices tied in a bag

Bring all ingredients to a boil, fish out the spice bag and pour the syrup over the corn in the jars. To make the corn look yellower put a pinch of turmeric on top of each jar before you seal it, then give it a shake.

PICKLED BEETS

As many beets as you like (or have), the smaller the better, but you can always cut big ones to whatever size you want after they've been cooked and peeled.

Wash and cook the beets till soft; put them in cold water and slip off their skins. Pack them in sterilized jars and pour over them enough syrup to cover; use the same as for the corn without the spices. If the amount given here isn't enough, make more. Lovina and Eli don't like their beets too sour: she makes her syrup with 1 cup sugar, 1 cup vinegar, 2 cups water, and $1/2$ teaspoon salt.

EVA'S PLAIN PICKLES

Wash cucumbers and let them stand in mild salt water overnight. Next day boil them in the same syrup as for corn till they change colour. Put them in sterilized jars, cover with syrup and put a piece of dill in the top of each jar. Seal.

NINE-DAY SWEET PICKLES

Eva says, "It's kind of a long-winded fuss making these but it's worth it." She loves to have a sweet pickle with her egg for breakfast.

Days 1 to 3: Put **5 quarts green cucumbers**, cut in pieces, in salt brine for 3 days. Use about **1 cup salt** in enough water to cover the pickles, stirring occasionally.

Day 4: Drain off the brine and put the pickles in clear cold water for the next 3 days, changing the water every day.

Day 7: Simmer the pickles for half an hour in weak vinegar water ($^1/_4$ vinegar to $^3/_4$ water) with a piece of alum the size of a walnut. Drain well and make a syrup of:

6 cups sugar	*Tied in a bag:*
6 cups vinegar	**2 tablespoons celery seed**
1 tablespoon salt	**2 tablespoons cinnamon buds**
	2 tablespoons allspice buds

Pour the boiling syrup over the pickles. Let stand 24 hours.

Day 8: Drain off the syrup, heat it, and pour over the pickles again.

Day 9: Repeat what you did the day before and then bottle the pickles. Wait a few weeks before you eat them. You'll be rewarded.

BABA'S DILL PICKLES
The best pickle this side of the Vistabula River

Gail Harwood, a lively and aspiring young writer, wrote to me: "As I grow older I realize that my grandmother is not getting any younger. So every two or three months I go back to the house in which I was born, back to the kitchen table where I licked the batter off the swirly-things, and back to the stories, anecdotes and folk wisdom of my grandmother. I think that hanging on to every story she tells me, and writing down every recipe, is my responsibility as a growing person and future culture-bearer.

"My family comes from that part of Lower Silesia which borders on Hungary to the south, the Ukraine to the east, and Czechoslovakia to the southwest, so cultural boundaries get a little mixed. My grandmother has no story to tell about her pickles. Suffice to say that four generations of the Harwood-Soltes-Kozak family complex have found these dills to be nothing short of hors d'oeuvres of the gods."

5 cups water
$^1/_2$ cup cider vinegar
$^1/_4$ cup salt
1 tablespoon brown sugar
8 grape leaves
2 quarts small cucumbers

8 heads and stems fresh dill
2 cloves garlic, crushed
2 teaspoons ground
  horseradish
2 teaspoons mustard seed

Boil the water, vinegar, salt, and brown sugar to make a brine. Line the bottom of pint jars with grape leaves. Halve the cucumbers lengthwise. Fill the jars to the top with the cucumbers. (Gail writes: "I take it that everyone knew to wash the cucs before cutting them. And it's also a good idea to quickly sterilize the jars in boiling water beforehand, especially if they have been collecting cobwebs in the basement all summer.") Put 2 heads and stems of dill in each jar, add garlic and seasonings. Pour the hot brine over the filled jars. Seal immediately and keep in a completely dark place for 5 to 6 weeks.

Gail says: "These pickles are in a class by themselves, above and beyond any store-bought stuff. I call myself the pickle-pusher because at least ten people at Wilfrid Laurier University have become addicted to Baba's pickles."

DELICATESSEN DILLS
1 quart

Sheila Hutton always makes 6 quarts of dills at a time, but you could start with one.

3¹/₂-inch cucumbers to fill a quart jar
2 whole branches dill
1 teaspoon pickling spice

6 cloves garlic, cut, but not too small
1²/₃ cups water
1²/₃ tablespoons pickling salt

As you pack the cucumbers into a quart jar, put in with them a sprig of dill and the pickling spice and garlic pieces; put 1 whole sprig of dill on top of the jar. Warm the water and salt till the salt is dissolved, it doesn't need to boil. Pour it over the cucumbers in the jar. Wait for several weeks before you start eating them. If you make 6 jars at a time use 4 quarts of water and 4 tablespoons of salt.

PICKLED CARROTS
2 pints

These look nice served among green pickles and they aren't hard to do.

Enough small carrots or carrot pieces to fill 2 pint jars
Water to cover
1 teaspoon salt
2 cups vinegar
1 cup water
1 cup sugar

Tied in a bag:
2 tablespoons mustard seed
3 whole cloves
1 cinnamon stick

Scrape the carrots, cover with water and boil until half done. Bring the other ingredients to a boil, put the drained carrots in the mixture and simmer till almost tender. Pack in hot sterile jars and pour the syrup over them. Seal.

LADY ROSE RELISH

Eva makes this for company. Norm makes it too with slight variations; because a large batch lasts a couple of years, she sometimes makes only half.

EVA'S VERSION:

3 quarts unpeeled
   cucumbers, sliced round
1 quart onions, chopped fine
1 large cauliflower,
   chopped fine
4 red sweet peppers,
   chopped
1 bunch celery, chopped

NORM'S VERSION:

2 quarts unpeeled
   cucumbers, chopped fine
2 quarts onions, chopped fine
1 large cauliflower,
   chopped fine
4 red peppers (1 hot,
   3 not hot)
1 bunch celery, chopped

Put all the vegetables in a porcelain or granite dish; sprinkle them with about a cupful (2 handfuls) of salt, stir to draw out the juices and let stand a few hours or overnight. Drain thoroughly.

Add:
3 cups white vinegar
3 cups water
1 tablespoon mustard seed
2 tablespoons celery seed
6 cups white sugar blended

with:
³/₄ cup flour
2 tablespoons dry mustard
2 teaspoons turmeric
2 teaspoons curry powder

Bring to a boil:
1¹/₂ quarts white wine
   vinegar
10 cups brown sugar
1 teaspoon mustard seed
   (optional)
1 teaspoon celery seed
   (optional)

Mix together:
³/₄ cup flour
2 tablespoons dry mustard
1 teaspoon turmeric

Boil all together and keep stirring so it doesn't sit on the bottom of the kettle, Eva told me. It should be quite thick when it's done and put away in sterilized jars.

Add a bit of vinegar to make a thin paste then stir it into the hot vinegar mixture; stir and boil a few minutes. Pour over the chopped vegetables and cook until thick – not long. Pour into sterilized jars, seal, and enjoy it with hot dogs, hamburgers, cold meats, or whatever.

JEAN SALTER'S PICKLING SPICE

Jean writes: "In England it is possible to buy packets of very good mixed pickling spice. To simulate this in Canada, we separated a packet out to its different components and have successfully made up our own for several years now."

15 dried red peppers
22 cloves
1 tablespoon + 1 teaspoon
  mustard seed
7 pieces of root ginger,
  each the size of a cashew nut

$^1/_3$ teaspoon blade mace
1 tablespoon + 1 teaspoon
  allspice, not powdered
3 tablespoons coriander seed

Tie them in 3 or 4 packets made with cheese cloth and drop into whatever you need them for.

JEAN'S SPICED VINEGAR

Bring malt vinegar to a boil with mixed spice (above), let stand for 1 hour before straining. The packet of spice can be used a second time.

JEAN SALTER'S RIPE TOMATO RELISH
about 4 pounds

Good to eat with cold meat or a pastie.

18 cups ripe tomatoes, peeled
  and quartered
$^1/_2$ cup onions, chopped or
  ground
$1^1/_2$ cups spiced malt vinegar
  (see above)

$1^1/_2$ tablespoons salt
$^1/_4$ teaspoon pepper
1 teaspoon paprika
$1^1/_2$ cups sugar

Cook the tomatoes and onions until a thick pulp is obtained. Add half the spiced vinegar, salt, pepper, and paprika; simmer until thick then add sugar dissolved in the remaining vinegar and cook until thick again. Bottle while hot.

JEAN SALTER'S RHUBARB RELISH

Jean told me that in England they keep picking rhubarb all summer. This is an interesting easy way to make relish.

2 cups rhubarb, cut in ¹/₂-inch
   pieces
1 cup pitted dates, chopped
1¹/₄ cups sugar
1 cup malt vinegar
1 onion, chopped

1 tablespoon salt
1 teaspoon ground ginger
1 teaspoon curry
1 tablespoon raisins,
   chopped

Put everything in a pie dish or roasting pan. Cook slowly in a 325°F oven for about 1 hour or until thick. Stir it fairly often. Pour into sterile jars and seal.

JEAN'S GREEN TOMATO RELISH

This is a great favourite in the Salter family.

3 cups green tomatoes
3 cups cooking apples
3 cups onions
1¹/₄ cups brown sugar
1¹/₂ cups raisins

1 tablespoon salt
1 teaspoon or less cayenne
1 teaspoon ground ginger
2 cups malt vinegar

Quarter the tomatoes, core the apples and peel the onions. Chop all fairly fine. Add the rest of the ingredients, bring to a boil, then simmer till thick. Seal in sterilized jars.

JEAN SALTER'S PICKLED ONIONS

Very sharp but good with cold meats and cheese. Jean writes, "I have found the perfect answer for peeling onions is to wear a snorkel mask."

Put small, whole onions in a bowl and sprinkle them with coarse salt. Leave overnight (covered with plastic wrap for self-protection). Wash off the salt next day and pack the onions in jars. Boil malt vinegar a few minutes, allow to cool before pouring over the onions to cover them. Add a good teaspoon of pickling spice (Jean's own page 54) including one red pepper per jar. Cover jars and leave to mature for several weeks.

PEPPER RELISH

Ruby says this is crisp, colourful, and it tastes good.

12 green peppers	3 pints vinegar
12 red peppers	3 cups sugar
15 onions	3 tablespoons salt
Boiling water	

Take the seeds and stems from the peppers and peel the onions. Put all through a food chopper then cover with boiling water; let stand a few minutes, drain and repeat the process. Put the drained onions and peppers in a kettle with the vinegar, sugar, and salt; cook gently for 15 minutes then put in sterilized jars and enjoy it all winter.

APPLE AND TOMATO CHUTNEY

At Rundles Restaurant in Stratford, the chef made this easy chutney to go with a meat pie. It's good with other things too.

2 quarts (4 pounds) red tomatoes	2 teaspoons peppercorns
4 onions, sliced	5 teaspoons salt
2 quarts (4 pounds) apples	1 tablespoon ground ginger
1 quart white wine vinegar	2¼ cups firmly packed brown sugar

Peel and slice the tomatoes and onions. Peel, core, and slice the apples, not too finely. Put sliced onions and tomatoes and apples into a large bowl; add the vinegar, peppercorns, salt, ground ginger and sugar; leave overnight or 4 to 5 hours. Pour into a pan over medium heat, stir until it is boiling, then simmer until thick and pulpy, about 1¼ hours. Don't boil it to a mush, the apples should keep their shape. Pour into sterilized jars and keep in a cold place.

PLUM CHUTNEY
3 to 4 quarts, but put in smaller jars

The 83-year-old friend who gave me this recipe told me that she and her mother and her grandmother would never be without it. The original recipe calls for a peck of plums. I've reduced it.

4 quarts plums	**1 tablespoon ground cloves**
7 cups brown sugar	**³/₄ cup white vinegar**
1 tablespoon allspice	**Salt to taste**
1 tablespoon cinnamon	

Gently boil all the ingredients, removing the plum pits as they start to float. Stir till it's as thick as you like, about 1 hour. Pour into sterilized jars and seal. It's delicious with meat or with toast.

KASHI CARTER'S BRANDIED PEACHES

These are a gourmet's delight. Every summer Kashi makes a crockful for special occasions.

6-quart basket peaches, peeled but not pitted   **5 to 10 pounds white sugar**

Put a layer of peaches in a stoneware crock, cover with sugar till you can't see the peaches, then another layer of peaches covered again with sugar until all the peaches have been put in and covered. Place a plate on the inside of the crock to keep the peaches down. Stretch plastic wrap over the top of the crock as a seal – you don't want those little summer fruit flies getting at this. Put on the lid of the crock and leave it on a window sill till Christmas. Serve the peaches whole with a meat course, preferably pork or chicken. The juice is good poured over ham, as a relish. Your guests will be flattered if you serve them these.

ADA'S BRANDIED RAISINS

Pleasant to use as a sauce on a number of things like ice cream or bland puddings.

| 2 cups raisins | 6 inches of cinnamon stick |
| 1/2 cup dark brown sugar | Brandy to cover |

Put all into a jar and don't touch it for 3 months. Better put it on the bottom shelf of a cupboard and surprise yourself with it one winter day.

DEVON TUTTI FRUITTI

Delicious on ice cream and will redeem any pudding. This one could be kept going for years, if you aren't greedy.

Prepare a large stone jar with a tight-fitting lid. Keep it in a reasonably cool place where no sneakers will get at it.

| 3 cups (1 pound) most small fruits as they come into season | 1 bottle of decent brandy (will preserve 5 pounds of fruit) |
| 2 cups sugar to 3 cups fruit | |

Begin with strawberries. Put 3 cups of firm berries in the stone jar; add 2 cups of sugar and then pour 1 bottle of brandy over them. Carefully tie down with double paper and string. (That should discourage intruders.)

When the raspberries come on, open the jar gently, stir well to the bottom. Add 3 cups raspberries and 2 cups of sugar and tie down again.

Follow with cherries (stoned) and do the same.

What's next? Plums, cut in half, peaches, coarsely sliced, apricots? (Don't use pippy or seedy fruit.) And remember when you have over 15 cups (5 pounds) of fruit in the jar you'll need another bottle of brandy.

Wait till Christmas to use it. Some people make it with rum instead of brandy. *Joyeux noël!*

BITTER ORANGE MARMALADE

Win Simpson comes from Scotland and this is her mother's recipe. Win writes: "I have written this out innumerable times for all the friends who think it is great. There is one snag: it can only be made once a year when the bitter oranges are in, which is usually the end of January or early February. I make two or three batches to last me through the year.''

11 bitter (marmalade)	**16 cups sugar**
oranges	**4¹/₂ quarts cold water**
2 or 3 lemons	

Wipe the oranges and lemons, cut them in half, take out the seeds, squeeze out the juice and slice or shred the peel finely. Soak the shreds if desired. (I usually prepare the fruit and leave to soak overnight then make the marmalade the next day.) Put water, shreds, and juice into a preserving pan and bring slowly to the boil. Put the membrane and seeds in a muslin bag to be boiled along with the juice, etc., then remove it before adding the sugar. Continue to boil until rather less than half the contents of the pan has boiled away. Add the sugar and stir until dissolved, then boil rapidly 8 to 10 minutes. Allow the marmalade to cool for 10 minutes, stirring occasionally before pouring into hot sterilized jars.

CHARLOTTE BUDGE'S PUMPKIN JAM

Pumpkin jam is a favourite in Neil's Harbour where the soil is too shallow for gardens and everything but fish must be brought in. I wrote Charlotte's recipe as she told it to me.

"Take half a big pumpkin, peeled, and with all the stuff took out of the middle. Cut it in strips and then in little chunks – they shrivel when they boil. Cut up 2 lemons, throw in an orange cut up the same way. Measure what you got and put in twice as much sugar. Let it stand overnight and in the morning it's watery. Put it on the stove to simmer for maybe 3 hours, but watch it and give it a stir now and then. Don't let it boil too quick any time or it will soak up all the juice.

"When it starts to turn a good orangey colour and the pumpkin gets clear so you can see through it and the syrup gets heavy when you try it on a dish, then it's done. And roight noice to have in the winter toime."

4

Meat, Fowl and Fish

When Peter and my niece Barbie, with their children Kennie and Patti, went to live in the fantastic six-level house that Peter built on a hilltop in the country, they wanted to do all the things they couldn't do in the city. They bred rabbits, they kept chickens, two ducks, guinea hens, beehives, a cat that had kittens, a dog, and a budgie. One day Peter went to an auction sale and came home with a cow named Agnes.

When he bid on Agnes, Peter wasn't told that she was the second wildest of the herd of 150 cattle being auctioned and that she was a bit pregnant with her fourth calf.

They kept Agnes in the garage and Barbie tried to make friends with her by offering her fragrant fresh grass; Agnes bunted Barbie and threw her six feet in the air. Barbie didn't try again to win Agnes' affection. She told me, "All we wanted was a gentle family cow and we got this wild thing that won't let you love her."

Peter built a shed for Agnes in the field they could see from the house. And there she produced Curly, a stalky white bull calf. No one dared go near the field where Agnes was grazing.

One night Agnes broke through the fence; with Curly following, she crossed the road and ran down to the Wagners' farm
where she kept circling the house and the barn till Peter and
Elmer Wagner finally cornered her. Next day a truck came
and took Agnes away to the butcher.

Barbie didn't mind the neat packages that came back to be
put in the freezer but Agnes' unwrapped liver, tongue, and
heart, placed on the kitchen counter, did give her a shiver.

All winter Peter and Barbie and Kennie and Patti ate Agnes.
There seemed to be so much of her. Barbie kept asking for
tough beef recipes; she explained, "Agnes is at her best in a
stew."

A year later they were still eating Agnes. Though most of
her place in the freezer was taken by Curly, there was still
some of Agnes. Barbie said, "We finally just ground her up."

AGNES-AT-HER-BEST

Barbie can put this stew in her oven, run Kennie into town for
his music lesson, and drive home to find Agnes simmering gently, tender at last.

2 pounds stewing beef	**2 to 4 carrots, sliced**
¼ cup flour	**1½ cups hot water**
¼ teaspoon each thyme, basil, celery seed	**2 bouillon cubes or equivalent**
⅛ teaspoon sage	**1 teaspoon Worcestershire sauce**
1¼ teaspoons salt	**¼ cup dry wine**
Pinch pepper	
4 onions, sliced	
6 potatoes, thinly sliced or chunked	

Dredge the pieces of meat in the flour mixed with herbs and
seasonings. In a roasting pan or casserole with a tight lid, put
layers of vegetables and meat, sprinkle on the seasoned flour
left from the dredging and pour in the blended liquids. Cover
tightly and bake at 325°F for 3 or 4 hours.

Barbie says if you don't like herbs you can omit them but
they seemed to suit Agnes.

RUNDLES CARBONNADE OF BEEF
4 portions

John Walker, the *chef de cuisine* of Rundles Restaurant in Stratford, prepared this in no time while we watched him. Best of all we ate it later with vegetables and fresh Irish Soda Bread (page 199). John told us some of the best French dishes are the simplest.

1 pound lean beef
1 bottle lager beer
Salt and pepper
3 or 4 tablespoons flour

2 tablespoons dripping or
  lard
1 cup finely sliced onion
2 tablespoons sugar

Cut the meat into half-inch slices – no thinner or they'll disappear. Marinate the meat in the beer overnight or for several hours. Strain off the beer – but keep it – and season the beef with salt and pepper. Pass it through the flour and sear it all round in hot dripping. Use tongs to place it in a casserole. Don't sear all the meat at one time; pay attention to each piece. Sauté the onions in the hot fat. Spread them over the meat in the baking dish, pour in the beer and the sugar, cover with a tight-fitting lid and simmer gently in a moderate oven, 350°F, for about 2 hours. Put the casserole on a tray to catch any boiling over.

If you've kept a piece of beef in your freezer longer than you should have, make a thick savoury gravy to give it more flavour.

If you don't have a timer on your oven to warn you to look after what's in there, use an alarm clock.

SCHNITZEL STEW

1½ pounds round steak
1 large onion, chopped
4 tablespoons butter
4 or 5 carrots, sliced
4 medium potatoes, sliced
1½ cups boiling beef stock or
  bouillon

Salt and pepper
1 tablespoon ketchup
1 tablespoon flour
½ cup sweet or sour cream
Parsley

Have the meat cut in 4 pieces a half-inch thick. Brown the meat and onion lightly in the butter. Add the carrots and potatoes. Pour on the beef stock, season, cover and simmer on top of the stove until the meat is tender, about 30 minutes. Blend together the ketchup, flour, and cream. Stir into the stew and bring briefly to a boil. Garnish with parsley and serve.

POT ROAST ON RICE WITH VEGETABLES AND HERBS
for 6 or more

Agnes Horst says, "I like a dinner where I can have the whole kaboodle in the oven ahead of time so I can do quilt-patching till the last minute."

4 to 5 pound pot roast
1 tablespoon flour
1 teaspoon salt
¼ teaspoon pepper
1 teaspoon mixed crumbled herbs (marjoram, basil, thyme)
Drippings or suet
2 or more onions, sliced thin
1 carrot per person, sliced

1 stem celery, sliced
½ cup peas or green beans, cut up
Half a green pepper (optional)
1 cup raw brown rice
½ teaspoon mixed herbs
2 cups boiling water or bouillon

Mix together the flour, seasonings, and 1 teaspoon herbs; rub thoroughly into the cut surfaces and sides of the meat. Heat the dripping or suet in a frying pan and sear all the surfaces of the meat, turning carefully so you don't let out the juices. In a deep roasting pan, or clay baker, spread the sliced vegetables and the rice mixed with the ½ teaspoon herbs. Pour in the boiling water and put the seared roast on top, settling it into the rice to get the lid to fit tightly. Put it in a 300°F oven and bake for 2 to 4 hours, adding more boiling water if necessary. The roast should be tender and tasty. A green salad completes the meal.

Stan and Harvey Hutton are twins who spent much of their childhood at our house across the street from theirs when I lived in Kitchener. They climbed our apple trees, had fun shows in our garage, made cookies in the kitchen, helped me do jigsaw puzzles, told me about their girl friends, and once threw over-ripe tomatoes at our white front door. They cleaned them off while listening contritely to a lecture on loyalty. Stanley is now married to Sheila; last time they visited me they brought with them their beautiful little son and a filebox of recipes. This is their favourite.

BRAISED SHORT RIBS IN A BEER OR WINE SAUCE
4 servings

You won't forget this: it has flavour.

1 tablespoon butter	2 bay leaves
1 tablespoon oil	1 teaspoon sugar
2 or more short ribs, cut into serving pieces	1 cup beer or red wine
	1 tablespoon corn starch
3/4 cup sliced onions	1/4 cup water
1 teaspoon salt	3 tablespoons sour cream
1/4 teaspoon pepper	
1/2 teaspoon whole allspice (optional)	

In a heavy pot or Dutch oven, brown the ribs on all sides in the butter and oil. Add the onions, seasonings, bay leaves, sugar, and beer or wine. Cover and cook over low heat 1 1/2 hours, or until tender. Remove the meat, skim the fat from the pan juices, stir in the blended corn starch and water. Cook over low heat till thickened, stir in cream and taste for seasoning. Serve with potatoes and/or dumplings, or noodles and vegetables.

LENDENBRATEN Sirloin Roast
serves 6

Wait till you taste the thick rich gravy that comes with this roast.

3 to 4 pound sirloin roast	1/2 cup boiling water
Salt and pepper	2 tablespoons flour
4 tablespoons butter	1 cup sour cream
1 onion, sliced	1/2 cup white wine (optional)
1 tomato, sliced	

Season the roast with salt and pepper; brown on all sides in the butter. Slightly brown the onion at the same time – or remove the meat temporarily till you brown it. Put meat, onion, and tomato in the pan, add boiling water, and put the pan in a 400°F oven for about 30 to 40 minutes, basting frequently. Remove the meat from the pan when it has reached the desired rareness – or doneness. To the drippings add flour, sour cream, and wine. Cook together briefly till the gravy is thickened. Slice the roast and pour the sauce over the servings.

BRAISED BRISKET
4 servings

My old friend Pop Swallow often said, "The tastiest part of the cow is the brisket." Layers of lean and fat give it a great flavour. Short ribs are almost as good. Get your butcher to saw the bones in 3-inch lengths. You'll need about 4 pounds for 4 people.

4 pounds brisket or short ribs	1 or 2 onions, chopped
4 tablespoons flour	1 stem of celery, chopped
2¹/₂ teaspoons salt	1¹/₂ cups boiling beef broth or
Black pepper to taste	consommé
¹/₂ teaspoon rosemary or thyme, finely crumbled.	4 to 6 carrots, cut in pieces
2 tablespoons beef or bacon drippings	

Dredge the brisket or ribs with the combined flour, seasonings, and herbs. Lightly cook the onion and celery in the drippings, then remove to a heavy pot or casserole with a lid. Brown the ribs on all sides in the same fat. Put the ribs in the pot with the vegetables, add the boiling broth and cover tightly. Bake in a 300°F oven for 2 or 3 hours, skimming off excess fat before thickening the juices by stirring in the seasoned flour (left from the dredging) mixed with cold water. Simmer till it thickens and serve with the meat and vegetables.

BRAISED DILL RIBS WITH CARROT GRAVY

Carol Dawson, the pretty sister of the Hutton twins, also used to come to our house every day; now she has a husband, Paul, and three little Dawsons, for whom she likes to cook this delicious Dutch oven meal, which can be easily expanded for company.

Short ribs (however many
  you need)
2 tablespoons salad oil
1 cup water
1 onion, chopped
1 cup grated carrots
2 tablespoons cider vinegar
1 tablespoon salt
$^1/_4$ teaspoon pepper
1 teaspoon dill seed
$^1/_2$ pound wide noodles
1 tablespoon butter
2 tablespoons all-purpose
  flour
Water

Brown the ribs on all sides in the oil; pour off the fat. Put all the ribs in a Dutch oven or heavy pot, add 1 cup water, onions, carrots, vinegar, salt, and pepper. Cover and simmer over low heat for 2 to $2^1/_2$ hours till the meat is fork-tender. During the last hour of cooking, add the dill seed. Boil the noodles in salted water, drain and stir in butter. Arrange noodles on a platter with ribs on top and keep warm in the oven. Skim the fat from the mixture in the Dutch oven, blend the flour with some water and stir into the mixture to make gravy, stirring until it thickens. Pour over the noodles or serve from gravy bowl.

CORNED BEEF

While my dermatologist, Dr. D. J. Grant, was removing a blemish from the bridge of my nose he talked with great enthusiasm about his way of preparing corned beef. Though his office was filled with waiting patients, he sat down and wrote the recipe for me.

Put a nice piece of brisket into an enamel or earthenware pot with enough water to cover it (so you'll know how much water you need). Remove the brisket temporarily and into the water stir:

2 tablespoons saltpetre
$^1/_3$ cup salt
$^1/_2$ a bud (approx. 5 cloves)
  of garlic
2 tablespoons mixed pickling
  spice

Drop the brisket back into the mixture, cover it and put it into your fridge for eleven days, turning it over every day. Then discard the marinade, put enough fresh water to cover the brisket into a cooking pot and simmer it for about four hours, till it is deliciously tender. If you want to add cabbage during the last half hour of cooking, Dr. Grant told me, that's good, too.

BEEF TONGUE

Probably the most delicate, tender, economical part of the animal. There is no waste except the skin which your dog might enjoy. You can make soup of the stock, serve the tongue hot or cold, with vegetables or a sauce. Mother used to pickle a tongue every Christmas time, my friend Connie sliced hers and set it in tomato aspic. I'm content to eat it with vegetables cooked in the broth.

Put a tongue in enough water to cover, season it with salt, pepper and whatever else you like – but if you use the broth for soup later you must be discreet. When the tongue has simmered long enough to be tender, a couple of hours, take it out of the stock and peel it. The skin comes off easily. (Give it to your dog before it dries and turns hard.)

BEVVY'S CANNED GROUND BEEF

A delicious Old Order Mennonite way of using ground beef when you butcher and have a lot.

15 pounds ground beef	**36 crackers**
$\frac{1}{2}$ cup salt	**3 or more cups water**
4 slices of bread	**4 eggs**
1 cup oatmeal	

Mix all this together very well and then pack firmly in jars with good screwing lids. Put the jars loosely lidded, in a large kettle in water up to the lid and boil gently for 3 hours – or less. Cool and fasten the jars securely and store them in a cool, dark place till you are ready to use them. You may have a problem cutting the meat out of the jars in neat, quarter-inch slices.

GRILLED CUTLETS, CHOPS OR STEAKS

At Rundles Restaurant in Stratford you'll be served the best lamb cutlets you've ever eaten. John Walker, the *chef de cuisine*, seasons half-inch cutlets with salt and pepper from a pepper mill, he brushes them lightly on both sides with oil or melted fat, places them on the greased bars of the grill, not too close to high heat, and lets them cook and brown for 5 minutes before turning them with tongs to do the same on the other side. John says about any cutlets, chops, or steaks: "Once you start cooking them, keep your hands off, don't fidget, don't turn till one side is done. Give the poor things a chance; you're not letting the meat cook if you keep turning it." (The same advice applies to barbecuing.)

John serves his cutlets, chops or steaks on very hot plates with quarter-inch slices of parsley, herb or garlic butter melting over them. And that really flavours them.

John Walker blends butter with various seasonings to give zest to meats, fish, vegetables and breads: he blends, shapes, wraps, labels, freezes, and slices it as he needs it.

PARSLEY BUTTER

Great with grilled steak, fish, asparagus, broccoli, anything that requires little cooking.

¹/₄ **cup butter**	**Salt and pepper**
Juice of ¹/₄ **lemon**	
¹/₄ **to** ¹/₂ **teaspoon finely chopped parsley**	

Combine all the ingredients with softened butter and blend well. Shape into a roll one inch in diameter. Place in wet greaseproof paper and let harden in the fridge – or keep it frozen till you want it.

HERB BUTTER

Very nice with lamb, zucchini, etc.
Made the same way as Parsley Butter but using a blend of thyme, oregano, and basil; you could vary the herbs, but don't use sage on lamb, save it for pork or goose.

GARLIC BUTTER

Great on steak or to make Garlic Bread.
Crush a clove or two of garlic till very soft before blending
with the butter.

OTHER BUTTERS

To the butter, lemon juice, salt and pepper, add very finely
chopped green peppers, or black olives, or anchovies, or
caviar, mushrooms, to give different flavours to various foods.
But you must use them discreetly.

RABBIT

When Patti and Kennie stopped raising rabbits they gave the
few that were left to neighbours who soon after invited them to
come over for dinner. Kennie passed his plate for a second
helping, "That's really good chicken," he said.

"That's not chicken," his hostess informed him. "That's
your old black rabbit."

Kennie and Patti looked at each other, dropped their forks,
burst into tears and ran home.

Perhaps you'd better make rabbit dishes with chicken; no
one seems to mind eating chicken. I don't have the heart to add
to the rabbit recipes I gave in *Food That Really Schmecks*.

GLAZED HAM

Buy the type and size of ham you like, put it in a roasting pan
and heat it in a 350°F oven for an hour – unless it is an uncooked one, then you must bake it 25 minutes to the pound – until it is done. Remove it from the oven and cut off the rind with
shears or a sharp knife. Score the fat diagonally about ⅛ inch
deep to make a diamond pattern. Spread over the ham
whichever glaze you prefer. Increase the oven heat to 400°F
and return the ham to the oven until the glaze is browned.

Don't apologize for serving small portions of meat, at today's
prices people are lucky to have meat. Give them more
vegetables.

BROWN SUGAR GLAZE WITH CLOVES

A lot of whole cloves   2 teaspoons dry mustard
1 cup brown sugar   A little ham fat

Stud the corners of the diamond pattern with the cloves. Combine the sugar, mustard, and enough of the ham fat from the roasting pan to make spreading easy. Spread it over the ham, return it to the 400°F oven and bake until the sugar forms a glaze.

BEER AND BROWN SUGAR GLAZE

1 cup brown sugar   1 teaspoon dry mustard
3 tablespoons breadcrumbs $^{1}/_{2}$ cup beer

Mix the sugar, breadcrumbs, mustard, and enough beer to make a paste that spreads easily over the ham. Return it to a 400°F oven and bake until a glaze is formed.

APPLESAUCE GLAZE

1 cup applesauce $^{1}/_{4}$ teaspoon nutmeg
$^{2}/_{3}$ cup brown sugar $^{1}/_{2}$ cup beer or ham dripping
$^{1}/_{2}$ teaspoon cinnamon Cloves (optional)

Mix all the ingredients together and spread over the ham which you may or may not have studded first with cloves. Return to the 350°F oven and bake 30 minutes longer.

CIDER AND HONEY GLAZED SPARERIBS, PORK HOCKS, AND PIGS TAILS

Glazed with cider and honey they are shiny, brown, and succulent.

As many ribs, hocks, or tails as you need for 6 people (a lot)
3 cups cider $^{1}/_{2}$ teaspoon thyme
$^{1}/_{2}$ to 1 cup honey $1^{1}/_{2}$ teaspoons dry mustard
2 tablespoons lemon juice   2 teaspoons sage
1 tablespoon salt

Spread the ribs, hocks, or tails in a large shallow pan; blend all the other ingredients and pour over the meat to marinate in a cool place for several hours or overnight, turning occasionally. Remove the meat from the marinade, saving the liquid. Spread the meat in a large baking pan, the less overlapping the better; put the pan in a 350 °F oven, set your timer for 20 minutes, then generously baste the meat with the marinade. Baste every 20 minutes for 1½ hours when all should be tender and the marinade turned into an irresistible glaze.

Of course these should be served with boiled or mashed potatoes and sauerkraut.

MARY ANN MARTIN'S BREADED PORK CHOPS

Prepare these ahead of time and cook them while your guests are breathing in their delicious aroma.

4 or 5 lean pork chops
1 cup white vinegar or wine
Flour to dredge
1 egg, slightly beaten
½ teaspoon salt
Pepper
½ cup fine biscuit or breadcrumbs

¼ teaspoon garlic powder
1 teaspoon dried parsley or herbs
1½ tablespoons oil
1½ tablespoons bacon fat or butter

Marinate the chops in the vinegar or wine for an hour at room temperature, or overnight in the fridge, turning several times. Drain and pat dry. Dredge the chops with flour, then dip in the slightly beaten egg, adding a bit of water to the egg if you need it. Combine the crumbs and seasonings. Roll the chops in the crumbs, coating them well on all sides. Let stand a few minutes, or put them in the fridge till you are ready to cook them. Heat the oil in a heavy skillet, adding bacon fat or butter for a better flavour. Put in the chops and brown nicely on both sides. Lower the heat, cover and cook slowly for about 45 minutes, or cover and put in a slow oven (250° to 300°F) until tender, adding a bit of water if necessary to prevent sticking. Turn the chops once. Uncover the last 5 minutes of cooking to crisp the neat golden coating.

BRINKEY'S SWEET AND SOUR PORK CHOPS

Ruby's friend pours this sauce over pork chops; Ruby says it's good on other meats, too.

¹/₂ cup white sugar
¹/₂ cup brown sugar
¹/₂ can tomato soup, undiluted

¹/₄ cup vinegar, lemon juice, or white wine
Pinch of chili powder

Blend all ingredients together, pour over chops, and simmer in a 300 °F oven till the chops are tender.

BROWN SUGAR AND BEER GLAZED PORK HOCKS
6 servings

Pork hocks are usually a bargain and there is no more tender, succulent meat than there is under that glazed brown exterior.

6 pork hocks (or one per person)
2 onions
2 cloves garlic
2 teaspoons salt
Pinch of pepper
2 bay leaves
6 cloves

3 tablespoons wine or lemon juice
Water
Glaze:
1 cup brown sugar
2 teaspoons dry mustard
¹/₄ cup fat from the hocks
¹/₂ cup beer or broth

Put the hocks in a kettle with onions, garlic, salt, pepper, bay leaves, cloves, and wine with enough water to cover the hocks. Bring to a boil, cover and simmer for about 2 hours, or until the hocks are very tender.

Arrange the hocks in a baking pan, mix together the sugar, mustard, dripping, and enough beer or broth to make a spreading mixture. Coat the hocks all round and broil until crisp, turning them to broil on all sides. Or simply put in a 400 °F oven and let nature take its course – but watch it.

And you should serve these with potatoes and sauerkraut.

TOAD IN THE HOLE

To put in 6 individual dishes or 1 large dish.

Batter:

1 cup flour

Salt and pepper

1 egg

1 cup milk

6 sausages or more

1 sliced onion or more

3 tablespoons butter

$\frac{1}{4}$ pound mushrooms

$\frac{1}{2}$ pound tomatoes, sliced

Mix the batter until it is smooth and shiny and let stand while you proceed. Put a sausage in each ovenproof dish – or put all in 1 large dish – and cook in a 400 °F oven for 10 minutes while you sauté the onion in butter; add the mushrooms to the onions, then the tomatoes, and cook for a few minutes. Spread the vegetables over the sausages and sprinkle with salt and pepper. Pour the batter over the vegetables and bake at 400 °F for about 30 minutes.

CHICKENS

Have you seen how they raise those flabby little pale grey chickens that you buy at the supermarkets? I can't bear to go into one of the long metal windowless buildings where, I'm told, they have thousands of chickens in wire cages hardly large enough for a bird to turn around because that might exercise muscles and toughen them instead of making them tender and fat so they won't take long to cook.

Only occasionally you can go to the farmers' market and find a firm yellow-skinned hen that's been brought up in a yard where it could wander all day and eat protein-packed grubs. Those are the chickens you can roast or boil with great expectation of flavour and a rich chicken stock to make soup or milk gravy. Those were the chickens of my childhood.

The modern anaemic cage-grown chickens have to get their flavour from whatever you cook with them: honey, orange juice, sour cream, wine, lots of butter, herbs, vegetables, paprika, soy sauce, mayonnaise, you name it. And with plenty of reinforcement they can be very good, too, inexpensive and easy to prepare.

EASY WAYS TO COOK CHICKEN

I often spend so much time looking up recipes that I don't have time to try them. I resort to coating chicken pieces in one of the following ways, and because it is so quick, so easy, and so good I wonder why I ever bother with any other. I sprinkle salt and pepper all over the chicken pieces, dip them in flour or crumbs or coat them as I choose, put them skin side up in a buttered baking pan with a lid, cover for the first half hour in 350°F oven, have a look and dab some more coating mixture over each piece then bake uncovered at 300°F for about half an hour longer, till the chicken is tender, golden, and crusty.

BUTTERED CHICKEN

Melt butter and coat the seasoned chicken generously before you bake it.

CHICKEN WITH MAYONNAISE

Coat the chicken with mayonnaise. Dip it in fine breadcrumbs as well, if you like.

CHICKEN WITH HERBS

Sprinkle herbs over coated chicken–it's as simple as that.

SOY CHICKEN

Beat a cupful of soy sauce and ¼ cup cooking oil together then dip in the chicken.

HONEY CHICKEN

Drizzle enough honey, brown sugar, and soy sauce to coat it lightly.

CHICKEN WITH ORANGE

Dip the chicken in butter, sprinkle with herbs then drizzle the pieces with orange juice.

Meat, Fowl and Fish / 75

CHICKEN IN CREAM WITH WINE (AND HERBS)

Dredge the chicken pieces in flour, spoon over them a cupful of sweet or sour cream diluted with ¹/₂ cup sherry or water. Add mushrooms if you like and/or sprinkle with herbs if you can't live without them.

CREAM OF MUSHROOM CHICKEN

Dilute a tin of mushroom soup with 1 cup of cream, pour it over the chicken, sprinkle it with paprika. When it's tender, sprinkle it also with parsley.

RUNDLES POULET SAUTÉ CHASSEUR
(Huntsmen's Chicken)

The *chef de cuisine*, John Walker, said this is a good way to put some flavour into those watery, limp pieces of chicken that have never seen the light of day.

1 frying chicken, or pieces
¹/₄ cup butter
Salt and pepper
¹/₄ cup chopped shallots or green onions
1 cup sliced or button mushrooms

¹/₂ cup dry white wine
1 cup demi glace or chicken broth
1 cup peeled and chopped fresh tomatoes
Chopped parsley and tarragon

Melt the butter in a pan over a fairly hot fire. Season the pieces of chicken and place them in the pan. Cook to a golden brown on all sides, cover with a lid and cook for a few more minutes. Lift the pieces with tongs into an entrée dish that can be put in the oven. Drop the shallots into the pan, cover and cook for a few minutes without browning them; add the mushrooms, cover and cook gently for 3 to 4 minutes. Drain off the fat, add the wine (and the demi glace if you have any – or chicken broth or bouillon). Add the tomatoes and simmer for 5 minutes. Correct the seasoning, pour the whole bit over the chicken in the entrée dish and put it into a 300°F oven until the chicken is tender or till you're ready to serve it. Sprinkle it then with parsley and tarragon.

Sorry about not giving you the demi glace recipe: John makes the French sauces so easily: by adding certain ingredients to other sauces he comes up with a new one. A demi glace is a derivative of sauce espagnole. (You'll have to go to Rundles to get a real Poulet Sauté Chasseur.) The day of our eighth lesson John made and served us Lobster Soufflé Suidoise, Poulet Chasseur with a green salad, Irish soda bread, and for dessert Gateaux Mille Fuille. The meal was a triumph. The French really care enough about food to spend time preparing it. Whenever it's served to me I make great resolutions, but at home my laziness overcomes me and I'm happy with pot pie.

CHICKEN POT PIE WITH PARSLEY DUMPLINGS
6 to 8 servings

Try to find a nice plump little slug-fed hen to give this delicate dish its flavour.

1 hen
Salted water
Much parsley

Peas, carrots, and one little onion, minced

Cut the precious little bird into serving pieces and put it in a pot; cover it with boiling salted water, or chicken bouillon if the hen is anaemic, let it simmer till tender. Drop in the finely cut vegetables while you stir up the dough for the *dumplings*.

2 cups flour
1 teaspoon salt
3 teaspoons baking powder
3 tablespoons shortening

3 tablespoons parsley, cut fine
¹/₂ teaspoon crushed rosemary (optional)
1 cup of milk, approximately

Sift together the flour, salt, and baking powder, cut in the shortening till it is crumbly, stir in the parsley and rosemary. Add enough milk to make a dough that can be dropped from a wet tablespoon into the boiling stew, letting the dumplings rest on the hen. Cover tightly, turn the heat down to simmer, and cook without looking for 15 minutes. Then behold! Lovely light dumplings. Sprinkle them generously with parsley and serve them with great satisfaction.

POULET ENDORMI (Chicken on a Bed of Rice)
enough for 9, if you have a big enough pot

I made this one day when Pierre and Janet were coming for dinner; the next night I had it again with Lorna and Ross; the night after that with Pam and Gerry. You can't trust rice: it never knows when to stop.

As many chicken pieces as you think you need (I added some after my second dinner)
1¹/₂ teaspoons salt
¹/₂ teaspoon pepper
Sprinkle of paprika
2 tablespoons cooking oil
2 tablespoons butter
1 cup sliced onion
1 clove garlic, minced
2 to 4 cups chicken broth or bouillon
1 cup white wine (in place of as much broth)

3 to 4 cups tomatoes, canned, frozen or fresh
1 bay leaf
¹/₂ teaspoon thyme
¹/₂ teaspoon tarragon
¹/₂ teaspoon oregano
1 cup sliced celery
1 cup sliced carrot
1 cup peas
1 cup raw rice
¹/₂ cup chopped parsley

Season the chicken with salt, pepper, and paprika. Heat the oil and butter in a frying pan and brown the pieces of chicken on all sides. Remove and keep warm. In the skillet put the onion and garlic, sauté until the onion is tender. Add 2 cups of the chicken broth and wine, and stir to loosen all the brown bits in the pan. Put in the tomatoes, and bring to a boil, then stir in all the rest of the ingredients, except the parsley which should be added just before serving. Scrape all into a baking dish, put the chicken on top, cover tightly, put the dish in a 325°F oven and forget about it for almost an hour, though it might be wise to look in at half time to add more chicken broth – rice being the greedy thing that it is. The dish will be fuller than it was when you started. It's great to have enough for three meals, or enough for nine people at one. Don't underestimate the chicken.

With this I served Pierre's favourite Schnippled Bean Salad.

BRUSSELS OR BROCCOLI DIVAN
for 7 or 8

This is a great company dish.

Chicken or turkey pieces
5 cups boiling water
2 teaspoons salt

1 quart Brussels sprouts or broccoli

Sauce:

¼ cup butter
3 tablespoons flour
2 cups hot broth or milk
½ teaspoon curry powder (optional)
1 cup grated cheddar cheese

1 cup sour cream
3 tablespoons dry sherry or white wine
1 teaspoon Worcestershire sauce

Simmer the chicken or turkey pieces in salted water until tender. Cook the sprouts or broccoli in salted water until just tender, then drain. Make the sauce: melt the butter, blend in the flour and curry; vigorously stir in the hot broth or milk, stirring until the sauce is thickened and smooth. Bone the cooked meat. Arrange the vegetables on a deep heat-proof serving platter or flat-bottomed casserole, sprinkle them lightly with half of the cheese, arrange the chicken slices over the top. Combine the sour cream with the sauce, stir in the sherry and Worcestershire sauce, pour it over the chicken. Sprinkle with the remaining cheese. Place about 5 inches below high heat in a preheated broiler until browned and bubbly or put in a 300°F oven till your guests have finished their apéritifs.

Norm's soy fried rice (**PAGE 83**) and squash, baked and whipped with butter and cream, make this a memorable meal.

CHICKEN VELVET

This is a super smooth way to serve all your nutriments in one dish. You can prepare it in advance and have it simmering gently to tantalize your guests as they arrive.

3 or 4 pound chicken or pieces

2 tablespoons cooking oil
2 tablespoons butter

Heat the oil and butter in a large frying pan and sauté the pieces of chicken over medium heat until browned on all sides. Meanwhile, in your blender put

2 medium tomatoes, quartered, or 1 cup canned	**1 clove garlic (optional)**
1¹/₂ teaspoons salt	**¹/₄ teaspoon pepper**
1 medium onion, quartered	**1 carrot, coarsely diced**
	1 stalk of celery, cut up

Blend for a few seconds then add:

6 sprigs of parsley	**1 cup sliced mushrooms**
¹/₄ cup dry sherry, white wine, or lemon juice	**(optional) and *not* put in the blender**
¹/₂ teaspoon rosemary	
¹/₄ teaspoon tarragon (optional)	

Cover and blend on high speed for 30 seconds. Pour over the browned chicken in the frying pan, cover and simmer for 45 minutes or until the chicken is tender, stirring occasionally. Add a cupful or two of sliced mushrooms, if you like, half an hour before serving time. Pour all into a large hot serving dish and be prepared to ladle the chicken and that lovely sauce over cooked rice, potatoes, or noodles. Serve with a green salad.

FREEZING FOWL

Wrap individual servings of fowl in foil, put all the wrapped pieces in a freezer bag. Don't let them get lost by themselves in the freezer or you won't find them till your annual cleanout.

ROAST CHICKEN, TURKEY, DUCK AND GOOSE – WITH STUFFING

If you have a really good way of roasting fowl stick with it, as I do. In *Schmecks* I've told about the tried and traditional way my family has always done it and I know no better way. Trying fancy, difficult recipes might have wonderful results but I don't roast a big bird very often and I like our good family way.

FOR LONERS OR COUPLES

You'll eat a lot better if you have a little broil, bake and toast oven that stands on your kitchen counter. Often you wouldn't bother to heat up your big oven to bake one serving of chicken and a potato, but if you have a small oven you'll find yourself able to cook all sorts of things in small quantities so much more quickly and just as effectively as you would in a big one.

The oven heats up almost instantly, you can bake a potato in half to three-quarters of an hour, as well as a piece of chicken. You can make a meat loaf, broil chops, steak, cutlets. You can even make half a dozen muffins. You can bake a soufflé, a casserole, reheat buns, biscuits, and vegetables. You can make toast. If you have one you'll think of all sorts of ways to use it. I got mine less than a year ago and I wonder why I waited so long.

MOTHER'S STUFFING FOR FOWL
for a 4 to 5 pound bird

Because I stuff a bird only for special occasions I always make Mother's stuffing because I like it so well, and my family would object to any other.

¹/₃ **cup butter**
1 onion, sliced fine
2 large stems of celery with leaves
Half a loaf, or a bit more, of not-too-fresh bread cut into cubes or torn into pieces, using the crusts

2 tablespoons cut-up parsley
Salt and pepper
¹/₂ **teaspoon dried sage or savoury**
2 eggs, slightly beaten
¹/₂ **cup milk**

Melt the butter slowly in a large frying pan; add the onion and cook gently till it is soft but not brown. Add the celery, cut up fine, and mix it with the onion. Turn off the heat, keep the pan on the warm burner and add the bread, stirring it with the onion and celery. Sprinkle over all, the parsley, seasonings, and herbs. Mix thoroughly. Beat the eggs and the milk together and pour them over the bread mixture; it should be moistened but not soggy.

You may increase the amounts for a larger bird. Also you may prepare your dressing ahead of time until you reach the point of adding the egg and milk. *Never, never* stuff your bird ahead of time. When you are ready to roast it reheat your bread, onion mixture, add the egg and milk, warm slightly and put it into the fowl just before you are ready to put it in the oven. Stuff the bird lightly, in the body cavity and around the neck, keeping the stuffing in with skewers or sewing it with a darning needle and string, as Mother always did.

WHOLE SALMON COOKED IN COURT BOUILLON

The best salmon I have ever tasted was made by John Walker during our Stylish Entertainment course at Rundles Restaurant in Stratford. A great dish for a supper party or a large family.

Court bouillon can be used to cook lobster or other fish as well as salmon.

1 quart water	**¹/₄ cup vinegar or white wine**
2¹/₂ teaspoons salt	**6 peppercorns**
¹/₂ cup sliced carrots	**¹/₂ cup sliced onion**
1 bay leaf	**Sprig of thyme**
2 or 3 parsley stalks	

Simmer all the ingredients for 30 to 40 minutes, then strain.

Meanwhile prepare a firm, fresh, unsmelly salmon: remove all the scales with the back of a knife so you won't cut the skin. Remove the gills, intestines, and blood from the backbone. Clean out the head, or remove it if the glazed eyes upset you.

Wrap the fish in a long piece of foil with the ends twisted like handles to lift the fish out of the bouillon after it's cooked. Seal the foil across the top and prick holes throughout its length to let the bouillon flavour the fish. In a pot long enough to hold the salmon without bending it, place the foiled fish in the strained bouillon. The liquid should cover the fish. Bring it slowly to the boil; skim, then simmer very slowly with a lid on so the steam stays in: 15 minutes for a 7-pound fish, 20 minutes for 14 pounds.

Unwrap, cut into the center bone in the thickest part and if it's done it will flake away. Salmon must be served at once – you can't reheat it and expect it to be as good – but you could rewrap it in foil with herb butter inside its cavity and keep it warm in a low oven for a very little while. Or serve it cold, letting it cool at room temperature and then skinning it.

Keen on presentation, John placed the salmon on a platter surrounded with little mounds of various *al dente* vegetables, sprigs of parsley, dill and twists of sliced lemon as garnish on the fish. Several people in the class took its picture. John said, "Don't spoil it with bits of this and that, the fashion today is to keep it simple, never elaborate." At the table the fish was served with Aioli Sauce (page 84) in a sauce boat, and mayonnaise for those who didn't like garlic.

SARDINE CRISPIES
for a loner

You might not believe it till you try it but sardines dipped in egg and dried bread or cracker crumbs then sautéed in oil and butter are so crisp and good that you'll want to eat them quite often.

I buy the tiny imported expensive sardines to eat as they are with lettuce; I also buy cans of the sardines packed in New Brunswick to use when I make something that combines them or cooks them. I thought one can would be enough for two meals of Sardine Crispies but I enjoyed them so much that I ate the whole lot with a green salad and the leftover egg in which the sardines were dipped, poured into the pan after the fish were crisp and golden. There wasn't any left for my cats, Willie and Cicely.

FRIED OR GRILLED FILLETS

Overcooked fish is dry and tough; cover the fillets for the few minutes it takes to cook them.

Cut the fish into serving portions, sprinkle them with salt and lemon juice and let stand for 10 to 15 minutes. Dip each piece in milk, then flour or bread crumbs. Fry the pieces in a lightly buttered skillet for only a few minutes on each side, depending on the thickness of the fillet. The moment the raw look or feel is gone, garnish with parsley or lemon slices and you'll have a delicacy.

To grill the fillets prepare the same way but put the pieces in a buttered pan, dot them with butter and put under a grill, turning only once when slightly browned on top.

MEAT ACCOMPANIMENTS

BUTTERED NOODLES

Quite often when I go to Bevvy's for supper she has a bowl of hot noodles with butter melted over them to be eaten with summer sausage and all the other things, like pickled beets and cheese, relish, celery and salad. Sometimes Bevvy stirs a cupful of cooked peas into the noodles.

Mother often used to melt butter in a frying pan, pour in the noodles and stir them around with lots of cut-up parsley. Sometimes she'd scatter brown buttered crumbs over them when she served them. Sometimes she left them in the frying pan until they were brown on the bottom, she'd flip them over and brown the other side as well. We always loved noodle days at our house.

The juice of a lemon sprinkled over buttered noodles is rather nice. Half a cup of hot cream poured over them isn't bad either.

SOY RICE
4 servings

This favourite of Norm's can be used as an accompaniment or could become a main dish by adding shrimp, or chicken, turkey, or ham.

2 tablespoons salad oil	Salt to taste
1 bunch of green onions, chopped with some of the green tops	2 tablespoons or more soy sauce
1 cup or more celery, diced	Chopped almonds browned in butter for topping
2 cups cooked rice	

Sauté the onions and celery in the oil but don't brown them. Add the cooked rice, salt, and soy sauce; mix and put in a buttered casserole. Bake at 350°F for half an hour, until thoroughly heated. Toss the buttered almonds on top just before serving. I bet you'll make this often.

ONION RICE

Norma Morrison finds this an easy casserole to serve with a salad and pork chops, or chicken.

2 cups hot water
1 cup long grain rice
2 tablespoons butter

1 envelope dehydrated
onion soup

Stir all together in a buttered casserole, let stand for 5 minutes, cover and cook in a 350°F oven until the rice is tender, about half an hour or longer.

AIOLI SAUCE (Garlic Sauce)

A richly flavoured smooth sauce that is delicious with fish or beef. Very popular in France, and at the Rundles Restaurant in Stratford.

4 fat cloves garlic per person
¹/₈ teaspoon salt
2 egg yolks

Freshly ground black pepper
1 teaspoon lemon juice
1 cup olive oil

Crush the garlic to a smooth paste in a mortar with salt; blend in the egg yolks until the mixture is smooth and homogenous. Add the olive oil drop by drop at first, then in a thin trickle, whisking the mixture till your arm feels it. The Aioli will thicken gradually until it makes a stiff, firm consistency. Season to taste with additional salt, a little pepper and the lemon juice; serve chilled in a sauce boat.

HOT HORSERADISH SAUCE

I don't like horseradish, but I won't deprive you of Ruby's recipes.

1 tablespoon butter
1 teaspoon flour
1/2 teaspoon salt
1/2 teaspoon paprika

1/4 cup cream or milk
1 egg yolk, slightly beaten
1/2 cup grated horseradish

Melt the butter, stir in the flour, salt, and paprika. Heat until it bubbles then remove from heat. Gradually add the cream, cook 1 to 2 minutes, stirring constantly. Stir several table-spoons of the mixture into the egg yolk, mix into the sauce, cook again for a minute or two, stirring all the time. Blend in the horseradish. Heat again and serve as a relish with hot roast or boiled beef.

HORSERADISH JELLO
8 servings

Ruby says this goes over big.
Dissolve 1 small (3 1/4 oz.) package of lemon jello in 1 1/2 cups boiling water. Chill until it is about to set then fold in:

1/2 cup mayonnaise
4 tablespoons prepared
   horseradish

1/4 teaspoon salt
1/2 cup heavy cream, whipped

If you like you might add 5 tablespoons of sliced, stuffed olives and 1/2 teaspoon paprika. Chill until set.

NORM'S NIPPY MUSTARD

Some people like this with ham, some with beef.

1/2 cup dry mustard
1/2 cup brown sugar
1/4 cup vegetable oil

1/4 cup horseradish
1/4 cup cider vinegar

Mix together the dry mustard and sugar. Stir in oil, horseradish and vinegar until it is smoothly blended. Spoon in-to small jars, cover tightly. Will keep for months.

5

Vegetables

While earning her way through university, my niece-in-law Nancy spent several summers working in a meat-packing plant. In her last year there she had to eviscerate chickens whose bodies were still warm and twitching. She'd come home at night, tired and unable to eat a good chicken dinner. Soon Nancy felt the same aversion for other meats. Eventually, travels in remote areas of the world, changing values, and a high regard for all life, brought her the conviction that vegetarianism was the only way for her.

People who are vegetarians seem to spend far more time – and perhaps more money – on food than people who eat meat. They must be sure they are getting enough protein from other sources; they have to know all about where the vitamins are and how many they are getting every day. They can't afford to be careless; what is more important than a healthy body and a lively mind? Nancy spends much time reading books on nutrition, shopping around in the right places for the right foods, and preparing them in the right way. Every Saturday morning she goes to the Farmers' Market and comes home with baskets of fruits and vegetables.

When Nancy is cooking, the smell of onions, garlic and "vegies," as she calls them, is as tantalizing as any meat dinner that I might prepare. She has several vegetarian cookbooks but mainly relies on her own inventiveness. She concocts some interesting recipes, bakes fruity muffins and crunchy cookies crammed with roughage and goodness. She eats great quantities of soy beans, cheese, nuts, whole grains. For a meal she alone consumes a bowlful of green salad that I would put on the table for four or five people.

Nancy is always healthy. She swims to the end of the lake and back every day, goes on long vigorous canoe trips, skis and skates in the winter. She has greatly influenced our family: we often have vegetarian meals. I feel guilty if I wear my beaver coat or mink stole – though the poor creatures have been dead a very long time. I think I would never buy another piece of fur or step on a caterpillar. But I still enjoy eating meat.

Inconsistent? Of course. So is Nancy – she wears leather sandals.

SAVOURY BEANS
6 or 8 servings

You'll get awfully sick of all the beans you froze last summer unless you have various ways of preparing them throughout the winter.

1¹/₂ **pounds string beans**	¹/₄ **cup boiling water**
¹/₄ **cup oil**	1 **teaspoon salt**
1 **clove garlic, crushed**	1 **teaspoon dried basil**
1 **tablespoon chopped onion**	¹/₂ **cup grated cheese**
³/₄ **cup diced green pepper**	
(optional)	

Cut the beans into 1-inch pieces, or leave them whole. Heat the oil and garlic in a heavy pan, add the onion and green pepper, cook slowly for 3 minutes. Drop in the beans, water, salt, and basil, cover and boil until tender, about 10 to 15 minutes. After removing from the heat, stir in half the cheese, turn the mixture into a serving dish and sprinkle with the remaining cheese.

The number of servings I'm suggesting in these recipes is approximate: more or less ³/₄ of a cupful, not nearly enough for a growing boy but too much for a little old lady. You can figure out how much you'll have by adding up the number of cupfuls in the recipe, not forgettting that some things swell and others shrink.

SWISS BEAN CASSEROLE
about 6 servings

A super dish for a buffet supper with cold meat and a salad.

About 4 cups green beans cut in 1-inch pieces or frenched
2 tablespoons butter
1 teaspoon salt
1 teaspoon sugar
2 tablespoons flour
¹/₄ teaspoon pepper

1 small onion, finely chopped
1 cup sour cream
Topping:
2 tablespoons melted butter
³/₄ cup breadcrumbs, or corn flakes, or Rice Crispies
¹/₂ pound cheddar, grated

Cook the beans in salted water until almost done. Melt the butter and stir in the salt, sugar, flour, pepper, and onion. Add the sour cream and mix well, then heat through. Fold in the drained beans and put all in a buttered casserole. For the topping mix the crumbs with the melted butter, then with the cheese. Sprinkle over the top of the beans. Bake in a 400°F oven for 20 minutes or a more moderate oven for longer. There won't be a bean left over.

BRUSSELS SPROUTS

Buy them on the stalk if you can and pick them off as you use them; they'll keep longer.

After cleaning the sprouts put them in boiling water for 8 to 10 minutes, take out of the water, drain well, then warm them in butter. Shake the pan over low heat, covered, to keep them from sticking. Never, never overcook them. You could make a Béchamel sauce for them or a Mornay. In other words, a white sauce or cheese sauce.

If you spend a bit more time to get really fresh vegetables you don't need to spend time making sauces to smother them. Plant a garden, go to your nearest market or make friends with a farmer who will sell you some to take home and put in a pot – for a very short time. Enjoy the flavour of the pure vegetable.

CAULIFLOWER

Cauliflower has so much flavour of its own it doesn't need much enhancement.

Break into flowerets and boil in salted water with a bit of lemon juice to keep the vegetable white. Boil about 10 to 15 minutes, till barely tender; the worst sin is overcooking and serving soggy, grey, water-logged cauliflower. Drain it the moment it's tender and serve it at once with melted butter, buttered crumbs, a white sauce, or cheese sauce. Half white sauce and half mayonnaise blended together gives it a piquant flavour.

TIRED VEGETABLES

If some of your vegetables are a bit tired you could always put a bouquet garni in the water when you boil them.

TURNIP

Mother always boiled turnip in beef broth and then added butter. You could also boil it thinly sliced, in salted water. Drain it, then mash it with sour cream, lots of pepper, and parsley.

SUGAR PEAS

These should be eaten fresh from the garden; they are hard to find at the market and their season is very short – more's the pity.

Cut off the stems, plunge the pods in boiling water until just tender, not very long, drain them and serve with lots of butter melting over them and salt and pepper. Some people put bacon bits over them too, but why detract from that precious delicate flavour? This is a once-in-a-summertime thing.

MAGDALINA HORST'S SCHNITZEL BEANS
6 servings

In Magdalina's old, old recipe the beans are supposed to be cooked for an hour, the tomatoes added and cooked for 2 hours longer. It can all be done in half an hour or less in these vitamin-saving times.

3 slices bacon, cut in narrow strips
1½ pounds green beans, cut in 1-inch pieces
3 large onions, sliced

1 teaspoon salt and pepper
1 cup hot water
4 medium tomatoes, cut in pieces

Fry the bacon until crisp, remove it but leave a tablespoon of the fat in the pan., Mix in the beans, onions, salt and pepper and the hot water and cook till the beans are almost tender before putting in the tomatoes and cooking until they are soft. Serve with crumbled bacon on top. This is a very good, savoury dish.

CABBAGE

Never be without a cabbage in your house; you can do so many things with a cabbage. The fresher and greener it is the better, but even if you've had it around for a while and its outer leaves look a bit dingy, there's nothing wrong with the rest of it. You can use it in salads, in soup, in a casserole, or as a vegetable with meat and potatoes. It used to be inexpensive.

FOR LONERS: In the fall I buy the biggest, heaviest cabbage I can find at the market, put it in a plastic bag and keep it in my cold storage room till it's small enough to put in my fridge. Every week I carefully take off a few of the outer leaves to make coleslaw, or hot slaw, or to shred and keep for several days in an airtight container in my fridge so I can easily mix as much as I want with salad dressing or other salad ingredients. One cabbage will last for months.

A doctor once told me that raw cabbage eaten every day would keep me vigorous: it's a rich source of vitamins A, B, and C, chlorine, calcium, sodium, and iron.

CHEESLAW
2 servings, but you can expand it

A quick schmecksy dish that is a complete meal – inspired by Mother's Hotslaw, my favourite way to serve cabbage.

4 cups sliced cabbage
1 or 2 tablespoons butter
¼ cup onion, finely sliced
  (optional)

Salt and pepper to taste
½ cup grated cheese

Slice the cabbage about ¼ inch wide then chop it a bit, but not fine, just so you don't have long strings to cope with. Put butter in a heavy pot, melt it, sauté the onions till soft. Put in the cabbage, salt and pepper; stir over low heat until the cabbage is softened and hot but not really cooked, the spines should remain almost crisp. Sprinkle the grated cheese over it, let it soften slightly then stir it to coat the cabbage.

To make Hotslaw, which is so great with potatoes and farmers' sausage, chops or ham: instead of the cheese you stir in a blend of 1 teaspoon sugar, 1 teaspoon vinegar, and ⅓ cup sour cream to coat the cabbage. Because she liked it so well Janet Berton, a great cook, asked me to make it three times during a week she was staying with me.

BUBBLE AND SQUEAK

Another good way to use that aging cabbage: quick, easy, and tasty. But my friend Kath told me that in Devon Bubble and Squeak is just a fry-up of leftovers.

Cabbage, as much as you
  think you need (it shrinks)
1 potato per person
Some onion if you like

1 tablespoon bacon fat and
  1 tablespoon butter
¼ to ½ cup boiling water
Salt and pepper to taste

Chop the cabbage, peel and slice the potato and onion, melt the fat in a large frying pan, add the vegetables and boiling water. Season with salt and pepper, cover the pan with a tight lid and cook over low heat until the potatoes are soft, about 15 minutes if you're single, longer if your frying pan is loaded. Stir the mixture occasionally and add more fat if necessary. If you'd like to brown it on the bottom, take off the lid after the potatoes are soft and let it develop a brown crust. This makes a good meal with cold meat or sausages and a salad or relish.

CORN FRITTERS

I could make a whole meal of these doused with maple syrup.

1 cup flour	**1¹/₂ cups corn, fresh, frozen,**
1 teaspoon baking powder	**or canned**
³/₄ teaspoon salt	**2 teaspoons melted**
2 eggs, beaten well	**shortening**
¹/₄ cup milk	**Deep shortening for frying**

Sift the flour, baking powder and salt; combine the beaten eggs and milk and stir into the flour mixture. Add the corn and melted shortening. Drop tablespoonfuls into hot fat and watch them for 4 or 5 minutes till golden. Drain on brown paper. Eat hot.

CORN CHEESE FRITTERS

Add ¹/₂ cup grated cheese to the above recipe if you want a different taste thrill.

BAKED CORN CUSTARD
6 to 8 servings

A loner can easily cut this recipe in half, but why not enjoy two meals of it? It's great with cold meat or bacon or with maple syrup!

Corn cut from 6 to 10 cobs, or about 2 cupfuls of kernels,	
fresh, frozen, or niblets	**Salt and pepper to taste**
2 egg yolks, lightly beaten	**2 tablespoons melted butter**
1 cup milk	**Pinch of curry powder**
1 tablespoon flour	**(optional)**
1 tablespoon sugar	**2 egg whites beaten stiff**

Stir everything but the egg whites together. Then beat the egg whites and fold them in. Pour all into a well-buttered baking dish and bake uncovered, in a 350°F oven for about an hour, or until the custard is firm and golden brown.

CHEESE SCALLOPED POTATOES AND CARROTS
10 servings

Norm often makes this attractive dish for a buffet supper, with cold meats and salad.

About 5 cups potatoes, pared and sliced thin
5 carrots, sliced diagonally (about 2 cups)
¹/₂ cup sliced onion
2 teaspoons salt
Boiling water

Cheese sauce:
3 tablespoons butter
2 tablespoons flour
1 teaspoon salt
¹/₈ teaspoon pepper
Dash of cayenne
1¹/₂ cups milk, heated
1¹/₂ cups grated cheddar

Parboil the potatoes, onion, carrots in salted boiling water for 5 minutes. Drain. Make the cheese sauce: melt the butter, stir in the flour and seasonings, then the hot milk. Stir till it thickens, remove from the heat and stir in half the cheese, leaving the rest for topping. In a buttered casserole, layer half the potatoes, onion, and carrots; top with half the cheese sauce; repeat with other half of vegetables and sauce. Sprinkle top with remaining cheese. Cover with foil and bake at 375°F for 30 minutes till tender. Uncover top for last 10 minutes to brown. Sometimes Norm makes this in a large, deep pyrex cake pan to expose more browned surface.

CORN AND CHEESE CASSEROLE

This is a good and easy way to use leftover corn, or the corn you froze last fall.

About 2 cups corn kernels
2 beaten eggs
1 cup milk
Salt and pepper to taste
1 cup grated cheese
3 tablespoons minced onion

Topping:
2 tablespoons melted butter
¹/₂ cup dried breadcrumbs

Stir all but the topping together and pour into a well-buttered loaf pan or small casserole. Melt the butter, stir in the crumbs to absorb all the butter and sprinkle over the corn mixture.

Bake at 350°F for about 40 minutes. This is a great thing to put in a little broiler oven if you have one.

CORN ON THE COB

If you know a farmer with corn in his garden start wooing him now. Beg him to call you when the corn ripens, go get it and cook it the minute you get home – even if it's mid-afternoon. And don't spoil it by overcooking.

Put enough water into a kettle to cover the corn after it's put in. Bring the water to a boil, add a teaspoon of salt or sugar for each quart and drop in the husked corn as quickly as you can. Return the water to the boil – watch it – and turn it off as soon as it's rolling. Let the corn stay in the water exactly 5 minutes then fish it out and serve it with lots of butter.

SCALLOPED SWEET POTATOES AND APPLES
6 servings

Eva grows her own sweet potatoes in her garden near Heidelberg. Must we import them?

6 medium sweet potatoes	**¹/₂ teaspoon ground mace**
1¹/₂ cups apple slices	**¹/₄ cup butter**
¹/₂ cup firmly packed brown sugar	**Buttered breadcrumbs (optional)**
¹/₂ teaspoon salt	

Wash and cook the sweet potatoes in boiling water to cover until just tender. Peel them and cut into crosswise slices ¹/₂ inch thick. Butter a 2-quart casserole and arrange half the sweet potatoes in the bottom, then half the apple slices, sprinkled with half a mixture of brown sugar, salt, and mace. Dot with 2 tablespoons of the butter. Repeat the layering, ending with apples, seasonings, and butter – or buttered crumbs. Cook in a 350°F oven about 50 minutes.

NEW POTATOES AND PEAS

Bevvy says this is a real summer dish – simple to make but with that little bit extra.

4 good sized new potatoes
Boiling water
Salt
1 or 2 cups fresh peas
¹/₂ teaspoon basil

Pepper
2 tablespoons butter
2 well-rounded tablespoons
   sour cream
Fresh cut-up parsley

Scrub the potatoes and cut them in quarters. Put them into a saucepan with about ³/₄ inch of boiling water and salt. Cover and boil till almost done then drop in the peas and sprinkle in the basil; when the peas are soft enough to suit you drain away any water that remains, add pepper, butter, and sour cream, and heat a few seconds. Turn into a serving dish and sprinkle with the fresh chopped parsley. Perfect with gravyless meat and a salad.

JILL'S POTATOES ROMANOFF
8 to 10 servings

Really special to serve hot as a casserole or cold as potato salad.

6 large potatoes
2 (10 oz) cartons sour cream
1¹/₂ cups shredded sharp
   cheddar
1 bunch green onions, sliced
   across stems

1¹/₂ teaspoons salt
¹/₄ teaspoon pepper
Paprika

Cook the potatoes in their jackets until barely fork tender. Peel and slice or shred coarsely into a large bowl. Meanwhile blend the sour cream, 1 cup of the cheese, the onion, salt, and pepper. Stir gently into the potatoes so you don't mush them. Put all into a buttered casserole, top with remaining cheese and sprinkle with paprika. Cover, refrigerate several hours or overnight, or freeze for future use. Bake uncovered in a 350°F oven 30 to 40 minutes, till heated through, no longer.

NOODLES ROMANOFF

Boil till just tender a package or two of noodles, and prepare them exactly the same way as Potatoes Romanoff except that you should use half milk instead of all that cream.

LIZA GINGERICH'S CANNED TOMATO CASSEROLE
6 servings or more

Every year – like all good Old Order Mennonites – Liza cans jars and jars of tomatoes from her garden. This is her favourite way of using them during the winter, all puffed up with a buttery flavour. Really good.

6 or more slices of generously buttered bread
1 quart canned tomatoes, or more

1 mild onion, finely chopped
1 teaspoon sugar
Salt and pepper
¹/₂ cup buttered crumbs

Put the buttered bread on a pan in 200°F oven until it is thoroughly dry and crisp – but not brown, though that wouldn't hurt it. Cut or break each slice into four and lay half the pieces in the bottom of a well-buttered casserole. Pour in half of the canned or frozen tomatoes; sprinkle with half the onion, sugar, salt and pepper. Cover with the rest of the bread squares, repeat the layers of tomato, onion, and seasonings. Spread buttered crumbs over all and bake in a 300°F oven for 1¹/₂ hours. Bring it out puffy and amazingly tasty. You can prepare this in advance and put it in the oven 1¹/₂ hours before mealtime.

HERBY ZUCCHINI TOMATO CASSEROLE
6 to 8 servings

A wonderful late summer dish that you can stretch or diminish to fit your largest or smallest casserole. A great way to use those overgrown zucchinis.

1 or 2 onions
2 tablespoons butter
Enough zucchini, cut in ¹/₂-inch slices, to completely cover the bottom of your casserole
4 tomatoes, cut in ¹/₂-inch slices
1 teaspoon salt

Pepper to taste
1 squashed garlic clove (optional)
¹/₂ teaspoon oregano
1 teaspoon basil
Topping:
1 cup breadcrumbs
1 cup grated cheddar
1 teaspoon blended herbs

Peel and slice an onion or two and cook long enough in the butter to soften it. Place the zucchini in the bottom of your casserole, put a slice of tomato on each slice of zucchini sprinkle with softened onion, seasonings, and herbs. Put more zucchini slices, tomato slices, and well-seasoned onions until you have filled up the casserole. Cover and bake in a 300°F oven for about 20 minutes, until the zucchini is slightly tender. Take off the cover and bake another 10 minutes till some of the liquid has evaporated. Mix the cheese with the bread crumbs and herbs, spread them over the top and bake about 5 minutes longer until the cheese melts and the crumbs are a tempting golden brown. This is great with a tossed salad, or baked potatoes and country sausage or pork chops, lamb cutlets – any meat without gravy.

SPINACH OR BEET GREENS WITH SOUR CREAM

This is the way I cook spinach – or beet greens – most of the time. Why fool around when you know such a good thing?

1 quart of fresh spinach (I've never had frozen spinach but it would do)	Salt and pepper
	1 teaspoon sugar
	1 teaspoon vinegar
1 chopped onion (optional)	¹/₂ cup sour cream
2 tablespoons butter or bacon fat	

Wash the spinach and cook it with water clinging to its leaves; when it is soft, drain it. Sauté the onion till soft but not brown in the butter or bacon fat; add the drained spinach. Sprinkle the salt and pepper, sugar, and vinegar over the sour cream, blend them together and stir into the spinach. If you have bacon you might use it crisply fried as a garnish. Done this way the spinach loses that iron good-for-you taste.

BAKED ONIONS

Put onions in the oven in their skins and in about half an hour they will be completely soft, juicy and mild, without any after effects. Perfect for loners with small broiler ovens.

ZUCCHINI SAUTÉ

Nancy can whip this up in about five minutes; the tantalizing aroma of the garlic lasts longer.

1 medium zucchini
1 tablespoon oil
1 tablespoon butter
1 or more sliced onions

1 or 2 cloves garlic (optional)
1 or more tomatoes, cut in
   wedges

Slice the unpeeled zucchini in ½-inch slices, heat the oil at medium heat and cook the onion and garlic till soft, push to the sides of the pan; drop in the zucchini slices so all the slices are in touch with the surface of the pan; cook till almost tender, drop in the tomato wedges and let them simmer. Don't over-cook the zucchini.

RATATOUILLE AUX PARMESAN

An impressive, colourful, French vegetable casserole: can be made the day before serving, hot or cold. John Walker, chef at Rundles in Stratford, performed this for us and we thought it was wonderful.

8 tablespoons olive or corn oil
2 onions, sliced not too fine
2 green peppers, roughly
   cubed
Salt and black pepper
2 aubergines (eggplant),
   cubed or sliced
2 courgettes (small zucchini),
   ½-inch slices

2 large garlic cloves, crushed
4 to 6 tomatoes, peeled,
   seeded, and chopped
Pinch of oregano
Pinch of basil or thyme
2 ounces parmesan
1 tablespoon chopped
   parsley

John told us this is a peasant dish. You should be able to see the form of the vegetables; if they're cut too fine they'll cook in-to a mush. Remember that.

Heat the olive oil, add the onions, and sauté lightly, add the green peppers and sauté them lightly as well, turning them over. Don't cook them. Season with salt and pepper. With a slotted spoon remove to a casserole. In the oil sauté the eggplant and zucchini with the well-squashed garlic; season lightly with the herbs; add the tomatoes and mix all together. Zucchini and eggplant take lots of seasoning because they don't have much flavour of their own. Don't *cook* them in the oil, just lightly sauté them; shake the pan. Place in the casserole with the onions and peppers and simmer gently, covered for 30 minutes, or put in a 350°F oven for half an hour, well covered. Stir, but not often, or you'll muck it up. The vegetables really stew in the oil; the only actual liquid they have is the tomatoes. The amount drops quite a lot as it cooks. Now uncover the dish and cook for about 10 minutes before serving; sprinkle with parmesan and brown under the grill then sprinkle over top the chopped parsley and enjoy the complimentary remarks you'll hear.

6

Lunches and Suppers for Families and Friends – or Just You

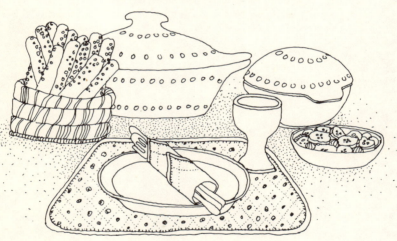

One of the girls in our gang at high school was flirty, pretty, and bound to get a husband. She scoffed at those of us who were studying to go to university. When we left for Toronto she went to Guelph to take the Wedding Ring Course at Macdonald Hall. As soon as she finished she married a lawyer whose father built them a big gabled house where she entertained elegantly with the help of her mother-in-law's maid.

Every Friday morning she sat down, as she'd been taught at Mac Hall, and made out menus for every day of the week to come. And she stuck to those menus. I don't know what she did when her husband called and said he couldn't make it home for lunch on Wednesday, or he was bringing a client home for dinner on Thursday, or if one of their children was invited to stay with a friend for supper and she had food left over. I often wondered what she did in emergencies but I never asked her.

She gained a reputation for being a great cook and hostess, was very proud of herself, and when anyone asked her for a recipe she always said her recipes were her secret and she wouldn't give them to anyone.

I now have a neighbour whose husband died soon after she had her third baby; she took a course at business college, got a job, paid a girl to look after the children till she came home at five. She planned all her meals ahead: she had to. She loved trying new recipes; when she invited friends for dinner she'd know a week in advance what she'd give them to eat and start preparing: her time was limited and scheduled.

Now she's retired and living alone – with all her time for herself. She often has friends in for dinner, still plans and starts days ahead to get ready a really classy repast with all the elaborate trimmings.

My sister Norma invites twelve to eighteen people for a buffet supper – then she's committed. She decides what she'll give them to eat and sticks to her decision, no changing her mind, no saying, "Well, maybe I'll have this instead of that." She buys what she needs, makes what she can in advance and at the last minute never seems flustered or hurried. She always turns out a meal that everyone raves about and her guests always ask, and are given, her recipes.

That's the way to do it. I know it works. Planning and preparing ahead is the way to enjoy entertaining.

I wish I would do it that way instead of the haphazard, rushed-at-the-last-minute method that is my habit. The result is that I avoid having parties. I don't invite people to come weeks ahead because it makes me nervous; with that much advance notice I have no excuse for not giving them the fabulous meal they expect from the author of a cookbook.

I like to call my friends at noon to come for supper that night; I tell them not to expect a production, just an unfancy, lazy meal. When someone visits me for a week or a weekend I run to the market, fill up my fridge with whatever is fresh in the season, and feel confident that no one will starve. All I have to do is make something out of what's there.

It's a poor system. It is no system. I don't recommend it. But my friends keep coming back; some even help me prepare whatever I have. Our joy is in eating and being together.

TO PLAN A MEAL

I know this is the way to do it. Sit down with a pencil and paper and dream about it, put down everything you can think of that you are going to need for your table and your menu. On another paper put everything you need to shop for. This planning could take quite a while of enjoyable sitting, relaxing time, and when you have finished you'll feel you are well on your way; you couldn't possibly flub it because it's all there: you just have to follow the blueprint. Save it for another time and add who your guests were so you won't repeat the menu when they come again.

If you're planning a party or even entertaining a few, you're going to have to go out to shop. You just can't give them limp lettuce and tired fruit. So while you're about it you might as well plan to splurge; pick up the few extras that you don't usually have in your pantry. Now is the time for experimentation. Now you can make that fancy dessert that you wouldn't dare to eat by yourself.

EVA'S ASPARAGUS CASSEROLE

This can be expanded or made as small as you like – a perfect meal by itself.

Noodles, cooked   **Cheese sauce**
Raw asparagus   **Grated cheese and**
Seasonings   **breadcrumbs**
Ground beef (optional)

Eva says, "Put noodles in the bottom of a buttered casserole, then put in as much asparagus as you need; over the asparagus spread a layer of ground beef, seasoned with salt and pepper; make a cheese sauce and pour it over – enough so you'll have plenty of moisture. Spread grated cheese mixed with breadcrumbs on top and bake in a 350 °F oven for 45 minutes or an hour, depending on how large a batch you make."

ASPARAGUS AND EGG CASSEROLE
4 servings

A great luncheon dish with hot biscuits.

2 slices of buttered bread broken into crumbs	2 tablespoons butter
1 pound of fresh cooked asparagus cut in 1-inch pieces	2 tablespoons flour
	¹/₂ teaspoon salt
	1 cup milk
4 hardcooked eggs, sliced	1 cup cheddar cheese, diced
	2 tablespoons butter for top

Put half the buttered crumbs in a buttered baking dish; spread the cooked asparagus pieces over the crumbs and the 4 hard-cooked egg slices over the asparagus. Blend the butter, flour, salt, and milk with the cheese and pour over all. Top with the remaining breadcrumbs mixed with 2 tablespoons melted butter. Bake at 350 °F for 30 minutes.

SPINACH SOUFFLÉ
12 servings

One of Norm's favourite luncheon or supper dishes. Served with a Greek salad, biscuits or rolls, and mushrooms in a cream sauce.

	1 cup flour
2 packages of spinach (fresh or frozen)	1 cup grated cheddar
	1 cup milk
3 eggs, beaten	¹/₂ cup butter, melted
Salt and pepper	1 teaspoon baking powder

Cook the spinach, drain it, and chop it a bit. Blend the beaten eggs, seasonings, flour, cheese, and milk; fold in the spinach.

Melt the butter in an 8″ x 12″ cake pan and pour the spinach mixture into it. Bake at 350°F for about 45 minutes. Let sit for a few minutes to simmer down before cutting it in squares.

SPINACH SOUFFLÉ FOR TWO

For two? I ate all of this at one sitting.

About ¹/₃ package raw spinach	2 egg yolks
¹/₂ cup milk	¹/₂ small onion, cut up
2 tablespoons butter	Salt and pepper
2 tablespoons flour	¹/₄ cup cheddar
	2 egg whites, beaten stiff

Cut the raw spinach leaves coarsely and drop them into your blender or food processor with all the rest of the ingredients but the egg whites. Blend until the spinach and onion are evenly fine. Pour all into a saucepan and stir over medium heat until thickened. Let it cool slightly. Beat the egg whites till stiff, then fold them into the spinach mixture and turn it into a buttered oven dish. Bake in a 325°F oven for 30 to 40 minutes, till it is firm when you insert a knife. It will puff up impressively and have real flavour when you serve it alone or with a mushroom or tomato sauce and toast or English muffins.

NANCY'S SPINACH QUICHE

For a Sunday brunch Nancy poured what I suspect was the making of a spinach soufflé into a deep pie dish lined with whole wheat pat-in pastry (page 252). She baked it and served it with muffins and a whopping tossed salad.

MARDI'S EGG AND MUSHROOM LUNCHEON DISH

Mardi keeps telling me how great and simple this is; her mother used to make it.

Mushrooms	Toast or patty shells
Hardboiled eggs	Butter
Cream sauce	

Sauté as many mushrooms as you think you might need (1 pound should be enough for 6 servings). Hard boil at least 1 egg per person. Sauté the mushrooms in butter until they are soft. Make a cream sauce using 2 cups of milk. Slice the eggs and stir them and the mushrooms into the cream sauce. Serve on buttered toast or in patty shells.

STUFFED ZUCCHINI

The zucchinis in Barbie's garden hide under the leaves and almost overnight seem to grow to the size of canoes. This is a good way to use one. You don't have to follow the recipe exactly but it will give you the general drift.

1 huge zucchini, or several
   smaller ones
1/4 cup oil
1/2 cup finely chopped onion
1/2 teaspoon finely chopped
   garlic
1/2 pound ground beef
1 egg, lightly beaten
1/4 cup ham, or bacon
   (or skip it)

1/2 cup fresh breadcrumbs
6 tablespoons parmesan
   cheese or other
1/2 teaspoon oregano
1/2 teaspoon salt, or more
1/4 teaspoon black pepper
2 cups tomato sauce or soup
   (optional)

Cut zucchini in half lengthwise and spoon out most of the pulp leaving the boatlike shell 1/4 inch thick. Chop pulp coarsely. Heat oil in a frying pan, add onions and cook until soft. Add zucchini pulp and garlic, cook 4 minutes, stirring often. Spoon this into a large sieve and set over a bowl to let drain. Heat 1 tablespoon oil in the pan, add ground beef and brown, stirring with a fork to break lumps. Drain the beef of fat. Combine vegetables and meat, beat in the egg, ham, breadcrumbs, 2 tablespoons parmesan, oregano, salt, and pepper. Spoon into zucchini boats, mounding slightly on top. Sprinkle top with remaining 4 tablespoons cheese. Place the zucchini in a baking dish, pour the tomato sauce around it, cover it with foil if the dish hasn't a lid. Bake at 375°F for 30 minutes. Ten minutes before serving, remove foil so the top will brown.

CHICKEN À LA KING
about 12 servings

When we were teen-agers a party wasn't a party unless we were served Chicken à la King. The girls always had two, the boys three. We were all skinny in those days.

12 flaky pastry patty shells	Salt and pepper to taste
2 tablespoons butter	1 cup green peas, cooked
1/2 cup flour	2 egg yolks, beaten
3 1/2 cups chicken stock	3/4 cup whole milk or cream
3 cups diced cooked chicken	1/3 cup pimiento, chopped
1 cup chopped mushrooms,	(for colour)
cooked in butter	

Melt the butter, add the flour, blend, then stir in the chicken stock and cook until thickened. Add the chicken, mushrooms, seasonings, and peas. Beat the egg yolks, stir in the milk or cream and blend with the chicken mixture over low heat until it is smooth and thick. Before serving stir in the pimiento. Fill the patty shells generously with some filling flowing over on the plate. A salad and rolls alongside and we were a happy gang.

SHRIMP CASSEROLE

Norm often makes this mild, delicious dish when she has people in for a buffet supper; it always goes over well with a tossed salad, vegetable, and relishes.

1/4 cup chopped onion	Dash of pepper and cayenne
2 tablespoons butter	3 ounces mushrooms
2 tablespoons flour	2 cups cleaned, cooked
2 cups milk, heated	shrimp
1/2 teaspoon Worcestershire	2 cups cooked rice
sauce (optional)	1/2 cup shredded old cheese
1/2 teaspoon celery salt	1/2 cup buttered bread or
1/2 teaspoon ordinary salt	cracker crumbs

Cook the onion in butter until tender but not brown. Make a thin cream sauce by blending the flour with the butter and onion, pouring in the milk and stirring till slightly thickened;

blend in the seasonings, and add the mushrooms, cooked first in butter. Stir in the cooked shrimp and the cooked rice. Pour into a casserole, top with a mixture of cheese and buttered crumbs. Bake in a 350°F oven for 20 to 30 minutes.

NANCY'S FAVOURITE LASAGNA

Nancy writes: "Even hardy meat-eaters love this rich, cheesy dish. When I'm in the mood for a treat, I always think about cooking this recipe." There are 4 basic steps:

1. Make tomato sauce.
2. Cook lasagna noodles (1 box) and drain.
3. Grate and slice cheeses.
4. Assemble

TOMATO SAUCE: I never worry about making too much of this sauce because it freezes well. Some day when I want to eat a good meal but am too lazy to prepare one I go to the freezer and thaw this sauce. Then I put it on top of spaghetti with mushrooms, or cook brown rice and mix the two together. This sauce is easily improvised, the secret is in the spices.

In a large pan boil slowly for about an hour.

3 cups stewed tomatoes (or fresh ones)	2 cups mushrooms, sliced
1 small tin (2 oz.) tomato paste	2 tablespoons basil
1 cup cut-up carrots	1 tablespoon oregano
1 cup chopped onion	1 tablespoon marjoram
1 cup chopped celery	1 teaspoon thyme
2 to 3 cloves garlic	1 teaspoon garlic powder
1 large green pepper, chopped	Salt and pepper

When sauce is cooked and cooled, mix it with: 1 pound ricotta cheese. If unavailable use any kind of cream cheese or cottage cheese. Set aside until you are ready to layer.

Slice thinly 1 pound mozzarella cheese, grate finely 1/2 pound parmesan or use packaged.

Begin to layer in a large and deep cake or loaf pan. I can often stretch this recipe into 2 pans and freeze one depending on the number of people I am feeding. On the bottom of a greased pan place a layer of cooked noodles, then smooth on a layer of sauce mixed with ricotta cheese. Then a layer of mozzarella cheese, and last sprinkle with parmesan. Continue these layers until the pan is nearly full. Bake at 350°F for 20 to 30 minutes. Needs only to be heated through and the cheeses melted.

SCALLOPED CORN BEEF

Lorna likes this easy-to-make supper dish with a green salad and mushroom muffins, (page 189), hot and buttery.

1¹/₂ tablespoons butter	¹/₂ teaspoon salt
¹/₂ small onion, chopped fine	¹/₈ teaspoon pepper
¹/₃ cup chopped celery	1 medium can corned beef
2 tablespoons flour	Buttered crumbs
1¹/₂ cups milk	

Melt the butter in a skillet, add the onion and celery; cook until the onion is soft and yellow. Add the flour and blend well, pour in the milk and cook to a smooth sauce. Season with salt and pepper, then stir in the corned beef broken into small pieces. Blend and place in a buttered baking dish. Sprinkle with buttered crumbs and bake in a 375°F oven for 25 minutes, while your muffins are baking as well.

VEGETABLE LOAF

This combination of vegetables and nuts is interesting and sufficiently satisfying to make you not miss the meat in what looks like a meat loaf.

4 medium-sized carrots	1 cup whole wheat
1 cup salted peanuts	breadcrumbs
3 large boiled potatoes	¹/₂ cup milk
2 medium onions	3 eggs, slightly beaten
2 tablespoons parsley	1 teaspoon salt
1 cup celery	Pepper to taste
1 cup spinach or cabbage	

In a chopping bowl or food processor chop up very fine the carrots, peanuts, potatoes, onions, parsley, celery, and spinach or cabbage. While you are chopping soak the breadcrumbs in the milk. Stir all together, add the slightly beaten eggs, salt, and pepper, and mix thoroughly. Butter a loaf pan and pat the mixture into it. (You might dot a bit of butter on top if you like.) Bake at 350°F for about an hour and a half. The top should be brown and the loaf firm. It is good hot or cold and might be served with mushroom or tomato sauce and a tossed salad. All very nutritious and delicious.

MEATLESS MEAT LOAF

I doubled this for three members of an Ashram in Toronto who stayed at my house after telling the K-W University Women's Club about their belief in yoga. They all rose at dawn to meditate and one young man offered to anoint my feet with oil.

1 cup chopped mixed nuts	1 onion, chopped
1 cup whole wheat	Salt and pepper
breadcrumbs	Squirt of Worcestershire
1 cup cooked rice	sauce
¹/₂ teaspoon crumbled dry	Water
basil	3 tablespoons melted butter
¹/₄ teaspoon crumbled thyme	

Mix all the ingredients, add a little water to moisten. Press into a buttered loaf pan, bake in a 375°F oven for 35 minutes, dotting with the melted butter. Serve with or without mushroom or tomato sauce, and a green salad.

NANCY'S CARROT LOAF

Nancy writes about this: "At the last minute, discovering I have few ingredients, I can always make this carrot loaf and ensure compliments from my guests. Served with hot muffins, it's a simple and delicious meal. It's also a great way to get rid of old tired carrots."

3 eggs, beaten
1¹/₂ cups stewed tomatoes
1 tablespoon honey
1 grated onion
2 or more cups grated carrots
¹/₂ cup raisins
¹/₃ cup soy flour (or
  whole wheat)

1 cup breadcrumbs
  (whole wheat)
¹/₂ teaspoon salt
3 tablespoons Brewers' yeast
  (optional for health freaks)
¹/₄ cup sunflower seeds
¹/₂ teaspoon marjoram

Beat the eggs, add tomatoes, honey, grated onion, carrots, and raisins. In another bowl mix: flour, breadcrumbs, salt, yeast, sunflower seeds, and marjoram. Combine the wet ingredients with the dry ones and stir well. Bake at 350°F for 1 hour or more until the eggs set. "If you have good luck turning the loaf upside down you will be very pleased with the visual effect," Nancy says.

VEGETABLE WALNUT LOAF

Nancy and her vegetarian friends really liked this when I tried it on them. It's light and has lots of flavour – almost meaty, I'd say.

1¹/₂ cups soft breadcrumbs,
  whole wheat preferred
1 cup walnuts
1 medium onion, cut in
  chunks
1¹/₂ cups cooked carrots
3 eggs, slightly beaten

1¹/₂ cups milk
1¹/₂ cups cooked or
  canned peas
1¹/₂ teaspoons salt
Pepper to taste
2 tablespoons melted butter

You may put all this into your blender or food processor until it is finely chopped – or you may do the job with a grinder or a sharp knife. Mix all together thoroughly, pack it into a well-buttered loaf pan, 9" x 5", and bake at 350°F for an hour. Serve with a sauce if you like and a good leafy salad.

SWISS FONDUE

A friend living in Lausanne, Switzerland, introduced me to Swiss Fondue. We would sit in a candle-lit restaurant with the bubbling cheese on the table between us and dip into it pieces of crusty French bread. According to Swiss tradition, whoever dropped a piece of bread from a fork into the fondue had to pay for the meal or give the other person a kiss. I seemed to always be the loser – one way or another.

1 clove of garlic	**1¹/₂ teaspoons corn starch**
1 cup dry white wine	**2 tablespoons Kirsch**
(preferably Neuchatel)	**Pepper to taste**
4 cups shredded natural	
Swiss cheese	
(preferably gruyère)	

Rub the inside of a saucepan or earthenware fondue dish or chafing dish with cut clove of garlic. Pour in the wine and heat but don't let it boil. Stir in about ¹/₄ cup of cheese, stir vigorously, keep adding in small amounts, stirring all the time until all the cheese is melted and the mixture is thoroughly blended. Add the corn starch blended with the Kirsch and stir until the mixture bubbles. Sprinkle with a bit of pepper. Keep the fondue hot but not simmering over an alcohol burner with a low flame, or a low candle. If it becomes too thick add a little more warm wine. Have French bread alongside torn into bite-sized pieces; put a piece on a fork, dip it in the fondue and don't burn your tongue when you eat it. You'll be amazed at how much you will consume. Don't underestimate.

CRÊPES GRUYÈRE

The mother of my friend in Switzerland one day took us to a restaurant in Montreux where the specialty was Crêpes Gruyère: pieces of cheese dipped in batter, deep fried crisp and golden, the cheese creamy soft inside. Maman was very fussy about what we ate with them: tender butter lettuce salad, white wine at room temperature, prunes stewed with an orange liqueur, and coffee. Of course the restaurateur would not give his recipe; I've been trying ever since that memorable day to find something like it. I think this comes close. I wish I could also reproduce Montreux' promenade view of the snow-capped Dents du Midi across the turquoise-blue waters of lovely Lac Leman.

Batter:
1 egg, beaten
1 tablespoon oil
¹/₂ teaspoon salt
³/₄ cup stale beer or white
  wine or milk
1 cup flour

**Pieces of gruyère or any
similar mild white cheese
cut in pieces 1″ x 3 ″ x ³/₄″**

Blend the first four ingredients then stir in the flour, using more or less till the batter is smooth and drops off the spoon with a splat, not a stream. Let the batter rest for a couple of hours, or overnight. Just before serving time, dip the pieces of cheese in the batter to coat them well, fry in hot fat until crisp and golden. As you eat them I doubt if you'll miss those mountains at Montreux.

If you don't want to use up all the batter with the cheese you might drop prunes or half-inch slices of apple or pieces of banana into it to make fritters.

Watch your deep fat frying. Don't do it unless you're going to stand right beside it every second. If your phone rings turn off the heat before you answer. Let the crêpes die a natural death; better sacrifice them than take a chance on burning your house. Ever notice how many fires are started by french fries?

And never, never, never put a lid on the hot fat pot: it can explode when you remove it. I have a friend who was horribly burned when he did it – and so was his kitchen.

ONION PIE
6 servings

A sort of quiche that would be great to serve to the girls when they come for lunch – or as a supper dish for the family.

1 cup crushed crackers   4 tablespoons melted butter

Combine and press in bottom and sides of a 9-inch pie plate, or use a pastry crust.

6 slices of bacon   2 eggs, slightly beaten
1 cup chopped onion   Dash of pepper
2 cups shredded cheese   Chopped pimiento (optional)
¹/₄ cup sour cream   Cheese slices

In a skillet cook bacon till crisp; pour off all the fat but 2 tablespoons. In the bacon fat cook onion until tender, not brown. Combine onion, bacon, and cheese, add sour cream, eggs, pepper and, if you want a touch of colour, the chopped pimiento. Put all in the pie shell, bake at 375° for 35 to 45 minutes. Take it from the oven and put slices of cheese – or more shredded cheese on top, then back in the oven for 2 or 3 minutes. Remove and let it stand for 10 minutes before serving. This recipe could easily be doubled for 2 pies.

JEAN SALTER'S CHEESE AND EGG PIE
6 servings

You might call it a quiche – but why? This is English.

9-inch unbaked pie shell	4 eggs
1¹/₂ cups grated cheese	2 cups milk
2 tablespoons flour	1 teaspoon salt
2 tablespoons butter	¹/₄ teaspoon pepper

Mix the cheese and flour and spread in the pie shell. Add butter in bits. In a mixing bowl beat the eggs, add the milk, salt, and pepper and stir until smooth. Pour over the cheese mixture in the pie shell. Bake in a 350°F oven for about 40 minutes or until it is puffed and brown. Remove, cool for 10 minutes before cutting into wedges for six.

JEAN SALTER'S SUSSEX PIE

A nice luncheon dish for two with a green salad.

1 onion, chopped	Salt and pepper
2 tablespoons butter	¹/₂ pound tomatoes
¹/₂ cup grated cheese	A little mustard
1 cup breadcrumbs	2 eggs, beaten

Fry the onion in butter. Mix the grated cheese and breadcrumbs, season with salt and pepper. Put alternate layers of sliced tomatoes, fried onions, cheese and breadcrumb mixture in a pie dish, ending with breadcrumbs. Pour the beaten eggs and mustard over all. Bake in a 425°F oven for 15 to 20 minutes. Watch that it doesn't burn.

RUBY'S FINNAN HADDIE CASSEROLE
4 servings

Ruby's children always loved finnan haddie dinners.

2 tablespoons butter
$^1/_2$ cup hot milk
1 cup rice, cooked light and
   fluffy
1 piece of finnan haddie,
   cooked

Lots of chopped parsley
2 hardboiled eggs, chopped
Salt and pepper to taste
Topping:
$^1/_2$ cup breadcrumbs
$^1/_4$ cup grated cheese

Mix all together in a buttered casserole and sprinkle the breadcrumbs mixed with the cheese on top. Bake in a 350°F oven till hot and nicely toasted.

SALMON OR TUNA WRAP-UP
6 or 8 servings

This will help the salmon or tuna go a bit farther.

2 tablespoons butter
1 onion, finely chopped
1 cup chopped celery
2 tins or 1$^1/_2$ cups salmon
   or tuna, drained
Salt and pepper
1 egg, slightly beaten

Biscuit dough:
$^1/_4$ cup butter or margarine
2 cups flour
3 teaspoons baking powder
$^3/_4$ teaspoon salt
$^3/_4$ cup milk

In the 2 tablespoons of butter, sauté the onion and celery till the onion is soft; mix it with the fish, adding seasonings to taste; stir in the beaten egg. Make biscuit dough. Cut the margarine into the dry ingredients, add the milk. Roll into an oblong about $^1/_2$ inch thick. Line a loaf pan with the dough, pour in the fish mixture and tuck the dough over it, leaving a vent down the centre. Or spread the fish mixture over the oblong of dough, roll it up like a jelly roll and drop it into a loaf pan. Bake for about 15 minutes in a 400°F oven; keep your eye on it. Serve with plenty of white sauce generously flavoured with chopped parsley, or herbs and chopped hardboiled eggs. And a green salad.

CAROL'S SALMON QUICHE
6 servings

A salmon couldn't have a better finale than this. It is super.

Pastry for a 9- or 10-inch
  pie plate
1 cup chopped or shredded
  cheddar cheese
2 tablespoons chopped onion
3 eggs

1 cup milk
2 cans (7³/₄ oz) salmon
  drained, reserve liquid
  (leftover fresh salmon)
¹/₄ teaspoon basil, tarragon,
  or oregano

Strew the cheese over the bottom of the pastry shell, sprinkle it with the onion, and arrange the flaked salmon over the onion to cover right to the edge. In a bowl mix eggs, the salmon liquid, and milk. Pour evenly over the salmon. Sprinkle with the basil, tarragon, or oregano. Bake at 375°F for about 55 minutes, or until set. Serve hot in wedges with a green vegetable, or salad – or both.

SINGLE SUPPER

Last night I thought I was making enough of this for 2 meals, but it was so good I ate all of it at one.

1 large tomato, frozen
  or fresh
2 slices of whole wheat
  bread, buttered
Cheddar cheese, sliced

1 or 2 eggs
Salt and pepper
¹/₄ teaspoon mixed dried
  herbs

I put a large tomato in a pie plate and stuck it under the grill while I buttered 2 slices of bread which I then put under the tomato cut in half to sop up the juices. Next I sliced enough cheddar to cover the bread and tomatoes completely and put that under the grill till it bubbled. Then I broke an egg into the middle of the dish, sprinkled it with salt, pepper, and herbs. I pricked the yolk so it ran over the tomato and cheese, and put it under the grill again – in my little toast 'n broil oven – till the egg became solid, but not tough. If I'd had a slice or two of bacon I would have grilled that on top of the egg at the same time. But you can't have everything.

If you're living alone what's wrong with a lunch of homemade cracker biscuits and cheese with a raw carrot or a piece of lettuce or a chopped vegetable salad, and an apple?

PAM NOONAN'S CABBAGE ROLLS

Pamela, who comes from Trinidad, said she was tired of being served crumbly Octoberfest cabbage rolls that were mostly rice; she devised this recipe of her own and brought a pot full of rolls to my house on a January day when her writer-professor husband Gerry and her son Johnnie very kindly shovelled deep snow off the roof of my cottage. Then we ate the best cabbage rolls I've ever tasted.

Rolls:
3 pounds lean ground beef
2 small onions, chopped
¹/₂ cup rice, cooked
**   in bouillon**
2 eggs, well beaten
Chopped chives
Salt, pepper, garlic salt,
**   and celery salt**
¹/₄ teaspoon cumin
¹/₂ teaspoon tarragon
³/₄ teaspoon tobasco
4 teaspoons soy sauce

Cabbage leaves, parboiled

Sauce:
2 cans (14 oz.) tomato sauce
¹/₂ cup tomato ketchup
¹/₄ cup vinegar
¹/₄ cup prepared mustard
¹/₄ cup barbeque sauce
¹/₂ cup brown sugar

Pam mixed well all the ingredients for the rolls then rolled two rounded tablespoons of the mixture in each parboiled cabbage leaf to make tight little bundles. She said you could secure them with toothpicks but she didn't bother. While she was making the rolls she was simmering the ingredients for the sauce. She put the rolls into her crockpot then poured the sauce over them. She let it cook for about 10 hours; the rolls were firm and delicious with plenty of sauce to cover each one. Pam said they could be cooked in a heavy pot on a stove in less time – but very slowly.

MAGGIE'S CABBAGE ROLL CASSEROLE

"Edna, who wants to fiddle around making all them cabbage rolls when they can make a casserole that tastes just as good?" Maggie asked me in her Neil's Harbour kitchen. Her son Keith echoed, "Mom, you said it."

1 pound hamburger	¹/₂ cup raw rice
1 tablespoon oil	1 can (10 oz.) tomato soup
1 onion, sliced fine	1 can water
¹/₈ teaspoon pepper	3 cups shredded cabbage
Salt to taste	Sour cream

In a large frying pan brown the meat in oil for a few minutes. Add the onion, salt, pepper, and rice; mix well. While gently browning add the soup and water. Put the cabbage in a baking dish, pour the rest over it and do not stir. Bake in a 325°F oven for 1¹/₂ hours. Put a dish of sour cream on the table to be spooned over each serving. "And that's some good," said Keith.

OLD STANDBY

There always comes a time – in my life, anyway – when I resort to this: made of leftover or fresh vegetables and ground meat, it's often surprisingly good.

No list of ingredients: I simply open my fridge and see what is in there that ought to come out. Then I supplement. In the bottom of a casserole I slice potatoes – raw or cooked ones – then a layer of whatever vegetables I have found: carrots, beans, peas, peppers, corn, parsnips, asparagus, even cabbage, broccoli, cauliflower, sprouts. The layer may be as thick as you like, but don't overdo it. If I want to use ground meat I fry it with sliced onion until it is slightly browned and spread it over the vegetables. If I use leftover meat I sauté the onion and mix it with the meat and leftover gravy. Finally, to give the dish the moisture it needs, I put enough tomatoes on top (raw, canned, or frozen ones cut in quarters). I forgot to mention: salt, pepper, and sprinkle with herbs each layer as you put it in. Cover the dish, put it in a 325°F oven for an hour or so and enjoy the illusion of a great meal coming up, because it will really smell good and often that's half the battle, isn't it? Or is it? Taste it and see. As long as there are no bones in the dish you can always scrape it into your blender and whizz it to an incredible soup.

PIZZA

I live miles from a pizzeria; when I want pizza I make my own. It is fun, easy and has many variations. Making the dough is a cinch – just like bread dough with whole wheat flour. For 2 large pizzas:

1¹/₂ cups lukewarm water
1 teaspoon sugar
1 tablespoon dry yeast
3 tablespoons vegetable oil

1 teaspoon salt
4 cups flour, all purpose or whole wheat or half of each

In a mixing bowl stir the sugar into the lukewarm water, sprinkle the yeast on top, let it stand for 10 minutes then stir thoroughly; add the oil, salt, and flour till you have a stiff dough. You might need more flour. Turn it out on a floured surface and knead till it's elastic and quite firm. Plop it back into the bowl, cover it with plastic wrap or a dish towel, put it in a warm place free from draughts and let it rise for a couple of hours, till it has more than doubled.

Meantime make the tomato sauce (unless you have some on hand):

1 cup sliced onions
2 tablespoons vegetable oil
1 teaspoon salt
1 teaspoon sugar
1 teaspoon oregano

¹/₂ teaspoon basil
¹/₄ cup parsley, chopped
1 can tomatoes, or equivalent in raw or frozen ones

Cook the onions in the oil for 5 minutes, add the rest of the ingredients and simmer for about ¹/₂ hour, stirring occasionally. It should be thick enough to spread on the pizza dough when it is ready.

Now comes the fun and the ingenuity and the gutsy taste of the pizza. Divide the dough in half, form each half into a ball and flatten it, roll it if you like, or keep stretching it with your hands as they do it on the TV ads, till you have at least a 14-inch circle. Put it on a large enough cookie sheet, if you don't have a regular pizza pan, as I don't. Crimp the edge so it will be high enough to keep the filling from bubbling out. Turn up your oven to 400°F and put the dough in for 10 minutes.

Now the filling: What do you like? What do you have? Try different things:

GROUND BEEF FILLING: I slather the tomato sauce over the pizza dough, cover it more or less with crumbled ground beef – raw or cooked – or leftover ground beef or other meat. Next I dot it all over with cheese: mozzarella if I have it because it melts so quickly; cheddar works well, too. Next I might have sliced mushrooms, slightly fried in butter, and/or some sliced ripe or green olives. Put it in the oven for about 20 minutes, enjoy its aroma, take it out and serve it at once with a tossed salad.

The dough might be thicker than what you get in a pizzeria – the way my just-out-from-Italy friend used to make it when I visited her. She'd go to an Italian bakery on Dundas Street in Toronto, bring home a chunk of dough and go on from there. Her pizzas were never spicy or hot and they were wonderful.

FILLING FOR VEGETARIANS: I slather the dough with tomato sauce, spread a cupful or more of cheese over it all – I've even used cottage cheese – then ripe olives, green peppers, mushrooms, sometimes asparagus, and a generous sprinkling of parmesan. If my guests hadn't been vegetarians I'd have sprinkled some bacon bits over it all.

ANCHOVY OR SARDINE FILLING: Tomato sauce on the dough, then if you have anchovies use them and be fancy. I had none so instead I boned a tin of Canadian sardines, laid them neatly in a sunburst pattern round the outer edge of the pizza, put olives between the fish tails in the centre, sprinkled all with grated cheese, then parmesan.

These are merely suggestions – look in your fridge or your

cupboard for inspiration. If you come up with something super write it down in your little black book so you'll be able to make it again.

PEPPERONI OR SAUSAGE FILLING: But who has pepperoni? Smoked pork sausage cut in slices and nicely laid on the tomato sauce, or little pork sausages previously cooked, or even sliced summer sausage or salami cut in V's and dotted on in a pattern then sprinkled with cheese.

When the pizza comes out of the oven, all bubbly and smelling divinely, cut it in pie-shaped segments with a sharp knife, or if the crust is too crispy, cut it with bacon sheers. My pizzas are not always a perfect circle – but who cares – they taste good.

They're great heated over the next day, too (or you might freeze one and use it later). I put mine in my electric frying pan with the lid on to heat instead of drying it out in the oven. It was a bit of a squeeze but it worked. And was wonderful.

ONE-DISH BARBECUE FRANKS

Lorna told me that not only kids love this flavourful frankfurter casserole.

10 small potatoes, unpeeled
3 tablespoons melted butter, margarine, or oil
¹/₄ cup coarsely chopped onions
1 tablespoon butter or salad oil
4 teaspoons white sugar
¹/₄ cup lemon juice
1 teaspoon dry mustard
4 teaspoons Worcestershire sauce
¹/₂ cup ketchup
¹/₂ cup water
1 package frankfurters

Cook the potatoes in 1 inch of boiling salted water, covered, for 15 minutes. Drain and place in a large baking dish; brush with melted butter or oil. Brown in 450°F oven, turning once. Meanwhile in a small skillet sauté onion in oil or butter, add remaining ingredients except franks. Bring to a boil. Slit the frankfurters. Turn oven to 350°F and arrange franks below the potatoes in the baking dish; pour the sauce over them. Bake 20 minutes, basting and turning once.

WHOLE WHEAT PANCAKES
for 6

Carol Hudgins is a nutritionist and she likes to invent things that are good for her three little children and her university professor husband, who looks very happy.

3 eggs, beaten slightly
Milk to fill 3 cups, including the eggs
1 cup whole wheat flour
$^1/_2$ cup white flour
2 teaspoons baking powder
2 tablespoons sugar
$^1/_4$ cup bacon fat

Pour the milk and eggs over the sifted dry ingredients and stir until the batter is lumpy-smooth, if you know what I mean. Fry in bacon fat in a 350°F frying pan. Serve with butter, maple syrup, and a wedge of lemon. Carol said her daddy always liked a bit of lemon with maple syrup. Also that a friend who had never liked pancakes liked these enough to eat six.

EGGS BENEDICT – WITH VARIATIONS

This is just a suggestion – great for a loner or for a special breakfast or a lunch with a green salad.

Make a rich cream sauce or a cheese sauce.

Fry as much bacon as you need, or sauté slices of ham and keep hot.

Split and toast as many English muffins as you need, or use toasted bread or buns.

Poach as many eggs as you need.

Now put them all together – the buttered, hot muffin on the bottom, next the bacon or ham, a slice of tomato if you have one, then the poached egg, and over all the rich creamy sauce. Sprinkle it with paprika, put a piece of parsley alongside and be grateful.

CHIVE BLOSSOM OMELET
serves 4

A springtime treat that can be made when the chives are in bloom – or before and after.

4 eggs	1 teaspoon chives, cut fine
4 tablespoons milk or water	2 tablespoons butter
1/2 teaspoon salt	12 chive blossoms
Pepper to taste	
1 tablespoon parsley, cut very fine	

Beat the eggs just enough to blend the whites and yolks well. Add milk or water, seasoning, parsley, and chives. Melt the butter in a heavy pan and pour in the mixture. When the edges begin to set reduce the heat. When the bottom is browned – watch it – sprinkle the blossoms over the omelet and fold it. Serve immediately on a heated plate. The blossoms add a delicious flavour and colour but the omelet without the blossoms can taste good at any time of the year.

LOW-CALORIE CHEESE SAUCE

This is a quick and easy one and almost as good as something richer.

2 cups water	1 teaspoon flavoured salt
2 tablespoons flour	1/8 teaspoon pepper
4 tablespoons instant dry milk powder or more	1 or 2 tablespoons very sharp cheddar or more

Put the water in your blender, measure in all the rest except the cheese and blend till it's foamy. Pour into a heavy saucepan at high heat, stirring all the time. It thickens in a few minutes. Take it off the stove, add the grated cheese and stir till it melts. That's it. If you want a thicker sauce add more flour. Use it without the cheese as a cream sauce. Or put in herbs or any other flavouring you like; the calorie count will stay down. Basic cream sauces can be flavoured with dill, curry powder, pimiento.

TOMATO CREAM SAUCE

So easy and so zestful – to put over an omelet or soufflé or anything that needs a delicious sauce.

Some cream of tomato soup (undiluted from a can) mixed with some sour cream. Try it and you'll see. Taste till you think it's just right to suit you.

SUPPER WITH LAURENCE

I am so lucky. Occasionally my much-younger-than-I friends call and ask if I'd like them to come to my house and make me a supper. The first one to do it was Ashley Lubin who made a Chinese meal. He brought all the ingredients, candles, roses, and a beautiful girl with a cloak of honey blonde hair and eyes the colour of forget-me-nots.

Next came Laurence McNaught: slim, with masses of curly black hair, soft brown eyes and a dreamy soft voice that reflects the accents of his Scottish father and Maltese mother. With him came Paul, tall and handsome. They had a swim first then drank wine and chatted till I wondered if the great bags of groceries they'd brought were forgotten.

It was eight o'clock when they started. Paul peeled and sliced 4 or 5 onions. Laurence sautéed them in oil with garlic, then added a large can of tomatoes and a small one of tomato paste. He tended it lovingly as it simmered while Paul cleaned and took mushrooms off their stems (and would have thrown them away but Laurence rescued them for his sauce).

Under Laurence's direction I chopped up cauliflower tops; Paul cleaned green peppers, putting the seeds into Laurence's brew – they said the germ, the essence of anything, is in its seeds which should never be discarded.

Next Laurence put 12 teaspoons cut parsley and almost a teaspoon of basil into his sauce, $1/2$ teaspoon coriander, $1/2$ teaspoon curry powder. "It smells kind of nice," he said, "reminds me of the sauce we made in Mexico by the side of a river with turquoise water."

Paul tasted as he crumbled some feta cheese, putting cauliflower bits on thin slices and handing some to me, until Laurence reminded him that he needed everything for his dish.

Laurence put the cauliflower into the pepper cups with the crumbled cheese, pieces of canned pimiento on top; he put the pepper lids back on, perfectly matched, then dropped them carefully into the tomato sauce. They floated – to his dismay. He patted them down, put them in the oven at 350°F for about an hour. Meantime Paul cooked noodles, putting a tablespoon of oil in the water so the noodles wouldn't stick.

At 11:15 our dinner was ready. Green peppers with the sauce spooned over the noodles, sprinkled with parmesan. With wine. And very good, too. For dessert Laurence brought expensive Byng cherries dipped in pure thick sweet cream. We finished dining at midnight. Nancy was amazed! She told me, "When Laurence has a dinner party at his house he starts preparing the food after everyone gets there. That is the evening's entertainment. We sometimes don't eat until 2 in the morning."

HAROLD HORWOOD'S CHINESE DISHES

Harold is a very special person: Newfoundland's award-winning novelist, naturalist, journalist, politician, teacher, explorer, he also does most of the cooking for his Beachy Cove household which is frequently expanded to more than fourteen because Harold takes in many strays and visiting writers. He learned about cooking in a Chinese restaurant.

While he was writer-in-residence at the University of Western Ontario, Harold came to my house one day with his wife Corky, little Andrew, baby Leah, and all the makings for a Chinese meal. He prepared it, we greatly enjoyed it, and he sent me his recipes for my cookbook. He wrote:

"Though the main part of the Chinese cuisine is an acquired skill that cannot be taught from recipes, Clear and Egg Drop Soup, Foo Yong (omelet), and barbecued meats can be done successfully by anybody."

All Harold's recipes use Chinese soy sauce. He says American or Japanese soy sauces are double in strength. If you use American sauce reduce to half the amount and add water to make up. Japanese soy sauce should be avoided altogether because it is not only double strength but also nearly saturated with salt.

CHINESE CLEAR SOUP

2 cups stock (beef, chicken, pork, or shellfish)
1 tablespoon Chinese soy sauce
3 or 4 medium-sized mushrooms, thinly sliced
1 cup thin egg noodles
1 small green onion with leaves
$^1/_4$ cup bean sprouts (optional)

To boiling stock add soy sauce and mushroom slices; boil for 3 minutes. Drop in the noodles and boil 3 minutes longer. Just before removing from the heat add sliced onion and bean sprouts.

EGG DROP SOUP

2 cups Clear Soup (above) with any or all of the vegetables and noodles
1 egg

While the soup comes to a boil, beat an egg with a fork until it is fairly thin; when the soup boils vigorously, pour the egg into it from a height of 2 feet or so, stirring the soup as you do it. Remove from heat at once and serve.

FOO YONG

Harold says this amount makes a refreshingly different breakfast or lunch for two.

3 eggs
1 teaspoon Chinese soy sauce
$^1/_2$ to 1 cup fresh sliced mushrooms or bean sprouts
2 tablespoons cooking oil

Harold directs: Start by pre-heating one of the large elements on the surface of your stove until it is red, and the top element of your oven until it's good and bloody hot. In a bowl beat the eggs with a fork until they reach the classic omelet stage; stir in the soy sauce until the colour is more or less even. Heat the oil in a large frying pan until it begins to smoke. Pour in the egg mixture and immediately remove from the heat. Over the surface of the uncooked egg sprinkle generously the mushroom slices or bean sprouts. Put the pan in the oven 6 inches under the heated top element; peek every few seconds to see when the eggs begin to bubble then take the pan out and fold the egg over like an omelet.

Harold says, "I recommend that you try not more than three eggs at a time. If you have to cook for a crowd, do the three-egg thing over and over again. Each panful takes only abut two minutes."

BARBECUE SAUCE

Harold writes: "You begin by making the sauce."

¹/₄ cup molasses
¹/₂ cup Chinese soy sauce
¹/₂ cup water
2 teaspoons powdered ginger

¹/₂ teaspoon powdered cloves
¹/₂ teaspoon powdered onion
¹/₄ teaspoon powdered garlic

Put everything in a large screw-capped jar and shake it up. That's all. Shake it again before using it, as the spices may tend to settle. To make Garlic Sauce for garlic ribs, you simply add more garlic.

BARBECUED CUBED PORK or BARBECUED SPARE RIBS

Start cooking cubed pork or spare ribs in hot oil in a wok or a large frying pan. (The wok is no advantage except for a mixed dish that requires various cooking times.) After three or four minutes of stirring the meat with a spatula, pour in the barbecue sauce (above) in a reasonable quantity and keep stirring over high heat until the sauce disappears and the meat is tender.

CHICKEN AND TURKEYS

Harold roasts fowl in a covered pan with the barbecue sauce poured generously over them, inside and out, basting them frequently, till they are brown and tender.

7

Salads and Salad Dressings

One day I asked Nancy and her friend Miriam from Chicago to give me some ideas for salads. Nancy said, "We always have the same thing, lettuce or spinach leaves, onion, garlic, tomatoes, bean or alfalfa sprouts if we can get them; with an oil and vinegar dressing, that's it."

"Yes, for me, too; it's always the same," Miriam told me. "Every day the same."

Though there is the possibility of infinite variety in salads, many people have the same salad every day. So do many restaurants, with dressings limited to oil and vinegar or Miracle Whip, the dominant taste being vinegar.

It was a happy day for me when I discovered that one table-spoon of commercial sour cream has two and a half times fewer calories than one tablespoon of salad oil (50 calories for sour cream, 125 calories for oil).

No Waterloo County dinner is complete without a sour-cream salad: a teaspoonful of sugar, a teaspoon of vinegar, salt, pepper and half a cupful of sour cream should be enough for three or four people when tossed with tender leaf lettuce with chives or onion, or thinly sliced cucumbers, or barely cooked schnippled (frenched) wax beans. The dominant flavour is subtle and creamy, not sour.

Any Mennonite woman will tell you to use a warm sour cream dressing for endive, spinach, cabbage, potatoes, or dandelion greens. Garnished with hard-boiled eggs and bacon bits: served with smoked pork chops or sausages, roasted pigs' tails or spare ribs with a schnitz pie for dessert you'll have a memorable meal.

I'm sorry I can't repeat all the salads I've written in *Food That Really Schmecks*. I haven't the same proselitizing en-thusiasm for the salads I'm giving you here, but I have tried to give you variety: accompanying salads, salads that are a whole meal, crisp salads that will keep for a week in your fridge and a few salad dressings.

I can't imagine anyone making a jellied or moulded salad for anything but a party. Like jewels in a crown, they look quite impressive and guests always say, "How pretty, I hate to cut into it." But served with hot things on a plate they melt and wet. I seldom make jellied salads, can't bear the suspense of knowing if they'll come out of the mould all in one piece; if they have substance the hazard is greater, if they are merely jelled liquid I'd rather drink liquid. I'll give you a few recipes that I've enjoyed at the homes of friends who are braver than I.

MOTHER'S GREEN LEAF SALAD

Mother often gave us this wonderful salad that seemed to be just right with whatever else she served. Sometimes she used only spinach leaves, or endive, a mixture of both with some let-tuce.

As many greens as you need for the number of people you're serving

1 slice of bacon per person to be served, cut in ¼-inch pieces

1 teaspoon brown sugar

1 teaspoon bacon fat per serving

½ teaspoon mild vinegar per serving

Salt and pepper to taste

3 tablespoons sour cream per serving, or less

½ hardboiled egg per person, sliced or chopped

Wash and drain the greens and remove coarse stems. Fry the bacon bits till crisp, remove and drain. To the bacon fat in the pan over low heat add the sugar and stir till it's more or less melted; stir in the salt and pepper and gently add the vinegar, being careful lest it might spit. (The sugar might become hard, if so, let it melt.) Blend well and let cool before you blend in the sour cream. It should be smooth and the thickness of mayonnaise; you might need more cream. Just before serving pour it over the mixed greens torn to bite-sized pieces. Toss gently to get some of the sauce on all the greens: not soggy – just nicely coated but not skimpy either. . . . Add more cream if you haven't enough. Garnish with the bacon bits and hardboiled eggs.

The oftener you make this the more adept you will become at judging the amounts for the dressing. It's really quite simple, unusual, and the best tossed salad I know.

SOUR CREAM

You can make your own sour cream from whipping cream by stirring in a tablespoon of buttermilk and leaving it at room temperature till it thickens.

FOR LAZY LONERS

Scrape, scrub, and eat a carrot every day. It's loaded with vitamins and minerals. Eat a stalk of celery with the leaves: it has calcium, sodium, potassium, phosphorus, iron, and vitamins A and C. Eat a banana. For lunch I often slice a banana over lettuce, sprinkle it with salted peanuts and dribbles of salad dressing. An apple done the same way is good with cubes of cheese.

CRANBERRY-CABBAGE SALAD
8 servings

A colourful, crisp, tart salad that goes well with chicken, turkey, or pork.

6 cups finely shredded red cabbage
1 cup drained cooked cranberries
Sour cream with Mother's Salad Dressing Concentrate (page 137)
1 cup sliced celery

Mix all the ingredients just before serving.

RICE AND CHICKEN SALAD
4 servings

Just as good made with ham, turkey, tuna, salmon, shrimp, or what have you.

1 to 2 cups cooked diced chicken, leftover, frozen, or a small tin
1 to 2 cups cooked rice
1 long stem of celery, sliced
A few slices of stuffed olives (optional)
$^1/_2$ green pepper, diced (optional)
1 tablespoon minced onion or finely chopped chives or green onion

1 cup green peas, raw, frozen, or cooked
2 tablespoons chopped parsley
1 tablespoon or more chutney or relish
$^1/_2$ to 1 cup mayonnaise
2 tablespoons sour cream

Mix all the solid ingredients. Keep the mixture in your fridge and add the chutney blended with the mayonnaise and sour cream just before serving on fresh lettuce or a ring of watercress with a garnish of radish, tomato, or olives. A few toasted almonds are a pleasant addition as well.

YOU-NAME-IT SALAD

You'll be amazed at what a good salad you can concoct by rummaging in your fridge and combining a few odds and ends. I'm not suggesting that you use all the ingredients at once.

Lettuce	Cooked or raw asparagus
Cabbage, shredded	Green peppers, pimiento
Celery stems and leaves	Chives, green onion and tops,
Crisp cauliflower	onion slices
Sliced olives	Spinach
Cooked corn, peas, or beans	Soya nuts or others
Tomatoes	Shredded coconut
Chick peas, kidney beans	What else is there?

Chop, not too fine, a combination you think you would like; mix it with mayonnaise or toss it with salad dressing, put it on a lettuce leaf, endive, or watercress, and you'll have a respectable, attractive, nutritious, non-fattening meal. There are so many variations that you could have fun trying something different every day.

RALPH'S GREEK SALAD

Ever since my brother-in-law visited Greece last summer he has been treating people to his own variation of a Greek Salad. He says it's all you need for a meal, with a fat hot bun. Combine in a bowl:

1 Spanish, Italian, or any mild onion, finely sliced in rings	Parsley, a few sprigs, not finely cut
2 tomatoes cut in wedges	2 or 3 inches of cucumber, sliced thin
1 cup crumbled feta cheese, or any other kind if you don't have feta	$^1/_4$ cup ripe olives cut in quarters
$^1/_2$ green pepper, sliced and cut in thin rings or squares, not too fine	

The Greeks Ralph visited didn't use lettuce but Ralph tears and tosses some in. He makes the dressing as close to serving time as possible:

1 garlic clove, mashed	**7 tablespoons olive oil, but**
1 tablespoon wine	**another oil will do**
vinegar	**Salt and pepper**

Mash the garlic clove and add it to the vinegar. (Use lemon juice if you don't have a mild vinegar.) Add 4 tablespoons oil and beat with a fork, add salt and pepper, then 3 more table-spoons oil. Blend very well before drizzling it over the salad greens, mixing it lightly.

Ralph likes this so well that he often serves it as an accompaniment to a dinner or buffet supper.

CRISP-KEEPING COLESLAW

This will keep for a week in the fridge, ready to serve whenever you need something crisp and refreshing. Very handy; Norm and Barbie often have this.

1 small head of cabbage	**$^1/_3$ cup water**
1 onion	**$^1/_4$ cup vinegar**
1 green pepper	**$^2/_3$ cup sugar (or less)**
2 stalks of celery	**1 teaspoon celery seed**
Salt and pepper to taste	**$^1/_4$ teaspoon dry mustard**

Shred the cabbage or chop it, slice the onion very finely and do the same with the green pepper and celery. Blend the other ingredients in a saucepan, bring them to a boil and let cool. Mix the dressing with the greens and let stand in fridge for 24 hours before you serve it. Put it in a china dish, not plastic or metal. Cover tightly. Drain the dressing off before serving but save it to pour on what is left over and put it back in the fridge. When you've used all the solids you may add more to the dressing.

MIXED COOKED VEGETABLE SALAD
at least 10 servings

This colourful salad keeps a long time, can be frozen, and may be served as a relish as well as a salad. Margaret Phelan sent me the recipe from her winter home in Arizona where she served it with a big roast beef dinner.

2 cups cooked, fresh, or frozen beans – or 1 can cut green beans	1 diced pimiento (canned or fresh)
2 cups cooked, fresh, or frozen peas – or 1 can small peas	1 green pepper, diced 4 stems of celery, cut fine 1 medium onion, cut fine
2 cups cooked, fresh, or frozen corn – or 1 can Mexicana corn	

Drain the cooked vegetables and mix with the celery, green pepper, and onion.

Dressing:
¹/₂ cup sugar, or a bit more
1 cup white vinegar or less

¹/₂ cup water
1 teaspoon flavoured salt
¹/₂ teaspoon black pepper

Bring to a boil, cool, then pour over the vegetables, toss lightly and marinate over night. Or longer. Drain off the dressing before you serve it but keep it to put back on the vegetables that are left. Very convenient to have in your fridge.

APPLE SALAD FOR HILDA
for 2 or 3 people

Every Monday when Hilda comes to my house she'd rather have an apple salad than anything else. It's refreshing and doesn't take long to make on a busy day.

2 or 3 large apples
1 thick stem of celery
Handful of walnuts
Enough mayonnaise to coat everything

¹/₄ cup cubed cheddar (optional)
¹/₄ cup raisins (optional)
¹/₂ cup sliced cabbage (optional)

Core and slice the apples, chop the celery and nuts. Mix with any optional ingredients and mayonnaise. Serve on lettuce. Mother's Concentrate (page 137) blended with sour cream is good with this.

JELLIED APPLE SALAD

If you want the same salad prepared ahead of time and for more people you might add ¼ cup of lemon juice to a package of lime or lemon jello, dissolved and chilled to the consistency of raw egg whites. Stir in the above ingredients, turn into a mould and chill until it is firm. Serve with lettuce and mayonnaise and fresh hot cheese biscuits.

NORA MYER'S JELLIED RHUBARB SALAD
6 to 8 servings

Very pretty and tasty on a cold luncheon plate served in Nora's and Ray's beautiful old stone house near Cambridge.

**4 cups rhubarb, cut in 1-inch
   pieces**
¹/₂ cup water
³/₄ cup sugar
**6 oz. package of strawberry
   jello**

1 cup cold water
1 tablespoon orange rind
**¹/₄ cup chopped nuts
   (optional)**
**1 cup finely chopped celery
   (optional)**

Simmer the rhubarb, water, and sugar until the rhubarb is tender, about 10 minutes. Remove from the heat, sprinkle in the jelly powder and stir till it's dissolved. Stir in the cold water and orange rind (and nuts and celery, if you want your salad to be crisp). Pour the mixture into a ring mould rinsed in cold water. Chill till firm. Turn out on a platter, put salad greens around, and cottage cheese in the centre.

Without the celery you could use it as a dessert with whipped cream and cookies.

Don't make company dishes except for company, then you won't tire of them. Some things should remain special. I once had a friend who wanted to have oysters every day. "Why not?" he said. "I can afford them." He also wanted every night to be like New Year's Eve.

To make your eating life interesting, meals should be made up of plain and fancy. Every day one thing should stand out.

FISH MOUSSE AT RUNDLES

This is a delicacy that should not be missed. It was served with crisp cucumber salad and soda bread before the main course. The fish used was leftover salmon.

1 pound flaked cooked fish	1 teaspoon paprika
1 cup milk	3 tablespoons flour
1 slice onion	1 teaspoon gelatine
1 bay leaf	3 tablespoons heavy cream
6 peppercorns	1 egg white
2 tablespoons butter	

Pass the fish through a blender for a second or mash it with a fork. Heat the milk with onion, bay leaf and peppercorns, infuse and strain. Melt the butter, add paprika, cook for 1 minute. Remove from the heat and blend in the flour, add the hot milk and cook to the boiling point. Put away for a while to cool in a bowl, not the pan it was cooked in. Mix the cold sauce with the fish a little at a time. Dissolve the gelatine over heat with a little water, add to the fish mixture. Whip the cream lightly; whisk the egg white and fold both gently into the fish mixture. Pour into a large mould or individual ones. The result was firm and tender, not stiff and rubbery.

Perfect.

TUNA FISH SPREAD, SALAD, OR DIP

This is a rich, flavourful concotion that can be used various ways and in small amounts.

8 ounces cream cheese	2 tablespoons finely chopped celery
2 tablespoons onion, chopped fine	2 tablespoons chopped pickle (optional)
1/8 teaspoon curry powder, no more	1/8 teaspoon pepper
1/2 teaspoon seasoned salt	1/2 teaspoon Worcestershire sauce
2 hardboiled eggs, chopped fine	4 tablespoons mayonnaise
1 can (6 oz.) flaked tuna	

Cream the cheese, add the remaining ingredients and serve on your favourite crackers or use a dollop on a salad plate with other salad things or use as a dip. A little goes a long way.

Before you serve guests – or your family – check your fridge to be sure you haven't forgotten something you've slaved over: that special sauce, or the melon balls.

CHIVE CHEESE DRESSING, SPREAD, OR DIP

This is one of my favourite things; I often make a meal of it spread generously on my own biscuits or crackers. Sometimes I use it as a salad dressing over chopped mixed vegetables. Or as a dip. Kath invented it because she doesn't like the texture of cottage cheese.

A good handful of chives, cut in ¼-inch pieces   **Creamed cottage cheese**
Salt and pepper to taste

Put the chives in your blender or food processor and gradually add the cheese as you keep blending, until the whole thing is a lovely soft green and smooth as sour cream. If you have dry cottage cheese, you could add sour cream or yogurt to give it the moisture it needs. I'm not fooling: this is terrific. And easy.

HERB CHEESE OR PARSLEY CHEESE

The same as chive cheese but use herbs or parsley instead of chives. Or try a combination.

FROZEN CHIVES AND PARSLEY

In the spring when the chives in your garden are flourishing, cut them and arrange them in bundles, wrap them tightly in plastic bags and freeze them to provide fresh greens through the winter. Simply hold the bundle and slice off whatever you need. Do the same with parsley.

TOSSED SALAD DRESSING

Phil Kitchen's Wellesley Township neighbours taught her how to keep a tossed salad crisp a long time before serving.

3 tablespoons sugar
¹/₂ cup vinegar
¹/₂ cup water

1 tablespoon salad oil
Seasonings to taste

Blend the sugar, vinegar, and water, then toss lightly with the salad greens and keep in a cool place, for several hours if necessary. Just before serving drain off the liquid, add to it the oil and seasonings and toss it again with your greens.

MOTHER'S SALAD DRESSING CONCENTRATE

A little of this thick, nippy dressing goes a long way when mixed with whipped or sour cream and seems to be just right with any salads that have fruit in them – or cabbage, or almost anything.

1 teaspoon flour
1 teaspoon dry mustard
Pinch of salt
¹/₂ cup water
1 egg, well beaten

¹/₄ cup brown sugar
¹/₄ cup vinegar
Sprinkle of cayenne pepper
Whipped or sour cream

Mix the flour, mustard, and salt with the water, add to the beaten egg and brown sugar. Slowly stir in the vinegar and sprinkle in the cayenne. Thicken the mixture in a double boiler, over hot water, stirring all the time. Chill it before you blend a little of it with the whipped or sour cream. How much cream you use depends on the size of your salad and how nippy you like your dressing. Taste it. The basic dressing keeps well for ages in your fridge, tightly covered. Also if it's mixed with sour cream it will keep as long as the sour cream would without it.

EVA'S MOM'S MAYONNAISE
makes about 1 quart

Rich, creamy, and popular long before Mr. Kraft flooded the world with Miracle Whip.

¹/₂ cup vinegar
1 cup water
2 tablespoons flour
1 cup white sugar

³/₄ teaspoon salt
1 tablespoon dry mustard
1 cup whole milk
2 eggs

Heat the vinegar and water. Blend the flour, sugar, salt, and mustard together to prevent lumping. Beat the eggs somewhat and blend with the milk then stir into the dry ingredients carefully, then into the hot water and vinegar. You don't need to do it in a double boiler if you keep stirring it over low heat. Keep stirring until it thickens; it won't take long. Let cool and it will keep in your fridge for a long time.

DRESSING FOR WARM POTATO SALAD

Warm, creamy, butter-yellow, there is none better than this. I wish I could convert the world to it so I'd never again be confronted by those stiff white blobs served up with an ice cream scoop.

¹/₄ cup butter
1 cup sour cream
2 beaten eggs

1 tablespoon vinegar
1 tablespoon sugar
Salt and pepper

Melt the butter and stir the sour cream, eggs, vinegar, sugar, and seasonings into it; cook long enough in a double boiler or heavy saucepan to make a sauce that is thick but not stiff. Taste it. Pour it over and mix it with 5 or 6 medium-sized, warm, sliced potatoes and onion or chives to be garnished with hard-cooked eggs. Don't be afraid to be lavish; you might need more cream.

MAYONNAISE

John Walker, *chef de cuisine* at Rundles told us mayonnaise will turn or curdle:
1. If the oil is added too quickly;
2. If the oil is too cold;
3. If the sauce is insufficiently whisked;
4. If the egg is stale.

He said he'd rather beat hell out of himself with a wire whisk than have to wash appliances.

Into my blender I drop all the following ingredients except the salad oil.

1 egg at room temperature	**¹/₂ teaspoon celery seed**
1 teaspoon salt	**(sometimes)**
1 teaspoon mustard	**Good sprinkle of paprika**
1 teaspoon sugar	**Pinch of basil leaves**
2 tablespoons wine vinegar,	**(sometimes)**
or white wine, or lemon	**1 cup salad oil, more or less,**
juice, or a combination	**added later**

Give the blender a swift whirl for a couple of seconds, then open the pouring hole in the lid and with the motor running drip in the salad oil very very slowly, ¹/₂ teaspoonful at a time until the mixture thickens. Stop the moment it does even if you haven't put in all the oil or suddenly the whole mixture might become liquid.

And then what? Put an egg yolk, at room temperature, into a bowl and very, very slowly stir the liquid dressing into it while you hope it will do the trick. If it doesn't, simply pour your liquid dressing into a bottle and use it as a liquid dressing. And start making nice thick mayonnaise all over again, being less heavy handed this time with the oil. Good luck. It really does work 99 times out of 100.

VARIATIONS: To this basic recipe I sometimes add other flavourings: chili sauce, nuts, blue or roquefort cheese, parsley, etc. But don't overdo it.

8

Baking with Yeast

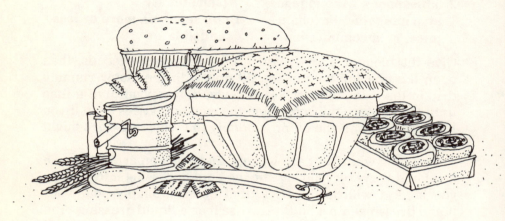

It pleases me mightily to think that I have sent hundreds, maybe thousands of people on the way to glory. I mean the glory of making, baking, and eating their own delicious, miraculous bread. Many, many men and women keep telling me with pride and enthusiasm that they started making their own bread from the Neil's Harbour recipe in *Food That Really Schmecks* and have gone on to its thirty variations of breads, buns, and rolls.

My sister, my neighbour Belle, and a number of other people had complained to me that they'd tried and tried to make bread without success; then at last they used my seemingly fail-proof Neil's Harbour recipe, and glory be, they had beautiful, tender, high, tasty golden loaves that stayed moist and delectable right to the end – which came all too soon.

I'm not boasting, I didn't invent it; I got the recipe from Clara May Ingraham who made it every week for her fisherman husband and thirteen children in Neil's Harbour, Cape Breton.

I'm not going to repeat the Neil's Harbour recipe here with its thirty variations, but I do have more recipes that I think are great and easy to make; some don't need any kneading, others can be kept in the fridge till you're ready to bake them.

I seldom now make an all-white bread. Having experimented with various flours and grains that are supposed to be more nutritious, I prefer the heavier, more gutsy, more flavourful loaves I make with whole wheat flour, wheat germ, rolled oats molasses, bran, cracked wheat, chopped grains, rye flour, etc. in various combinations.

As well, I've been making some light, lovely quick rolls, pretzels, English muffins, buttercakes, luscious mince meat and spicy hot cross buns, sourdough pancakes, Arabic bread, Christmas stollen, kuchen, and piroschky. Merely listing them here excites me to get up and make some.

PATTI'S QUICK-TO-MAKE BREAD
3 loaves

When Patti was twelve she made delicious crusty loaves of bread. I asked for her recipe and discovered it was almost the same as the basic Neil's Harbour Bread recipe in *Food That Really Schmecks*, with Patti's own simplification.

1 cup lukewarm water	1/4 cup white sugar (or honey)
1 teaspoon white sugar	1 tablespoon salt
2 tablespoons yeast granules (2 packets)	1/2 cup salad oil or melted shortening
2 cups lukewarm water (or more)	About 9 cups all-purpose flour or whole wheat

Dissolve the teaspoon of sugar in the cup of warm water, sprinkle the yeast over it and let stand for about 10 minutes, then stir till the yeast is dissolved. Stir in the 2 cupfuls of warm water, salt, honey, oil, and – one cupful at a time – enough flour to make a soft dough. Mix thoroughly. When the dough loses its shiny wet look it should be ready. (The Neil's Harbour Bread is kneaded at this point but Patti didn't bother.) Cover the bowl with plastic and let the dough rise in a warm place away from draughts till doubled in bulk, about 1½ hours.

Divide the dough and shape into 3 or 4 loaves, put them in buttered loaf pans. Let rise again until doubled. Bake in a 400°F oven for about 30 minutes. Tip the loaves from the pans to a rack and let cool slightly before devouring.

VARIATIONS: You can vary this recipe by adding wheat germ, or herbs, or raisins, or anything you think might be interesting.

If your bread seems pale on the bottom or does not give a hollow sound when you flick it with your finger, put it back in the pan and into the oven a few minutes longer. No harm will be done, bread is very obliging.

Some evening when there's a crummy half hour between your favourite TV programs, stir up a batch of bread or buns. Let the dough rest till you're ready to go to bed; punch it down, put it in loaf pans and into your fridge or a cold place. In the morning take it out and let it rise to double in bulk; it will take quite a while to come up to room temperature – but you don't have to watch it, you can get on with your other work or your novel.

BUNS AND ROLLS AND PIZZA

Instead of making several loaves of bread, make little balls of some of the dough; drop them into buttered muffin tins or put them side by side in a cake pan. Let them rise to double and bake at 400°F for about 15 minutes. Or take a grapefruit-sized chunk, flatten it with a rolling pin, stretch it thin to make a pizza crust.

HAMBURGER BUNS

Roll some of the bread dough ¾ inch thick, cut it with a tuna tin, let the buns rise and bake them at 400°F for 15 minutes. Only one drawback: after tasting homemade hamburger buns no one will want the store bought variety again. Especially if you've made them with whole wheat flour.

HOT DOG ROLLS

Roll the bread dough ³/₄ inch thick, cut in strips and round the edges; let rise and bake at 400°F for 15 minutes.

LETTING BREAD RISE IN A WARM PLACE: Bread rises best in a temperature of 80°F (22°C); If it is much cooler the rising is sluggish and takes longer; if too hot the yeast will die. An overheated apartment would be perfect. Or a hot summer day. Belle turns on her oven to its lowest setting for 5 minutes, then turns if OFF and puts the dough in with the door shut. A friend puts hers on a heating pad, well wrapped and turned low. I put mine on a sunny window ledge or on a shelf above an electric heating unit. Mother used to put her bowl of dough on a board on top of a radiator. Find your own spot.

BUY YOUR YEAST in bulk and keep it for months in your fridge or freezer. It's much less expensive than those little 1 tablespoon-size packets.

IF YOU ARE INTERRUPTED while mixing or kneading your dough, don't worry about it: it will be easier to handle when you get back to it. Cover it if you're having a long-winded phone conversation. If the dough has risen smooth and puffy above the rim of your bowl and you can't carry on with the process just then, don't let it run over; simply punch the dough down and let it rise a second or even a third time. It will rise more quickly each time – but not forever. Nor will it rise much after you put it in the oven.

BUTTERMILK SCONE LOAF
2 loaves

Chewy, light, with great flavour – especially when toasted.

2 cups buttermilk, or sour milk	¹/₄ cup shortening
¹/₂ teaspoon baking soda	¹/₂ cup lukewarm water
¹/₄ cup white sugar	1 teaspoon sugar
2 teaspoons salt	1 tablespoon yeast granules
	6 cups all-purpose flour

Scald the buttermilk or sour milk, stir in the baking soda, sugar, salt, and shortening and cool to lukewarm. Dissolve the yeast and proceed as in Patti's Bread recipe. Instead of putting the loaves in pans you might shape them into 3 large round balls and put them on a cookie sheet.

BUTTERMILK IN A RECIPE: Whenever I get a new cookbook I go through it and put an S beside those recipes that need sour milk or buttermilk and a Y for a yeast dough.

TO MAKE BUTTERMILK: Simply add ½ cup buttermilk to 1 quart fresh milk – real or powdered – and let it stand at room temperature till it thickens, then refrigerate it.

TO MAKE SOUR MILK: Put 1 tablespoon of lemon juice or white vinegar in the bottom of a cup, fill the cup with milk, stir and let stand at least 10 minutes to clabber.

POWDERED MILK doesn't have to be scalded but in bread recipes it should be heated to lukewarm.

WHOLE WHEAT FLOUR may be substituted for all-purpose flour in yeast recipes, but the resulting loaves might not be as light or as high.

THE AMOUNT OF FLOUR OR LIQUID in a recipe that seems exactly right at one time may not seem right at another because the absorptive quality of the flour varies with temperature and humidity. Merely add a bit more flour or liquid until the dough is easy to handle and has lost its wet look. Better too moist than too dry. And don't be nervous, you'll soon get the feel of it. Remember that bread-making is fun and therapeutic; be light-hearted about it and your bread will be light.

½ cups lukewarm water, 1 tsp. sugar, 1 pkg. yeast
(1½ cups)

2 cups hot water, 3 tbsp. sugar, 1 tbsp. occt, 3 tbsp.
lard, 2 cups cold water, 11 cups flour

Dissolve 1 tsp. sugar in lukewarm water. Add yeast
& let stand 10 min. Dissolve 3 tbsp. sugar, salt, lard
in 2 cups hot water. Add cold water & stir in yeast.
Add 7 cups flour. Let stand 15 min. Add rest of
flour & work to nice soft dough. Knead it well.
Let stand till double in bulk. Work down let stand

Let stand until ~~rises~~ then divide into
4 loafs. & let stand to rise.
Bake 350° - 30 min.

TO MAKE AN EXTRA LOAF OF BREAD: Simply add 2 to 3 cups more flour and more liquid, plus a bit more of whatever flavours it. The yeast will take care of the rest.

EVA'S WHITE BREAD
4 loaves

Eva's bread looks better than any I've ever seen: golden, crusty, high – perfect; and inside it is moist, has a smooth, even texture and tastes good enough to eat without any trimmings.

1 teaspoon sugar	**3 tablespoons lard**
$^1/_2$ cup lukewarm water	**2 cups cold water**
$1^1/_2$ tablespoons yeast	**11 cups all-purpose flour**
2 cups hot water	**(Eva uses her own wheat**
3 tablespoons sugar	**and has it ground: pure)**
1 tablespoon salt	

Dissolve 1 teaspoon sugar in $^1/_2$ cup lukewarm water, add yeast and let stand 10 minutes. Dissolve the 3 tablespoons sugar, salt, and lard in the 2 cups hot water. Add the cold water; and when the mixture is lukewarm, stir in the dissolved yeast and 7 cups of flour. Let stand 15 minutes. Add 4 more cups flour and work to a nice soft dough, not sticky. Don't be afraid to knead it well. Let it stand in a warm place, covered, in the bowl for $1^1/_2$ hours till double in bulk. Work down, let stand another hour then divide into 4 well-buttered loaf pans. Let stand one hour or till well risen and then bake at 350 for 30 minutes – or until brown and with a hollow sound when you tap it.

BARBIE'S NO-KNEADING BRAN BREAD
1 loaf

Great flavour. Barbie tosses this off in no time, and it's eaten almost as quickly. I mixed it in my food processor.

1 cup scalded milk	**1 tablespoon yeast**
2 tablespoons butter	**1 teaspoon sugar**
3 tablespoons molasses	**$^1/_2$ cup lukewarm water**
1 teaspoon salt	**$2^1/_2$ cups all-purpose flour**
$1^1/_2$ cups bran	

Scald the milk, add the butter, molasses, salt and bran; let cool to lukewarm. Dissolve the yeast with the sugar in the lukewarm water, let stand 10 minutes, stir and add to the milk mixture. Stir in the flour, half a cupful at a time. Beat it in until it is too stiff to beat then just mix it well. (I put everything in my food processor and let it whirl till a ball of dough was formed. Fantastic!) Cover the bowl, put it in a warm spot, covered, and let it rise till it doubles, about 1½ hours. Stir it again and scrape the dough into a well-buttered loaf pan. Cover and let rise again until doubled. Bake in a 400°F oven for 20 minutes, or till it is brown on all sides. Remove at once from the pan, put on a rack to cool – then try to control its demise.

I can't imagine making a yeast thing that yields only one loaf. I like yeast things so much that I always want to double the recipe: the surplus can be a treat for my neighbour or tucked away in the freezer for that day when it will be a pleasant surprise to discover it.

BARBIE'S CHEESE BREAD
2 loaves

When Barbie wants to give her family a real treat this is it.

2 cups milk, scalded
1 tablespoon soft shortening
1 tablespoon salt
2 tablespoons sugar
2½ cups finely grated strong cheddar
2 tablespoons dry yeast
1 teaspoon white sugar
½ cup lukewarm water
6 cups all-purpose flour, approximately
1 teaspoon dry mustard
½ teaspoon paprika
¼ cup cheese and butter for topping

Scald the milk, add the shortening, salt, 2 tablespoons sugar, 2½ cups cheese; stir and cool to lukewarm. Dissolve the yeast and teaspoon of sugar in the ½ cup lukewarm water, let stand 10 minutes and stir. Add to the milk mixture. Stir in the flour, one cupful at a time, with the mustard and paprika. When the dough is smooth and elastic knead it, return it to the bowl and let rise in a warm place till doubled in bulk; cover the bowl with a towel or plastic. Shape into loaves, let rise in buttered loaf pans till doubled. Bake in a 375°F oven for almost 40 minutes, covering loosely with aluminum foil if they start to brown too much on top. Remove from the oven, brush the tops with melted butter and sprinkle with ¼ cup grated cheese. Return to the oven for a moment to melt the cheese. Cool on a rack, then watch the loaves disappear.

JEAN SALTER'S WHOLE WHEAT AND CRACKED GRAIN BREAD WITH BRAN
4 loaves

This is the flavourful, nutritious, chewy bread I make most often.

4²/₃ cups boiling water
2 cups cracked wheat, or Red River Cereal, or 5- or 7- or 12-grain cereal
1 cup bran
4 tablespoons vegetable oil
1 tablespoon salt
(I put in ½ cup molasses, Jean doesn't)

1½ cups dried skim milk powder (optional)
4 tablespoons wheat germ
1 teaspoon sugar
1 cup lukewarm water
2 tablespoons dry yeast
9½ cups whole wheat flour

Pour boiling water on the cracked grain and bran; leave until lukewarm. Add salt, oil, molasses, skim milk powder, wheat germ, and stir. Dissolve the sugar in the cupful of lukewarm water, sprinkle the yeast on top and let it stand for 10 minutes till the yeast floats; stir and add it to the lukewarm grain mixture. Add the whole wheat flour 1 cupful at a time, beating it in thoroughly at first then mixing till it is smooth. The dough should be quite soft. Turn it out on a floured surface, sprinkle flour over it and knead it. You'll probably have sticky hands because the dough should be quite moist. When it feels smooth and all together, plop it back into the bowl to rise, covered in a warm place, for 1½ hours or until doubled. Shape into loaves and place in 4 well-buttered pans. Let rise again until doubled. Bake in a 400°F oven for about 40 minutes. Remove from the pans and cool on a rack. Try to resist eating it hot with butter melting into it – that's when I eat 3 or 4 slices. And do I not gain weight? I won't tell you.

VIM AND VIGOUR BREAD
4 loaves

This should keep you healthy and enthusiastic.

$3^1/_2$ cups milk, scalded
2 cups rolled oats or wheat flakes
1 cup wheat germ
1 cup bran
$^1/_2$ cup honey or molasses
$^1/_2$ cup oil or shortening
1 rounded tablespoon salt

1 cup sunflower seeds
1 teaspoon sugar
$^1/_2$ cup lukewarm water
2 tablespoons yeast
8 or 9 cups whole wheat flour or half whole wheat, half all-purpose

Pour the scalded milk over the rolled oats, wheat germ, bran, honey, oil, salt, and sunflower seeds; let cool to lukewarm. Dissolve the yeast and proceed as in Jean Salter's recipe (previous page).

MAGGIE'S MOLASSES PORRIDGE BREAD
3 loaves

This bread has that down-east molasses flavour, doesn't need kneading, is very moist, chewy, with a hard crust. Super. Maggie says, "You got to freeze this fast or they'll eat it before your back's turned."

2 cups boiling water
2 cups rolled oats
1 cup wheat germ
1 cup molasses
$^1/_2$ cup shortening
$1^1/_2$ tablespoons salt
1 cup lukewarm water

1 teaspoon white sugar
2 tablespoons yeast
$7^1/_2$ cups all-purpose flour, or half whole wheat
$1^1/_2$ cups more lukewarm water

Pour the boiling water over the rolled oats, add the wheat germ, molasses, shortening, and salt; stir and let stand till the mixture is lukewarm. Dissolve the sugar in 1 cup lukewarm water, sprinkle the yeast over it and let stand about 10 minutes, then stir it into the oats mixture. Stir in the flour, then add the $1^1/_2$ cups lukewarm water and mix well. Let rise in a cold place overnight if you like, or let it rise in a warm place till it doubles in bulk. Spoon it into 3 buttered loaf pans and let rise to the top of the pans. Bake in a 400°F oven for about 45 minutes. Watch it. Take it out of the pans and cool on a rack.

BEER AND RYE BREAD
2 loaves

A firm solid loaf with a subtle flavour.

1 tablespoon yeast
1/2 cup lukewarm water
1 teaspoon sugar
1/2 cup all-purpose flour
1 tablespoon salt
1 cup sour milk or buttermilk

1 bottle beer
1 1/2 cups white flour
5 cups rye flour
3 tablespoons caraway seeds (optional)

Sprinkle the yeast over the water and sugar; let soften 10 minutes, then stir. Stir in 1/2 cup flour and let stand until bubbles form. Add the salt, milk, beer, white, and rye flour, and caraway seeds, mixing the dough till it is thick. Knead on a lightly floured surface until smooth and elastic. Return to the bowl, cover, and let rise in a warm place until doubled, about 1 1/2 hours. Punch down and form into 2 loaves. Place the loaves in buttered pans, cover and let rise again until doubled. Bake in a 400°F oven for 15 minutes; reduce heat to 350°F and bake until the loaves test done.

COCOA RYE BREAD
2 or 3 loaves

Sophie says, "This moist dark rye bread has so much flavour you'll want to eat it just so."

1 teaspoon sugar
1/2 cup lukewarm water
2 tablespoons yeast
1 cup molasses
1 rounded tablespoon salt
1/4 cup shortening or oil
2 1/2 cups lukewarm water

4 cups rye flour
1/2 cup cocoa
5 cups white or whole-wheat flour
1 cup raisins (optional)
1 cup walnuts (optional)

Dissolve the spoonful of sugar in the ¹/₂ cup warm water and sprinkle the yeast over it; let stand for 10 minutes till the yeast rises, then stir. Add the molasses, salt and shortening to the 2¹/₂ cups lukewarm water. Stir the rye flour and cocoa together then beat into the molasses mixture. Add the dissolved yeast and 1 cup of whole wheat or white flour and beat until the dough is smooth. Keep adding the flour until the dough is firm enough to turn out on a floured surface. Knead the rest of the flour into it till the dough is smooth and elastic. Put it back in the bowl, cover, and let rise in a warm place – it will double in about 2 hours. Punch it down, shape it into 2 or 3 loaves and place in well-buttered loaf pans – or if you want round flatter loaves, put them into pie plates or on cookie sheets. Let rise again, about 1 hour. Bake in a 375°F oven for 35 to 40 minutes.

If you add the raisins and walnuts with the flour you'll have a delicious tea bread.

ARABIC BREAD

For several years at Conestoga College, Barbie taught newcomers to Canada how to speak English; her grateful pupils often brought her presents. One day a Lebanese brought two puffy loaves of Arabic bread made by his wife. Barbie and her family liked the bread so well that she asked the man – in eloquent sign language – if his wife would show her how to make some. He seemed very pleased, kept smiling, nodding his head, and next day brought her a large sackful of loaves – at least twenty. Barbie persisted till she got her idea across and arranged to go to his home to see the bread being made. It was quite simple: Barbie now makes Arabic bread quite often. She makes about 30 loaves and freezes the surplus. You could try ¹/₃ of the recipe till you get the hang of it.

1 tablespoon sugar	**12 cups all-purpose flour**
6 cups lukewarm water	**2 tablespoons salt**
3 tablespoons yeast	

Dissolve the sugar in the lukewarm water, sprinkle the yeast over it and let stand until the yeast is bubbly. Put the flour and salt into a large bowl or plastic dishpan. Stir down the dissolved yeast and pour it into the flour; blend thoroughly. If it is sticky add a bit more flour; if it is too dry add more water. The dough should be smooth and firm but not stiff. Knead it a bit in the bowl. Leave it, covered, in a warm place and let the dough rise until doubled, about 1 hour.

Now, turn on the top element only of your oven and put a rack on the bottom position. Punch down and break off gobs of dough about the size of tennis balls. With a rolling pin roll each ball on a floured surface until very thin, about ½ inch thick. Carefully slide the sheets of dough on the lower rack in the oven at about 450°F degrees. You might have room for 4 loaves at a time. while you are rolling out more, bake the ones in the oven for about 10 minutes, until the tops are lightly brown and puffy. Flip them over and let them brown on the other side. Place the baked loaves on a cloth and cover them with another cloth. (Barbie uses a table cloth which she doubles over them.) When the buns of bread are still warm, Patti and Ken like to push them down gently: they deflate like a balloon and are flat, 2-layered, and soft. (Like Yorkshire pudding with a top, bottom, and nothing in t' middle.)

They must be eaten warm, split, spread with butter on the inside, and cheese, or a cooked hamburger, or tomato, or hard-boiled egg mixture, or any sandwichy sort of thing. One loaf becomes like the outer parts of a sandwich but more interesting delicious and chewy.

MARY ANN MARTIN'S MAGIC BUNS, DOUGHNUTS, AND ROLLS

One hot summer day Eva and her sister Hannah took me to Mary Ann's farmhouse where the dough was rising; in a very short time we were gorging on perfect plump cream buns, chelsea buns, long Johns, honey glazed doughnuts and rolls.

1 teaspoon sugar	**¾ cup sugar**
½ cup lukewarm water	**¾ teaspoon salt**
2 tablespoons yeast	**2 eggs, beaten**
½ cup lard or shortening	**6 or 7 cups all-purpose flour**
3 cups water	

Dissolve the teaspoon of sugar in the ¹/₂ cup lukewarm water, sprinkle the yeast over it and let stand 10 minutes till the yeast rises, then stir. Blend the lard, 3 cups water, ³/₄ cup sugar, and salt; heat to lukewarm on the stove. Add the beaten eggs, then the dissolved yeast mixture. Add enough flour for a soft dough. Set in a warm place till doubled in bulk. Mary Ann put her dough in a plastic pail with a lid and on that hot summer day it rose like magic. Punch the dough down and shape into whatever buns, rolls, or doughnuts you want to make.

CREAM BUNS: Like those we used to get at the baker's shop after school. Super. Shape the pieces of dough into balls the size of a pingpong ball, set on greased cookie sheets 2 inches apart, and let rise till doubled in size. Bake in a 400°F oven for about 15 minutes. Watch them, they shouldn't be tan. When they are cool, slit them almost in half and slather the bottom half with cream filling.

1 tablespoon shortening or butter
1 cup icing sugar

¹/₂ teaspoon vanilla
A few grains of salt
Warm water

Rub the shortening and sugar into crumbs, add the vanilla, salt, and enough warm water to make a soft spreading mixture. Mix with a knife then beat till light. Be generous when you slather it on the bottom half of the buns. They can be frozen.

CHELSEA BUNS: Mary Ann melted 3 tablespoons butter in a cake pan, generously sprinkled brown sugar and raisins over the bottom of the pan. She rolled out a piece of dough about ¹/₂ inch thick, slathered it with melted butter, sprinkled it with brown sugar, cinnamon and raisins, then rolled it up like a jelly roll, cut it in pieces about 1-inch thick, dropped each piece cut side down into the pan till it was filled. She let it rise till at least doubled then baked it in a 350°F oven for about 25 minutes, till golden.

EVA'S STICKY BUNS: Eva told us she makes her buns exactly as Mary Ann makes her Chelsea buns but instead of putting butter, sugar and raisins in the bottom of the pan she pours in a blend of maple syrup and cream!

LONG JOHNS: Mary Ann rolled out some of her magic dough about ¹/₂ inch thick, cut it in strips 1″ by 4″, let the strips rise till doubled, then quickly fried them in hot, deep fat till they were golden brown. When they had cooled on a rack, she slit them lengthwise and not quite through, slathered them with the same cream filling she'd used for the cream buns, and sprinkled the tops with icing sugar.

DOUGHNUTS WITH A HONEY GLAZE: Some of Mary Ann's dough was rolled and cut in circles with a doughnut cutter, let rise till they were big and puffy, then fried in deep hot fat. When the doughnuts were cool she dipped them in the glaze:

1¹/₂ tablespoons honey   **1 cup icing sugar**
3¹/₂ tablespoons boiling water

Stir all the ingredients till blended. Dip the warm doughnuts into the warm glaze and let cool and dry on a rack.

PLAIN BUNS: To make all this variety Mary Ann mixed up a second batch of dough. The dough she had left was rolled into small balls and dropped into greased muffin cups, allowed to rise, then was baked in a 400°F oven about 15 minutes, till golden. What a feasting day we had.

NUTTY SWEET BUTTERY BUNS

Next time you make white bread or Mary Ann Martin's Magic Buns try making some of the dough into these delicious tear-apart buns. Eva calls them Pull Buns.

Combine 1 cup sugar, ¹/₂ cup finely chopped nuts, and 2 teaspoons cinnamon; melt ¹/₂ cup butter. When the dough has risen in the bowl take out a good-sized gob of it and roll it into a cylinder about 1¹/₂ inches in diameter. Cut the roll into pieces the size of ping pong balls. Drop each ball into the melted butter to coat it, then into the sugar and walnut mixture. Place the coated balls in circles in a well buttered large pie or cake pan or heap them in a large loaf pan or tube pan. You may have several layers of balls. Sprinkle any remaining sugar mixture and butter on top. Cover and let rise until doubled. Bake at 375°F for about 20 minutes or slightly longer if you have several layers. Watch them so the sugar won't burn. Invert on a rack letting the pan rest over the buns for 2 minutes before removing it. Turn right side up on a serving plate and let the lucky eaters pull off the warm, sugary, luscious buns.

LORNA'S MINCE MEAT BUNS
1 dozen rolls

These are divine: tender, moist, light and deliciously flavoured with mince and Grand Marnier, or what have you.

1¹/₂ cups mince meat	**1 tablespoon orange-**
¹/₄ cup chopped pecans	**flavoured liqueur**

Make Mary Ann Martin's Buns (page 151) to the place where the dough has risen to double in the mixing bowl. Divide it in 3 and with ¹/₃ make Lorna's Mince Meat Buns. Unless you want 3 dozen. (With the other ²/₃ of the dough you may try another kind of bun.)

On a floured surface roll ¹/₃ of the dough to a 12″ x 9″ rectangle. Spread with mince meat and chopped pecans, leaving a 1-inch border. Sprinkle the mince meat with 1 tablespoon orange liqueur (Grand Marnier or Cointreau). Beginning at the long side roll the rectangle like a jelly roll. Cut the roll into 1-inch slices with a very sharp knife and put each piece into a buttered muffin cup. Let rise for 1 hour. Bake at 350°F for 20 to 25 minutes, until lightly browned.

GLAZE: Combine 1 cup icing sugar with 1¹/₂ tablespoons warm water and dribble some over each slightly cooled bun. How could 1 dozen of these be enough?

EVA'S MINCE MEAT BUNS

Almost the same as Lorna's, but Eva doesn't dribble on the liqueur. She puts her buns into a pan beside each other and over them pours a syrup before putting them in the oven. The syrup is made with ³/₄ cup brown sugar, 1 cup water, butter the size of an egg. she cooks this to a syrup, cools it before pouring it over the risen dough in the pan. Better try both.

RUBY'S BUTTER PUFF ROLLS

The dough for these great tasting rolls can be kept for a week in your fridge and baked whenever you want them, fresh from the oven. The recipe is exactly the same as Mary Martin's (page 151) but uses ¹/₄ cup less sugar and ¹/₄ cup more shortening.

Put the dough into your fridge, or a cold place, till you want to bake the rolls; it will rise slightly but should be covered. Break off pieces of cold dough, shape into balls and put them into buttered muffin tins or roll the balls of dough in melted butter and put them beside each other in a cake tin, or make any of Mary Ann's varieties. Let them rise for at least an hour, maybe longer. Bake at 400°F for about 15 minutes.

GRANDMA STRATTON'S BUNS

When I came back from Arizona there was a tin box with my accumulated mail and in it I found half a dozen buns made by Lynn Wolff at least two weeks before; they were still moist and delicious. She enclosed her recipe which was the same as Mary Ann's (page 151) but had no eggs, 1 cup of lard instead of one half, and 4 cups of water, and 9 cups of flour. Lynn said, "In case you have aspirations, my father holds the record of eating the most fresh-out-of-the-oven buns, over a dozen in one sneaking session."

LARDY CAKES

When I visited Kath in Devon we would drive the six miles to Totnes to go shopping along its lovely ancient street. I could never resist the bake shops where I always bought richly delicious Lardy Cakes.

Take a piece of proved dough (that is, bread or bun dough that has risen). In Totnes it was always white. Roll it flat into a square. Dab pats of lard all over the dough. Scatter over this some brown sugar, raisins, and currants. You can also sprinkle on grated nutmeg and cinnamon, chopped peel, whatever you like and in any combination you like.

Then fold the corners into the centre like an envelope; then fold it in half.

Roll flat again and repeat the whole process twice more. Put into a greased tin and bake in a hot oven. This can also be cut into small squares or oblongs and baked on a baking sheet in a 400°F oven.

RALPH'S HOT CROSS BUNS
1¹/₂ dozen

My brother-in-law Ralph is always so pleased with his Hot Cross Buns that they are soon gone to his friends, relatives and neighbours – and next day he whips up another batch.

1 cup scalded milk
¹/₂ cup sugar
1¹/₂ teaspoons salt
¹/₄ cup shortening
1 teaspoon sugar
1 tablespoon yeast
¹/₂ cup lukewarm water
2 eggs, beaten
2 cups all-purpose flour

1 tablespoon cinnamon
¹/₂ teaspoon cloves
¹/₄ teaspoon nutmeg
3 cups whole wheat flour
1 cup raisins or currants
1 cup mixed peel

Scald the milk, add the ¹/₂ cup sugar, salt and shortening; stir till they dissolve; cool to lukewarm. Sprinkle the teaspoon of sugar and the yeast over the ¹/₂ cup of lukewarm water and let rest for 10 minutes before stirring. Add the dissolved yeast to the lukewarm milk mixture, stir in the beaten eggs then beat in 2 cups of flour sifted with the spices; add the raisins and peel. Stir in the remaining flour then knead till the dough feels smooth and elastic. Plop the dough back into the bowl, cover it and put it in a warm place to rise till double in size, about 1¹/₂ hours.

When risen, punch the dough down, take it out of the bowl on the floured surface and roll it into a roll, not too skinny and about 18 inches long. Cut the roll into 18 pieces, roll each piece into a ball and place about 2 inches apart on a buttered cookie sheet. Let rise to double again. With the back of a knife, indent lightly a cross on the top of each bun; let rise a few minutes more then bake at 400°F for about 10 minutes. As soon as you take them out of the oven, glaze the buns to give them a shine. While the buns are baking bring ½ cup of water and 4 tablespoons icing sugar to a boil, simmer for 2 or 3 minutes. You don't have to make these only at Easter; they are wonderful any time.

ENGLISH MUFFINS
about 18

I was thrilled to find I could easily make my own English Muffins instead of having to buy those weary old store packages. Hot, tender, and moist between a crisp brown top and bottom, they are failproof and freeze like a breeze – if they last that long.

1 cup scalded milk
1 tablespoon sugar
1½ teaspoons salt
¼ cup vegetable oil
½ cup lukewarm water
1 teaspoon sugar

1 tablespoon yeast
1 egg (optional)
4 cups all-purpose flour, whole wheat, or both
About 4 tablespoons cornmeal

Scald the milk, stir in the tablespoon of sugar, salt, and vegetable oil. Pour into a large bowl and let stand till tepid. In the ½ cup of lukewarm water sprinkle the teaspoon of sugar and the yeast and let stand for 10 minutes. Stir the yeast then pour it into the lukewarm milk mixture. Beat in the egg and 2 cups of flour till the batter is smooth. Cover the bowl and let it stay in a warm place until doubled and bubbly, about 1½ hours. Stir down the bubbles and add the other 2 cups of flour, more or less, till the dough is no longer sticky. Knead it on a floured surface till it feels elastic – not dry or stiff, but not sticky either.

Let it rise again until doubled. If you can't wait that long – as I never can – sprinkle your surface with cornmeal and roll out the dough to ³/₄ inch thickness. Sprinkle it with cornmeal, cut it in 3-inch rounds. With the leftover bits squeezed together and cut, you'll have about 18 muffins. Cover and let them double in size.

Heat a griddle or electric frying pan to medium, brush lightly with shortening and place the muffins on the hot surface. They should brown on one side in about 5 to 8 minutes, but watch them. Turn over and brown on the other side. They'll puff up as they cook, be white on the sides, crisply brown top and bottom. Heavenly smell. Cool them on a rack until you can handle and eat them. Tear them apart, never cut them. With butter melting into them they need no embellishment. If you can restrain yourself from eating all at a sitting they'll keep in your fridge for a week, tied in a plastic bag and be fresh when reheated. Also they're wonderful split and toasted – and they freeze. But mine have never lasted that long.

COUSIN HILDA'S COFFEE CAKE

This is Mother's interpretation.

**1 yeast cake (1 tablespoon
dry yeast) soaked in ¹/₂ cup
lukewarm water for
10 minutes**

Put into a double boiler **1 cup of milk**; let it get scalding hot but not boiling. Put into a large mixing bowl:

2 eggs, well beaten   **³/₄ teaspoon salt**
¹/₃ cup white sugar   **¹/₃ cup shortening**

Pour the scalding milk into this and stir well until dissolved. Add 1 cup lukewarm water and when the whole mixture is lukewarm stir in the yeast. Sift and add 3 cups flour and mix well; keep adding more flour to make a soft dough, about 6¹/₂ cups. Hilda uses 6 cups and then feels her way; she puts the dough on a board and mixes in the flour, I use only a spoon and mix it in well.

Let it rise until double the amount, then press it down and stir it. Let it rise until double again. Put it into greased cake pans, round or square, and let it rise again until double.

Topping: Melt ¼ cup butter on low heat. Mix 1 cup brown sugar and 1 tablespoon corn starch. Let this melt slowly in the butter. If too thick add a bit of cream but it must be fairly thick or it will run when hot. Spread it gently over the risen coffee cakes without disturbing them. Sprinkle with a mixture of brown and white sugar and cinnamon. Bake the cakes at 375°F until they are nicely browned, maybe 15 to 20 minutes. You can tell when they look right.

HILDA'S CHRISTMAS STOLLEN
4 stollen

Every year before Christmas Hilda makes about twenty stollen to give to her friends as a Christmas treat; I'm always glad when she gives me one, tightly wrapped in foil. She makes six or eight for herself too and freezes them. Hilda told me that in Sachsen (now part of East Germany), where she was born, they didn't make cookies at Christmas but saved all their money for the goodies that went into the stollen.

1½ cups scalded milk	1 teaspoon salt
1 cup warm water	1 teaspoon nutmeg
1 tablespoon sugar	1 teaspoon coriander seeds,
2 tablespoons dry yeast	crushed
8 cups all-purpose flour	½ cup all-purpose flour
1 pound unsalted soft butter	½ cup candied orange and
1 cup sugar	citron peel
4 eggs	2 cups seedless raisins
Peel of 1 lemon, grated	1 cup almonds, chopped
Peel of 1 orange, grated	¼ cup rum

Scald the milk and let cool to lukewarm. Dissolve the tablespoon of sugar in the warm water, sprinkle the yeast over it and let stand 10 minutes, then stir well. Add the yeast mixture to the lukewarm milk with 1 cup of flour. Beat well and let rise in a warm place until light and bubbly. Cream the butter and sugar, add the eggs one at a time, beating hard each time. Add the grated lemon and orange peel and the salt. Add the creamed mixture to the yeast mixture with the remaining 7 cups of flour, nutmeg and coriander. Knead until smooth and elastic, about 15 minutes. Sprinkle the additional ½ cup flour over the candied orange and citron peel, raisins, and almonds. Mix well and knead into the dough with the rum until evenly distributed.

Let rise until double in bulk then punch down and divide the dough into 4 pieces. Roll each into a circle and spread with melted butter. Press down the centre of each circle with a wooden spoon handle, fold the circle over to double. Brush the top with melted butter, place on a greased baking sheet, cover and let rise until doubled. Bake at 350°F for 45 to 50 minutes. Cool on a rack then sprinkle with icing sugar.

BUTTERCAKES

Among the events of our very young lives was being taken to Toronto for the day in the Brisco, my father's first car. The drive took four hours – one way. But all I remember of the day in the city was standing in front of Child's Restaurant, watching the girl inside the window baking buttercakes on a big black pan, then going inside with Mother and Daddy, sitting at a table and eating the buttercakes, hot from the griddle and dripping with butter. We always said we wished we could eat them every day of our lives.

1½ cups scalded milk	1 teaspoon sugar
1½ teaspoons salt	2 tablespoons yeast
2 tablespoons shortening	½ cup lukewarm water
2 tablespoons sugar	4½ cups flour

To the scalded milk add the salt, shortening, 2 tablespoons sugar; stir then cool to lukewarm. Sprinkle the teaspoon of sugar and the yeast over the ½ cup lukewarm water and let rest for 10 minutes before stirring and adding to the tepid milk mixture. Stir in the flour and beat it until you're almost tired. Cover the bowl of dough and let it stand in a warm place to rise until doubled. Now comes the magic moment! Scoop up as much dough as a tablespoon will hold, drop it on a lightly-greased hot griddle or electric fry pan and bake until the bottom is golden, then flip it over and brown the other side. Bliss, heavenly bliss will follow when you break them apart and let the butter melt into them.

Too bad I didn't learn to make them when I was young and skinny.

FLEISCH PIROSCHKY (Meat Buns)

Katie Enns told me the Russian Mennonites usually serve these with borscht; I think they'd be good with a salad meal, too.

1 cup milk, scalded	1 teaspoon sugar
2 teaspoons salt	1 tablespoon dry yeast
¹/₂ cup shortening	3 cups flour
¹/₂ cup lukewarm water	

Blend the salt and shortening with the scalded milk and let it cool to lukewarm. Dissolve the sugar in the warm water, sprinkle the yeast over it and let it stand for about 10 minutes till the yeast bubbles up; stir the yeast down, add it to the lukewarm milk mixture then stir in the flour to make a soft dough. Let it rise, covered in a draught-free, warm place until doubled.

MEAT FILLING FOR PIROSCHKY

1 onion, chopped fine	1 or 2 hardboiled eggs,
¹/₂ tablespoon each oil and	chopped (optional)
butter	Salt and pepper to taste
2 cups ground cooked beef	Leftover gravy or sour cream

Sauté the onion in the butter and oil until yellow; add to the ground meat and eggs, salt, pepper and enough gravy or sour cream to moisten (or instead, use 1 cup mashed potatoes).

Pinch off pieces of dough and flatten them into rounds with your hands. Put 1 tablespoon of filling on the round, seal the edges together to form an oblong bun and place on a well-greased cookie sheet. Let stand about 10 minutes then bake at 350°F for 25 to 30 minutes until golden brown.

APFEL PIROSCHKY FILLING

1½ cups shredded or sliced apples	**½ teaspoon cinnamon**
1 tablespoon flour	**1 small egg**
⅓ cup sugar	**¼ cup cream**

Combine and beat well; proceed as for Meat Piroschky.

Cooked dried apples or cooked prunes and raisins could be used instead of the raw apples.

PRETZELS

When we were kids there was a scary little old man with a stubbly face, ruffled grey hair and a dirty white apron, who had a bakery of sorts near the Kitchener market. Mother would never buy anything from his shop, but sometimes Daddy used to go there and bring home big fat wonderful chewy hot pretzels. They were shiny brown on the top, sprinkled with coarse salt, soft in the middle, and suspiciously dark on the bottom. Daddy said the black wouldn't hurt us, the pretzels were baked in a brick oven. We blissfully ate them before they were cold.

I have been trying unsuccessfully ever since those long ago days to find pretzels like them. Only once, in a store in Columbus, Ohio, I saw big hot pretzels and bought one to eat on the spot. But it lacked the chewy quality and flavour of the old man's.

Recently I've been trying to make some. They're not like the old man's, either but they're not bad. When I took them from my oven I couldn't resist eating one after another until I was horrified to realize I'd eaten nine. I took five to Belle, next door; she sceptically tried one, then immediately ate the rest.

1 cup milk, scalded	**2 eggs (save yolk of one for topping)**
¼ cup butter	
1½ tablespoons sugar	**3¾ cups flour or more**
1 teaspoon salt	**2 tablespoons sugar in boiling water**
1 tablespoon yeast	
¼ cup lukewarm water	

To the scalded milk add the butter, sugar, and salt; let cool to lukewarm. Sprinkle the yeast over the lukewarm water and let stand for 10 minutes; stir well before blending it into the other tepid mixture. Beat slightly one whole egg and the white of another and stir into the yeast mixture before adding the flour, one cup at a time, beating well after each addition until it gets thick. Knead the dough on a floured board for several minutes; put it back in the bowl, cover and let it rise in a warm place until doubled. Punch down, roll out on a floured surface about ³/₄ inch thick.

Now the fiddling starts – but you soon get the knack of it. Pinch off pieces of dough, roll each piece into a rope ³/₄ inches thick and about 8 inches long and form a pretzel. Let them rise till they look puffy.

Put several quarts of water and 2 tablespoons sugar in a large pan, bring to a slow boil, drop in the pretzels one at a time, adding however many you have room for without touching each other. Simmer the pretzels for 5 minutes from the time they rise to the surface of the water, turning them once during the cooking. Lift them out of the water with an egg turner and place gently on a rack to drain. Beat the reserved egg yolk and lightly brush over the top of each pretzel, then sprinkle each with coarse salt.

When enough pretzels have been cooked to fill a buttered cookie sheet, bake them in a 400°F oven for about 15 to 20 minutes, or until the top is golden brown and you can't wait any longer to get at them. They must be eaten fresh and hot.

If you get tired of shaping the pretzels you could make circles, pinching the ends together: they are not unlike bagels.

LESS-BOTHER PRETZELS
1 dozen

When Ernie Ritz was mayor of Wilmot township he told me about the fat chewy pretzels made by his son's wife Kathryn. They must be eaten hot from the oven – and that is no problem.

2 tablespoons yeast
1¹/₂ cups warm water
1¹/₂ teaspoons salt

4¹/₂ cups flour
¹/₄ cup soda dissolved in 1 cup water

Dissolve the yeast in lukewarm water, letting stand about 10 minutes; add it and the salt to the flour, mix well and let rise about 15 minutes. Roll the dough into strips about 8 inches long, place them in the soda solution for 2 minutes. Shape the strips like pretzels, place them on a greased pan, sprinkle with coarse salt and bake them at 325°F for 10 minutes. Keep watching so they won't dry out. Eat them at once or they're no good.

SOURDOUGH STARTER

Sourdough is a fun thing to have – besides a tangy good thing to eat in bread, rolls, biscuits, pancakes, etc. If you're out of yeast and miles from a supply, you can always start some as the pioneers did. Simply put 1 cup of milk in a bowl or a crock (nothing metal) and let it stand at room temperature for 24 hours. Stir in 1 cup of flour, cover the bowl with cheesecloth and put it outside on your porch or balcony for several hours to expose it to the wild yeast cells that are floating around in the breeze. You could do this for several days to be sure you have a catch. (But not in the winter.) Bring it back into your kitchen and leave it, uncovered, in a warm place for several days, depending on how long it takes to bubble and smell sour. (If it starts to dry out stir in a bit of tepid water.) You'll know when it's ready to use: it smells sour and bubbles like yeast.

Sometimes you have to try several times before you get a catch of wild yeast. If you grow impatient you can always start sourdough by combining a tablespoon of regular yeast with the milk and flour, letting the mixture stand in a warm place till it bubbles and becomes sour, in about 48 hours.

Put the starter in a covered container with plenty of room for expansion and store it in your fridge – for years, if you keep it going. Each time you use it you must replenish it by adding equal quantities of milk and flour and letting it stand in a warm place for 24 hours.

Sourdough starter should be used at least once a week (giving you a great excuse to keep making those lovely, flavourful things). If you don't use it for 2 or 3 weeks, spoon out and discard about half of it and replenish. It should improve with age. If you're going away on a holiday for several weeks and you can't take it with you, put it in your freezer and when you come home – happy day – get it out and let it stand in a warm place for 24 hours to get the yeast action started again.

BASIC SOURDOUGH to make PANCAKES, WAFFLES and HOT ROLLS

You'll say you've never had pancakes like these – or hot rolls either. You can make these if you go on a camping trip; make or take your sourdough with you.

¹/₂ **cup starter**	**2 tablespoons sugar**
2 cups milk	**1 teaspoon salt**
2 cups flour	**1 teaspoon soda**
2 eggs	

Blend the starter, milk, and flour, and leave at room temperature overnight or for several hours. Then add eggs, sugar, salt, and soda and mix well – but don't beat it.

To make pancakes, drop large spoonfuls of the batter on a greased griddle. Turn over when the top side is full of broken bubbles and is no longer glossy. Serve with syrup and purr your pleasure. (You may stir in fresh or frozen blueberries if you like.)

SOURDOUGH WAFFLES: Use the same batter as for pancakes but add 2 tablespoons of salad oil before you drop the mixture on the waffle iron.

OATMEAL or WHOLE WHEAT PANCAKES AND WAFFLES: Simply substitute 1 cup oatmeal or whole wheat for 1 cup of flour.

SOURDOUGH HOT ROLLS: Any leftover pancake batter? Make these delicious rolls.

To at least 1¹/₂ cups leftover pancake batter, or the whole recipe, stir in enough flour to form a stiff dough. Turn out on a floured board and knead until it is smooth and shiny. Put it in a bowl, and let it rise in a warm place for about an hour. Punch it down, knead again and roll out to ³/₄ inch thickness. Cut with a glass or tuna tin, dip top and bottom in melted butter and place in a greased baking pan. Cover, let rise until nearly double, another hour. Bake in a 375°F oven for about 30 minutes. Serve warm and buttery. Wow!

SOURDOUGH ENGLISH MUFFINS: Instead of dipping the hot rolls (above) in butter and baking them in the oven, dip the tops and bottoms in cornmeal, let rise till doubled and bake on a frying pan or griddle for 8 minutes, each side.

9

Cape Breton Oat Cakes,
Bannocks and Pork Buns,
Tea Biscuits, Onion Squares and Scones,
Wheat Thins, Cheese Wafers,
and Savoury Crackers

Here's something I'm really excited about. One of the most interesting and practical discoveries I've made since I started writing this book is learning how to make my own wheat thins, savoury crackers, cheese wafers, etc. They are so crisp, nutritious and tasty that for me they've become an addiction. I never let my biscuit box stay empty longer than it takes me to whip up another batch of four or five different flavours.

I eat some every day with cheese, or soup, or a dip, with salad, or spread with cottage cheese blended with chives. If I'm not very firm with myself I'll snack on them mid-morning or at bedtime. "No harm done," I rationalize. "They're not sweet."

It's great fun to experiment with various grains, flours, and flavours. I've made an infinite variety. Every batch is different and seems better than what went before. They don't look as neat, square, and perfect as those you buy in costly little boxes, but whenever I serve them my guests exclaim, "Aren't they *good*! I didn't know you could make them; I must have your recipe."

They are so quick and easy: you just mix them like pastry, roll them thin, slip the sheet onto a cookie pan and indent them with a wheel or a knife. I'm not good at figuring expenses but I'm sure they cost less than a quarter as much as the factory-made products: a batch with four cups of flour fills my round tin that is 8 inches across and 4 inches high. That's almost 200 biscuits!

I can hardly wait till you try these and I get your reaction.

One more thing: Whenever I go to Cape Breton I gorge on the good things my lady friends there bake so quickly and easily: oat cakes, bannock, tea biscuits and pork buns. Try them and you'll see why I come home with recipes and avoirdupois.

WHOLE WHEAT THINS – BASIC RECIPE

From this basic recipe you can make biscuits galore, with as many flavours as you can imagine.

4 cups whole wheat flour
1 teaspoon salt, (optional)
1 tablespoon sugar

³/₄ cup shortening
²/₃ cup water or milk, more or less

Mix the dry ingredients. Cut in the shortening until it is finely blended. Pour in the water and stir till it forms into a soft ball, like pastry. (If you have a food processor all this can be done in a few seconds.) Divide the dough into 4 parts; roll each part as thin as parchment. (I roll mine on a lightly floured pastry cloth and it never sticks.) Slide the sheet of dough on an unbuttered cookie tin and indent it in squares with a pastry wheel or a knife. To prevent bubbling, prick the dough all over with the tines of a fork – let it bounce.

Bake in a 400°F oven for almost 10 minutes, until crisp and

pale. Slide the sheet to a cooling rack and break the biscuits where you have marked them.

Easy, isn't it? And you don't even have to wash the cookie pan.

DIFFERENT FLAVOURS

With one batch of the Basic Recipe you can make biscuits with four or more different flavours. After you have divided the dough pat each piece into a ball, flatten it to an oval and generously sprinkle over it whatever flavour you please. Then roll the dough thin as you can and the flavouring will be smoothed out and rolled into it.

SAVOURY CRACKERS: Sprinkle the dough with savoury salt.

CELERY MORSELS: Sprinkle with celery seed.

SESAME SEED OR POPPY SEED CRISPS: Sprinkle with sesame or poppy seeds.

ONION NIBBLES: Sprinkle with toasted onion flakes – very popular – or dehydrated onion soup.

GARLIC GOBBLES: Sprinkle with garlic powder or salt.

CHIVE BITES: Sprinkle with dried chives or mix finely-cut fresh chives with the dough.

HERB TASTIES: Sprinkle with the herb of your choice.

BOUQUET GARNI BISCUITS: Sprinkle with a combination of herbs.

CAYENNE CRACKERS: Sprinkle with cayenne or paprika.

BEEF BITES: Sprinkle with Beef Bouillon mix or Chicken Broth mix.

Got the idea now? Just open your cupboard door and look around, make up your own names and your own flavours. It is surprising what you'll come up with.

SOY FLOUR SNACKS

The protein-seekers will find these a godsend; Nancy tasted them and said, "Oh good." Substitute 1 cup soy flour for one of whole wheat in the Basic Recipe (page 168). Add any flavouring you like.

CRACKED WHEAT THINS

Pour a cup of boiling water over a cupful cracked wheat, or Red River Cereal, or 5-, 7-, or 12-grain cereal. Let it soak for half an hour or so, then follow the Basic Recipe (see page 168), using one less cup of flour. Add the soaked grain last; you might need a bit more water to get the right consistency. Add flavours if you like but they don't need them.

SOY NIPS

Using the Basic Recipe (page 168) substitute 2 or 3 tablespoons soy sauce for as much water. The biscuits will be dark brown. Don't overbake them or they'll lose the subtle flavour and taste burnt.

WORCESTERSHIRE WAFERS

Substitute 2 tablespoons of Worcestershire sauce for water in the Basic Recipe (page 168).

CHEESE WAFERS

These are tenderly crisp and deliciously cheesy – everyone's favourite.

2 cups flour, white or whole wheat
¹/₂ teaspoon salt
¹/₂ cup margarine
1 cup finely grated cheese
¹/₄ cup water, or slightly more

Blend the margarine with the flour and salt; blend in the cheese and gradually add as much water as you need to have the dough form a ball. Then do what the Basic Recipe (page 168) tells you. Watch them in the oven, don't let them brown. (Sprinkle them with sesame seeds or anything that won't detract from the cheese flavour. But why bother?)

THE ULTIMATE BISCUITS

After making dozens of batches of biscuits I finally put in everything the nutritionists say is good for you. They are crisp, crunchy, with a toasty brown flavour having no need for embellishment.

1 cup rolled oats
$^1/_2$ cup bran
$^1/_2$ cup cracked grain
$^1/_2$ teaspoon salt
$^3/_4$ cup margarine or butter
1 cup boiling water

$^1/_2$ cup wheat germ
1 cup sunflower seeds
1 cup whole wheat flour
$^1/_2$ cup all-purpose flour

Measure the oats, bran, cracked grain, salt and margarine into a bowl; pour in the cup of boiling water and stir till the margarine is melted and well blended. Let stand until lukewarm. Stir in the wheat germ, sunflower seeds and the flour. Proceed as in the Basic Recipe (page 168). This dough is a bit harder to handle but the result is worth the risk.

FRUITY TEA BISCUITS

This is a super recipe: tasty and tender. You might think it is too big; cut it in half if you want to, but I'll bet you won't cut it a second time. You can always freeze the biscuits if you can't stop eating them.

4 cups flour (part whole
  wheat, optional)
1 teaspoon salt
1 cup white sugar (or less)
1 teaspoon baking powder
$^1/_2$ teaspoon soda

1 cup shortening
1 cup orange or mixed peel,
  or raisins or currants
$1^1/_2$ cups buttermilk or sour
  milk

Sift the dry ingredients; cut in the shortening till well blended (I let my Mixmaster or food processor do it.) Stir in the peel or raisins. Add the buttermilk and stir just long enough to moisten the flour, adding more milk if necessary. Drop large blobs from a tablespoon on an ungreased cookie sheet and bake in a 450°F oven for about 15 minutes, till slightly golden. Serve with a cup of tea.

STRAWBERRY OR PEACH SHORTCAKE

If you want the best strawberry shortcake you've ever tasted use the Fruity Tea Biscuit recipe, omitting the fruit and using 2 tablespoons baking powder, 1 teaspoon soda, and 2 cups buttermilk. Spoon the batter into a 9″ x 13″ pan, sprinkle the top with white sugar and bake in a 400°F oven for almost half an hour. Serve warm, smothered with squashed, sugared berries or sliced peaches.

BUTTERMILK BISCUITS

To make unsweetened biscuits to serve with a salad or jam simply omit the sugar and fruit from the Fruity Tea Biscuit recipe.

CLARA MAY'S PORK BUNS

In Neil's Harbour I loved to sit on the old rocker beside the big black woodstove and watch Clara May do her baking. So did her grandchildren. She didn't follow a recipe; she couldn't read; nor did she measure anything exactly; she knew by the feel. These are the amounts she told me:

¼ cup salt pork	½ teaspoon salt
Boiling water	¼ cup shortening
About 3½ cups flour	1 cup big sticky raisins
2 rounded teaspoons baking powder	1½ cups cold water

Clara May cut the salt pork into little chunks the size of small peas; she poured boiling water over them and then let them drain while she sifted the flour, baking powder, and salt into a bowl. She cut in the shortening. "You got to work it in with your hands till it feels roight good," she told us. With a fork she stirred in the big sticky raisins and the well-drained pork chunks then poured in about a cupful of cold water. "Stir it till the dough follows the fork around the bowl," she showed us. "Sometimes it needs more water." She gradually added at least another ½ cupful. "Ye want a soft dough but it must hold its shape." She broke off pieces of dough, rolled them around in her hand to a ball and put them on ungreased cookie pans about 1¹/₂ inches apart.

Clara May opened the oven door, stuck in her hand to feel. "Henry, the fire needs more wood." She looked round the kitchen. "Where is that man? Lil, go get your father. You want a hot oven for pork buns to get noice and fat and a little bit brown." She answered my question, "How long?" "I don't know, I just look after I wash up the dishes and clean off the table, maybe 10 or 15 minutes."

When the biscuits were baked and cooling on the table a grandchild reached to take one. "Now you git," Clara May screamed. "I wants them for supper." She put them in tins, then in the cupboard behind the stairs. "If I don't hide 'em," she said, "them grandchildren would have 'em et faster 'n you could skin a codfish."

SUDDENLY BISCUITS

While Kath was visiting me we suddenly needed some biscuits to go with a salad; she noted the ingredients as I whacked them together. Success!

2 cups white flour	**1 teaspoon salt**
1 cup whole wheat flour	**1 tablespoon white sugar**
1 cup bran	**¹/₂ cup oil**
¹/₂ teaspoon soda	**1 cup buttermilk**
1 teaspoon baking powder	

I blended all the dry ingredients, whipped the oil into the buttermilk with a fork until it was creamy, poured it over the flour mixture and stirred it till all the flour was absorbed–no longer. I dropped tablespoonfuls on an ungreased cookie sheet, baked them in a 400°F oven for about 20 minutes and served them hot, with butter.

QUICK, SUPER CHEESY BISCUITS

Whenever I want to have something special to go with a salad–or just to eat with great enjoyment–I whip up a batch of these.

1 cup all-purpose flour
3 teaspoons baking powder
$^3/_4$ teaspoon salt
1 cup whole wheat flour
$^1/_4$ cup margarine

1 cup coarsely grated
  cheddar
$^1/_2$ cup currants or raisins
  (optional)
1 cup milk

Sift the all-purpose flour, baking powder, and salt, stir in the whole wheat. Cut in the margarine till it disappears. Stir in the cheese and raisins or currants. Add the milk, using just enough to hold everything together. Don't handle the dough any more than you need to. Drop gobs of it on an ungreased baking sheet and pop it in a 450°F oven for about 12 minutes. The edges will be golden and you will be unable to resist a quick taste. Don't burn your tongue.

LORNA'S CHEESE DROP BISCUITS

These must be eaten very hot.

1 cup flour
$^1/_4$ cup butter
2 teaspoons baking powder

1 cup grated cheddar, very
  strong
$^1/_2$ cup ice cold water

Mix the flour, butter, and baking powder like pastry. Add the cheese, then the ice water. Grease a cookie sheet and drop the biscuits from a spoon, about 12. Put a dab of butter on top of each biscuit before baking, at 400°F for 10 to 15 minutes.

MARTINA SCHNEIKER'S SCONES

Martina says she can never make enough of these.

3 cups sifted all-purpose
  flour
2 teaspoons baking powder
1 cup sugar
1 teaspoon salt
$^3/_4$ cup butter or margarine
1 cup raisins

1 egg, well beaten
Milk, almost a cupful

Topping:
1 egg yolk, beaten
2 tablespoons milk

Sift the flour, baking powder, sugar, and salt into a bowl. Cut the butter into the mixture until it is fine, add the raisins and mix well. Beat an egg in a measuring cup, add enough milk to fill the cup, stir into the flour mixture. Knead lightly, roll out to ³/₄ inch thickness, cut into triangles. Brush tops with a beaten egg yolk blended with 2 tablespoons of milk. Bake at 450°F for 10 to 12 minutes. Eat warm.

ONION SQUARES

A flavoursome treat to be eaten with a salad, soup, or as a snack.

2 cups sliced onions **3 tablespoons butter**

Sauté the onions in the butter until they are tender but not brown. Let cool.

2 cups sifted flour
2 teaspoons baking powder
1 teaspoon salt
¹/₄ cup shortening
Sprinkling of your favourite
  herbs or chopped parsley

1 cup milk

Topping:
¹/₂ cup grated cheese or
  ¹/₃ cup sour cream

Sift the flour, baking powder, and salt together, cut in the shortening until the mixture is fine. Add the herbs and/or parsley and milk and stir only until the flour is moistened. Spoon into a well-buttered 8-inch-square pan, spread the sautéed onions over the top and sprinkle with the cheddar or slather with sour cream. Bake about 20 minutes in a 425°F oven. Cut in squares and serve hot.

CAPE BRETON OATCAKES

Wherever I've gone in Cape Breton I have been treated to oat cakes – golden, crisp, and more, more and morish. Mary McLeod at The Point in Ingonish was famous for hers: guests used to tuck them away in their pockets so they wouldn't have to wait till the next meal to get more. Miriam McLean, in The

Bonnie House of Airlie near North Sydney, made fine oat cakes, too, and so did Clara May at Neil's Harbour. Jessie McEvoy who lives on a farm near Cape North served oat cakes with tea then took me to hunt crowberries behind the barn and beyond where she showed me the great field stones that mark the graves of her grandparents; she told me, "Instead of being buried in Dingwall graveyard they wanted to lie forever among their own mountains."

3 cups rolled oats	1 teaspoon baking soda
3 cups white flour	1¹/₂ cups lard or shortening
1 cup brown sugar	³/₄ cup cold water
2 teaspoons salt	

Combine all the dry ingredients. Cut in the lard then work it in with your fingers till it's really well blended. Add water a little at a time until the dough is right to roll, like pastry. Use rolled oats on the board instead of flour, and don't skimp it. Roll about ¹/₈ inch thin. Cut in squares with a knife and bake at 350°F for about 12 to 15 minutes. Watch them, they're too precious to let burn. Eat them with coffee or tea – or walking along a country lane by the sea.

JEAN SALTER'S OATMEAL BANNOCKS

Crisp and toasty to eat with cheese or fruit; very popular.

3¹/₂ cups quick but not instant oats	2 tablespoons flour
1 teaspoon salt	¹/₂ cup shortening
	About ¹/₂ cup water

Combine the oats, salt, and flour. Cut in the shortening and add enough water to dampen and form a ball. (A food processor does this in a jiffy.) Leave to swell for 10 minutes. Divide the dough in two and roll each part to ¹/₈ inch thickness; slide onto an ungreased cookie sheet, indent into squares with a pastry wheel or knife. Bake in a 350°F oven for about ¹/₂ an hour, but watch that they don't turn brown.

SWEET OATMEAL COOKIES

Jean says just add 1 cup of sugar to the bannock recipe.

CAPE BRETON BANNOCK (with my options)

In their home on the edge of the sea at Neil's Harbour, Archie and Irene Walker get lots of visitors; Irene says this bannock is her standby. No wonder they have lots of visitors.

Combine the following:

1 ¹/₂ cups bran
1 ¹/₂ cups flour (1 whole
    wheat, ¹/₂ white)
1 ¹/₂ teaspoons salt
¹/₂ cup wheat germ (optional)

1 teaspoon baking soda
1 teaspoon baking powder
2 tablespoons brown sugar
2 handfuls coconut

Cut in with a knife:

¹/₄ cup oil (or more)

Add my options if you like:

1 cup sunflower seeds, or
    1 cup raisins or currants

Stir in:

1 ¹/₂ cups buttermilk, or more
    to make a firm dough.

Gently form dough into a large ball and place it on a buttered pan; press it out to an oval 1 or 1 ¹/₂ inches thick. Cut a cross on top for good luck, and bake at 400°F until it is toasty brown – Irene said 45 minutes but mine was done in 20.

10
Muffins in Half an Hour

Your phone rings in the afternoon and a friend says, "Put on the kettle, dear, we'll be with you in half an hour for a cup of tea."

You answer, "Great, I'll be so glad to see you," and you mean it but you're also frantically thinking, "What in the world will I feed them?"

The answer is muffins: quick, easy, delicious, and foolproof.

Turn on the oven. Give your muffin tins a good buttering. Sift the dry ingredients into a bowl, blend the liquids, mix them together with a few strokes of a spoon. Drop the batter into the tins, put them in the hot oven for 20 minutes while you tidy up and listen for the timer that tells you the muffins are baked.

Your friends coming in the door say, "Wow! Something smells good in here."

Muffins can't miss. Overbeating is their only hazard. The batter should look lumpy and drop from the spoon in a blob. If you use an electric mixer or blender for anything but blending the liquid ingredients, or if you stir until the batter is smooth and elastic – forming long strands when the spoon is lifted – your muffins have had it. You can bake them, of course, but they'll probably have tunnels and holes, be tough, dry and insipid. If you blend the ingredients just enough to barely moisten the flour, your muffins will have a smooth, moist, even texture and a puffy top, golden, and glossy. Served hot you don't have to split and butter them – unless you crave extra calories.

Never serve a cold muffin. If there are any left over they can be frozen for the next emergency. To reheat them, wrap loosely in foil and put them in a hot oven for 5 minutes, or use a bun warmer, or a heavy covered pot turned low on top of the stove, or a broiler-oven. Most of your friends will eat three or four, which doesn't leave many for next time, does it?

If you have to buy muffin tins be sure to get seamless ones.

BRAN MUFFINS

For breakfast every morning? These light and tender ones are good any time of the day.

1 cup whole wheat or all-purpose flour	1 teaspoon baking powder
1 cup bran	1 egg
1/4 cup wheat germ	1/2 cup oil or shortening
1 cup brown sugar (or half molasses)	1/2 cup milk
3/4 teaspoon salt	1 teaspoon vanilla
	1/2 cup raisins or chopped dates

Thoroughly mix all the dry ingredients; blend the egg, oil, milk, and vanilla. Pour the wet into the dry mixture, add raisins or dates and stir till just combined. Half fill 18 greased muffin tins and bake at 375°F for about 20 minutes. Cool on a rack.

BANANA BRAN MUFFINS

Pieces of banana stirred into bran muffins, instead of raisins, make a nice change.

JEAN SALTER'S BRAN MUFFINS AND BRAN LOAF

Without eggs or shortening, the outside is chewy, the inside moist and delicious.

1 cup bran	1 cup brown sugar
1 cup mixed dried fruit or raisins	1 cup flour
1 cup milk	1 teaspoon baking powder

Mix together first four ingredients and soak for 1 hour, if you can wait that long. Add flour and baking powder and stir to combine. Spoon into buttered muffin tins and bake at 350°F for about 20 minutes.

For the Bran Loaf spread the batter in a buttered loaf pan and bake at 350°F for about 40 minutes. Test it.

NORM'S BLUEBERRY MUFFINS

I've eaten a lot of blueberry muffins in my day, but none as good as these.

³/₄ cup white sugar	1¹/₂ cups pastry flour
¹/₄ cup butter (and Norm uses butter)	2 teaspoons baking powder
1 egg, well beaten	¹/₂ cup milk
¹/₂ teaspoon salt	1 cup blueberries, fresh or frozen

Cream the butter and sugar, add the egg and beat till creamy. Add the sifted dry ingredients alternately with the milk. Lightly fold in the berries. Drop into buttered muffin tins. Bake at 375°F for 15 to 20 minutes, and you'll have a dozen superstars!

SUMMER BERRY MUFFINS: Instead of blueberries fold in 1 cup of whatever berries are in season: rhubarb, strawberries, raspberries, currants; if large cut to size of a raspberry. Some berries tend to turn the batter gray, but they taste good.

SURPRISE MUFFINS: Half fill buttered muffin tins with blueberry muffin batter (without the blueberries); drop in a rounded teaspoon of jam or a piece of fruit (half-thawed raspberries are great). Cover with the rest of the batter and bake at 350°F for 18 to 20 minutes.

PEACH MUFFINS

Plump, tender and delicious – absolutely marvelous – these should be eaten on the day they are baked. Lorna's husband Ross, who never eats more than one of anything said, "Girls, do you realize we have each eaten three?"

1¹/₂ **cups flour**	1 large egg
1¹/₂ **teaspoons baking powder**	¹/₂ cup milk
1 teaspoon salt	¹/₄ cup melted butter or
¹/₄ cup white sugar	vegetable oil
¹/₄ cup brown sugar	1 teaspoon almond flavouring
1¹/₂ cups fresh, sliced	White or powdered sugar for
peaches	topping

Sift the flour, baking powder, and salt into a bowl; stir in the sugar. Slice the peaches – you don't need to peel them. Beat the egg, add the milk, shortening, and almond flavouring, beating all together. Pour the egg mixture over the dry ingredients, stir until barely moistened, then lightly fold in the sliced peaches. Drop spoonfuls into well-buttered muffin tins. Bake in a 400°F oven for about 20 minutes, or until golden. Dip the tops into powdered sugar while hot and serve before they cool.

If you think some might be left over or if you want to freeze them, dissolve 2 teaspoons of Fruit Keep in 3 tablespoons of water, stir in the sliced peaches to coat them and drain well before adding them to the muffin mixture. If you don't, the peaches will turn brown and their flavour is medicinal. Too bad.

MAPLE SYRUP MUFFINS

These glazed muffins look company-fancy; they're light as angel food and their flavour is divine.

¹/₄ cup soft shortening,
  margarine is fine
¹/₂ cup white sugar
1 teaspoon salt
1¹/₂ cups flour
1 tablespoon baking powder
³/₄ cup rolled oats

¹/₂ cup milk
¹/₂ cup maple syrup
Glaze:
1 tablespoon butter
¹/₂ cup icing sugar
1 tablespoon maple syrup,
  or a bit more

Soften the shortening, blend in the sugar and salt; add the flour sifted with the baking powder and blend with a pastry cutter till the mixture is crumbly; mix in the rolled oats. Blend the milk and syrup together in a measuring cup, pour the mixture over the dry ingredients and stir just enough to moisten. Drop into muffin tins and bake at 350°F for 20 minutes.

While baking, make the glaze and spread it over the muffins when they come out of the oven and have cooled just a little bit. Serve them warm. Your guests will apologize for being such gluttons – but no one can resist these.

VERY RIPE BANANA MUFFINS

Delicate, tasty and tender.

3 ripe bananas, 1 cupful
¹/₃ cup melted shortening or
  oil
¹/₂ cup sugar
1 teaspoon salt
1 egg, well beaten

1 teaspoon vanilla
1¹/₂ cups all-purpose flour
1 teaspoon baking powder
¹/₂ teaspoon soda
¹/₂ cup chopped walnuts
  (optional)

Mash the bananas, add the shortening, sugar, and salt; beat till they blend. Add the egg and vanilla and beat again. (You may do that much in your mixer or blender if you like, but no more.) Sift the flour, baking powder and soda into the banana mixture, add the nuts, stir with a few strokes of your spatula or spoon – only enough to moisten the flour. Drop spoonfuls into greased muffin tins and bake in a 350°F oven for 15 or 20 minutes. You should have 18 muffins. Tip the muffins onto a rack to cool only slightly before you gobble them with that cup of tea.

When I visited Marnie Paisley at her winter home near Tucson, Arizona, she invited sixteen ladies for afternoon tea. In the morning we made four kinds of muffins for the event. I didn't have my muffin recipes with me and had to guess what to put in them; I must have guessed right: all the ladies wanted all the recipes.

ORANGE AND GRAPEFRUIT PEEL MUFFINS

These were the hit of the day: bitter-sweet, made with the peel of a grapefruit and an orange that Marnie and I had for breakfast.

Peel of 1 grapefruit and 1 orange	**¹/₂ cup shortening**
1 to 2 cups buttermilk	**2 cups flour**
1 cup sugar	**2 teaspoons baking powder**
1 teaspoon salt	**¹/₂ teaspoon soda**

Cut up the complete grapefruit and/or orange skins into your blender or food processor, pour in the buttermilk and whirl till the skin is finely ground. Add the sugar, salt, and shortening; the mixture will be a mush. Into a bowl sift the dry ingredients. Pour the rind mixture over the flour and stir just enough to blend – you may need more buttermilk. Spoon into buttered muffin tins and bake in a 400°F oven for 20 minutes. They'll be light, have great flavour, will stay moist, reheat well, and freeze perfectly.

APPLE CINNAMON MUFFINS

Very moist and refreshing, the ladies liked these, too. Marnie served pieces of cheese along with them.

¹/₂ cup margarine or butter	**2 cups flour – 1 whole wheat, 1 white**
³/₄ cup sugar	**1 teaspoon soda**
1 egg, beaten	**1 teaspoon cinnamon**
1 cup buttermilk	*Topping:*
1 teaspoon salt	**1 teaspoon cinnamon**
1¹/₂ cups apple, unpeeled and sliced	**2 or 3 tablespoons sugar**

Blend the margarine, sugar, and beaten egg till smooth; add the buttermilk, salt, and sliced apples, mixing well. Add the flour, soda, cinnamon, sifted together, and stir just enough to moisten. Spoon into buttered muffin cups (at Marnie's we used small ones), sprinkle with cinnamon and sugar mixed together, and bake at 400°F for 20 minutes.

DATE AND ORANGE MUFFINS

These are Ruby's favourite muffins. And no wonder.

1 whole orange	1¹/₂ cups flour
¹/₂ cup orange juice	1 teaspoon soda
¹/₂ cup chopped dates	1 teaspoon baking powder
1 egg	²/₃ cup white sugar
¹/₂ cup butter or margarine	1 teaspoon salt

Cut the whole orange into pieces to remove the seeds. Drop the pieces into the blender with the additional ¹/₂ cup orange juice and whirl till the peel is finely chopped. Drop in the dates, egg, and butter; give the blender a very short whirl. Into a bowl sift the flour, soda, baking powder, sugar, and salt. Pour the orange mixture over the dry, stir lightly, just enough to moisten. Drop spoonfuls into buttered muffin tins and bake at 400°F for about 15 minutes. They are super.

RUBY'S OATMEAL MUFFINS

At Marnie's I put dates in these and they weren't quite as light and buttery as when I make them without but still very popular.

1 cup rolled oats	¹/₂ cup melted shortening or oil
1 cup buttermilk	
1 cup sifted flour	¹/₂ cup brown sugar
1 teaspoon salt	1 egg, beaten
¹/₂ teaspoon soda	1 teaspoon vanilla
1¹/₂ teaspoons baking powder	1 cup chopped dates (optional)

Combine the oats and buttermilk, let soak while you heat your oven, butter your pans, assemble and mix all your other ingredients. Sift the flour with the salt, soda, and baking powder. To the oatmeal mixture add the melted shortening, brown sugar, beaten egg, vanilla, and dates. Pour in the sifted dry ingredients and stir only long enough to moisten. Spoon into buttered muffin pans and bake at 400°F for 15 to 20 minutes, until golden. Eat while they are hot.

GINGER RAISIN MUFFINS

One day when four friends were coming to my cottage I didn't have an egg to put in my muffins, so I had to invent some without eggs. The man of the company ate 4, the ladies 2 apiece – and they were fat ones (I mean the muffins). The ladies at Marnie's ate quite a few of these too, but they were smaller (again I mean the muffins).

¹/₂ cup shortening (I used margarine)	1 cup whole wheat flour
¹/₂ cup packed brown sugar	1 cup all-purpose flour
1 teaspoon salt	1 tablespoon baking powder
¹/₂ cup milk	2 teaspoons ginger
¹/₂ cup molasses, blended with the milk	¹/₂ teaspoon cinnamon
	¹/₂ teaspoon nutmeg
	1 cup raisins

Cream the shortening with the sugar and salt, blend with the milk and molasses. Stir together the cup of whole wheat flour, baking powder, ginger, cinnamon, and nutmeg. Pour the liquid ingredients over the dry – or the dry into the liquid – drop in the raisins, and stir just enough to moisten the flour. Spoon into the well-buttered muffin tins and bake at 400°F for about 20 minutes.

DOUGHNUT MUFFINS

Both Norm and Eva gave me this recipe. Because they are irresistible I am giving you Eva's version – which is exactly twice as large as Norm's and makes 3 dozen.

3¹/₂ cups pastry flour, not
sifted (Norm uses sifted all-
purpose)
1 tablespoon baking powder
1 teaspoon salt
¹/₂ teaspoon nutmeg

1¹/₂ cups white sugar
2 eggs
²/₃ cup shortening or lard
(Norm uses vegetable oil)
1¹/₂ cups milk
2 teaspoons vanilla

Combine the flour, baking powder, salt, nutmeg and sugar. In another bowl beat up the egg, oil or shortening, milk and vanilla. Add to the dry ingredients and stir just enough to moisten. Fill buttered muffin tins ²/₃ full and bake at 350°F for 15 to 20 minutes. Tap the tins to dislodge the muffins. Eva says they eat theirs dunked in maple syrup just like you would doughnuts. Norm's half-size recipe says: "Melt 1 cup of butter and roll the hot muffins in it to coat them all over, then immediately roll them in a mixture of 2 cups sugar and 2 teaspoons cinnamon to coat them like a doughnut. Eat them hot. They are scrumptious."

COFFEE WALNUT MUFFINS

These are the quickest of all.

1 tablespoon instant coffee
powder
¹/₂ cup hot water
¹/₂ cup whole milk or cream if
you have it
1 egg, beaten
¹/₂ cup melted shortening, or
vegetable oil if you're
really in a rush

2 cups flour
3 teaspoons baking powder
¹/₃ cup sugar
1 teaspoon salt
¹/₂ cup chopped walnuts

Dissolve the coffee in the hot water, add the cream, beaten egg and shortening. Sift the flour, baking powder, salt and sugar into a bowl. Stir in the walnuts. Pour the liquid ingredients into the dry and mix just enough to moisten them. Spoon the batter into buttered muffin tins and bake in a 400°F oven for 20 minutes. Makes 12. The flavour is great.

MRS. CLEASON SCHMIDT'S BOILED RAISIN MUFFINS

The flavour is enhanced by boiling the raisins before you put them into the batter.

³/₄ **cup raisins (or 1 cup)**	¹/₂ **teaspoon salt**
1¹/₂ **cups water, boiling**	1 **teaspoon vanilla**
¹/₂ **cup shortening**	1¹/₂ **cups flour**
³/₄ **cup brown sugar**	1 **teaspoon baking powder**
1 **egg, well beaten**	1 **teaspoon soda**

Simmer the raisins and water in a covered pot for about 20 minutes, then let them cool. Cream the shortening and sugar together, beat in the egg, salt, and vanilla till creamy. Add the cooled raisins and water. Sift the flour, baking powder, and soda into the mixture and stir only until moistened. Spoon into buttered muffin pans, about 1¹/₂ dozen. Bake at 350°F for 20 to 25 minutes.

GRAPENUTS MUFFINS

A hard crispy crust and mysterious little crunchy bits in a soft moist inside make these disappear far too quickly – but you can make more in 25 minutes. Keep the oven hot.

1¹/₄ **cups flour**	1 **teaspoon salt**
2 **teaspoons baking powder**	¹/₃ **cup oil**
2 **cups grapenuts**	1 **cup milk**
¹/₂ **cup sugar**	1 **teaspoon vanilla**

Mix all the dry ingredients. Blend the oil, milk, and vanilla; pour the mixture over the dry ingredients and stir just enough to moisten. Spoon into well-buttered muffin tins, sprinkling more grapenuts on top. Bake in a 400°F oven for about 20 minutes. Cool on a rack. Serve warm. They'll be chewy and won't need any butter.

GRANOLA MUFFINS

Made in exactly the same way as grapenuts muffins but with granola instead of grapenuts, ¹/₃ cup molasses and ¹/₄ cup brown sugar instead of ¹/₂ cup white sugar. You might need a little less milk or a little more flour. Great flavour.

SEVEN GRAIN CEREAL MUFFINS

Harold Horwood, Newfoundland's leading author, spoke at the Kitchener Public Library one freezing rainy day. While he was driving and walking on the ice to my cottage I put these muffins in the oven. With Dubonnet and pieces of cheese we both ate four and he took the rest home to Corky, his wife.

1 cup 7-grain cereal or Red River Cereal
1 cup buttermilk
1 teaspoon salt
$^{1}/_{2}$ cup oil
$^{1}/_{2}$ cup brown sugar
1 cup raisins

1 cup flour (I used whole wheat)
1 teaspoon baking powder
$^{1}/_{2}$ teaspoon soda
2 teaspoons ginger
$^{1}/_{2}$ teaspoon cinnamon

Put the cereal into a bowl, pour the buttermilk over it, add the salt, oil, sugar, and raisins; mix them and let rest for about half an hour, unless you are in a rush. Sift the flour, baking powder, soda, ginger, and cinnamon into the cereal mixture; stir just enough to dampen all the flour, adding a bit more milk if you need to. Spoon into greased muffin tins; it will make a dozen fat ones. Bake in a 400°F oven about 20 minutes and eat them hot, hot. The cereal I used had hard crunchy bits in it but the texture of the muffins was light as a feather. Harold told me he uses molasses instead of sugar in all his muffins.

PEANUT BUTTER MUFFINS

Peanut butter freaks will love these. Let your growing boys try them.

$^{1}/_{2}$ cup peanut butter
3 tablespoons vegetable oil
1 teaspoon salt
$^{1}/_{4}$ cup sugar, brown or white
1 egg

$1^{1}/_{2}$ cups milk
1 cup all-purpose flour
1 tablespoon baking powder
1 cup whole wheat flour
Peanut butter to spoon on top

Blend the peanut butter and oil, salt and sugar; beat in the egg, stir in the milk. Sift the white flour and baking powder into a bowl, stir in the whole wheat flour, then combine with the peanut butter mixture just enough to completely moisten the flour. Spoon into buttered muffin tins. Put about 1 teaspoonful of peanut butter on top of each muffin. Bake at 400°F for 20 minutes. Serve warm, with a knife to spread the hot peanut butter over the muffin – quite a nice touch.

MUSHROOM MUFFINS

If you want muffins that are fantastic to eat with a salad or soup, try these.

1 egg

1/3 cup melted shortening or oil

1/4 cup milk

1 can (10 oz.) condensed cream of mushroom soup (undiluted)

2 cups pastry flour

3 teaspoons baking powder

1/4 teaspoon salt

2 tablespoons cut-up parsley or chives (optional)

Beat the egg, blend in the shortening, milk, and soup. Sift together the flour, baking powder, and salt. Add the liquid mixture to the dry ingredients along with the parsley or chives, and stir only until the flour is moistened – remember the rule. Fill the buttered muffin tins 2/3 full and bake for 20 minutes at 425°F. You'll have 12 to 14 muffins that everyone will rave about.

I haven't yet had a chance to try them but I think they'd be good with cream of tomato, chicken, celery or asparagus soup as well, don't you?

11
Quick Breads

If you are the kind of person who likes to give a cup of tea and a little something edible to everyone who knocks at your door you might be wise to develop a repertoire of quick breads. They can be mixed up as quickly as muffins, take longer to bake, but stay moist longer, need no icing as cakes do, and take up less space in your freezer. Sliced thin, lightly buttered, or spread with cheese, they rest neatly on a saucer with a tea cup and are a pleasure to eat.

Their variety is infinite; you can put all sorts of things into them: dates, walnuts, sunflower seeds, honey, zucchini, raisins, bran, wheat germ, spices, oranges and lemons, bananas, cranberries, carrots, apples, currants, molasses, poppy seed, apricots, prunes.

Also they make a great little gift to take to your neighbour or a friend in distress.

BEULAH'S PRESERVED GINGER LOAF

From Mother's old hand-written recipe book. Light as a feather and ready for love.

$^1/_2$ cup butter
1 cup sugar
3 eggs, beaten
$^1/_2$ cup milk
$^1/_2$ teaspoon salt
2 cups flour

1 teaspoon baking powder
1 cup raisins
$^1/_3$ cup preserved ginger, chopped
1 cup chopped nuts ($^1/_4$ for topping)

Cream the butter and sugar, beat in the eggs, milk, and salt. Stir in the sifted flour and baking powder, just enough to moisten; blend in the raisins, preserved ginger and $^3/_4$ cup nuts. Sprinkle $^1/_4$ cup nuts over the batter and bake in a 250°F oven for over an hour.

QUICK PLUM BREAD

I made this tangy loaf to take to a friend but I cut off a slice to taste it first – then I cut another slice, then another – till I had to make another loaf for my friend.

2 cups flour
$2^1/_2$ teaspoons baking powder
1 teaspoon salt
$^1/_2$ cup sugar
$1^1/_2$ cups fresh or frozen plums, pitted and quartered

$^1/_2$ cup chopped nuts
1 egg
$^3/_4$ cup milk
Rind of 1 orange, 1 lemon, or grapefruit
3 tablespoons vegetable oil

Into a mixing bowl sift together the flour, baking powder, salt and sugar. Stir in the plums and nuts. Into your blender break the egg, add the milk, orange, lemon or grapefruit rind and the oil; give it a whirl till the rind is very fine. Pour the wet mixture into the dry one and mix only till the flour is moistened, no more. Spoon it into a well-buttered loaf pan, sprinkle the top with sugar and bake at 350°F for almost an hour, but test it with a toothpick before that. Cool on a rack. The crust will be chewy, the inside moist, the flavour will tempt you to eat more and more and more.

DATE LOAF WITH RAISINS

Marnie Paisley inherited this old favourite from Miss Emma
Kaufman who was known by many people in the world of the
YWCA in Canada and Japan.

1 teaspoon soda	4 tablespoons butter
1 cup dates, cut in pieces	1 egg
1 cup raisins	1¼ cups flour
1 orange rind, grated	½ teaspoon salt
1 cup boiling water	½ cup broken walnuts
1 cup white or brown sugar	

Sprinkle the soda over the dates, orange, and raisins and pour
the boiling water over them. Let cool. Cream sugar and butter,
beat in the egg and stir into the date-raisin mixture when it has
cooled. Sift the flour and salt into the bowl with the rest and
stir only until it is blended. Fold in the nuts. Pour into a loaf tin,
well buttered, and bake at 350°F for about 55 minutes. This
keeps well for some time; it freezes well, too.

JEAN SALTER'S BRAN LOAF

Turn to Jean's Bran Muffins (page 180); sometimes she puts
the batter into a well-buttered loaf pan instead of muffin tins.
She bakes it in a 350°F oven for about 40 minutes. Butter it
while it is still warm and there won't be any left when it's cold.

MARNIE'S CRANBERRY NUT BREAD

The red cranberries show up in each white slice – pretty as
well as tasty. I won't guarantee it but you might try it with a
cupful of cranberry sauce if you don't have raw cranberries.

2 cups flour	1 egg, well beaten
1 cup sugar	¾ cup orange juice
1½ teaspoons baking powder	Rind of 1 orange, chopped
½ teaspoon soda	½ cup chopped nuts
1 teaspoon salt	1 to 2 cups fresh cranberries,
¼ cup shortening	coarsely chopped

Sift the flour, sugar, baking powder, soda, and salt; cut in the shortening till the mixture is crumbly. Blend the beaten egg with the orange juice and rind. (I put mine in my blender.) Pour all at once into the dry ingredients, mixing just enough to dampen. Gently fold in the nuts and the cranberries. Spoon the batter into a greased loaf pan, spreading the corners and sides slightly higher than the centre. Bake in a 350°F oven for about 1 hour, till the crust is golden and an inserted toothpick tells you it's baked through. Remove from the pan to cool on a rack.

CRANBERRY MUFFINS: If you'd rather have muffins, drop the batter into muffin tins and bake at 400°F for 20 minutes.

CARROT BREAD

A visitor from France said this bread, on the fifth day of its life, had a subtle flavour – and ate several slices. (When Joyce Carter called to say she was bringing her friend to meet me, I had rejuvenated my little old loaf by dribbling over it a shot glass of Cointreau.)

1 cup sugar
¹/₂ cup salad oil
2 eggs, beaten
1 cup shredded carrots
¹/₂ cup milk
1¹/₂ cups sifted flour
1 teaspoon baking powder

1 teaspoon soda
¹/₄ teaspoon salt
1 teaspoon cinnamon
¹/₂ cup chopped walnuts
¹/₄ cup Cointreau, rum, or
  brandy (entirely optional)

Mix the sugar and salad oil, add the beaten eggs, stir in the shredded carrot and milk. (If you have a blender put everything in it and give it a whirl till the carrots are chopped.) Sift the flour, baking powder, soda, salt, cinnamon into the carrot mixture and stir just enough to blend, adding the walnuts as well. Bake in a buttered loaf pan for about 55 minutes in a 350°F oven.

You don't need the Cointreau if you eat this when it's fresh – actually you don't need it any time because the loaf stays moist. Do fashion editors make me show-off? The first time Joyce came to my cottage she wore white gloves, now she and her husband, Clay Derstine, come in their bare feet.

ORANGE RAISIN OATMEAL BREAD

Liz Elstner is a pretty young lawyer who says she saves time, energy, and money by making two loaves at a time.

2 cups raisins	2¹/₂ cups rolled oats
Boiling water	³/₄ cup oil
3³/₄ cups flour	2 eggs
2¹/₂ teaspoons salt	2 large oranges, juice and
5 teaspoons baking powder	rind
1³/₄ cups sugar	1¹/₄ cups milk

Plump the raisins by pouring boiling water to cover them; let stand 10 minutes, then drain and pat dry with a paper towel. In a large bowl combine the flour, salt, baking powder, sugar, rolled oats, and raisins. Beat together the oil, eggs, orange juice, rind, and milk; pour over the dry ingredients, stirring only until they are moistened; you may need more orange juice or milk. Spoon the batter into 2 greased loaf pans, spreading evenly to all corners. Bake at 350°F for 50 to 60 minutes – or until done when tested with toothpick stuck in the centre. Cool on a rack for 10 minutes before removing from the pans. Eat one, freeze one.

SALEMA HOLLINGER'S MOLASSES WHOLE WHEAT BREAD

A light, quick bread, tender and moist, with no shortening, and that old-fashioned flavour.

1 teaspoon salt	1 beaten egg
1 teaspoon soda	¹/₂ cup molasses
³/₄ cups all-purpose flour	¹/₂ cup brown sugar
2 cups whole wheat or	1¹/₂ cups buttermilk
graham flour	

Mix the salt, soda, and two kinds of flour together. Beat the egg with the molasses and brown sugar, then add the buttermilk. Pour the liquid ingredients into the dry and stir only until moistened. Pour into a buttered loaf pan, bake in a 350°F oven for about 40 minutes, till the bread tests done. Butter it and serve it while still warm if you want to hear your guests purr with great satisfaction.

PRUNE BREAD

A good thing to make with those cooked prunes you forgot about. Almeda says, "You could even use schnitz and guetcha (dried apples and prunes, cooked together)."

²/₃ cup cooking oil
1¹/₃ cups sugar
2 eggs, slightly beaten
²/₃ cup buttermilk
²/₃ to 1 cup chopped cooked
   prunes

1²/₃ cups flour
¹/₂ teaspoon salt
¹/₄ teaspoon cinnamon, or
   more
1¹/₃ teaspoons soda
¹/₂ cup chopped nuts

Beat together cooking oil, sugar and the beaten eggs; stir in the buttermilk and whatever prunes you've found, but not much more than a cupful. Sift together into the liquid mixture, the flour, salt, cinnamon, and soda; add the nuts. Pour the batter into a well-buttered loaf pan and bake at 350°F for half an hour, then reduce the heat to 325°F and bake another half hour. Let cool in the pan a few minutes before turning out on a rack. It will be moist, light and tasty, will do you no end of good.

GRANOLA OR GRAPENUTS RAISIN BREAD
1 long or 2 small loaves

Ruby says this loaf is full of surprises – depending on what you've put in your granola.

1³/₄ cups all-purpose flour
1 cup sugar, brown or white
4 teaspoons baking powder
1¹/₂ teaspoons salt
1¹/₂ teaspoons cinnamon
1 cup whole wheat flour
1¹/₂ cups granola
   (or grapenuts)

1¹/₂ cups raisins
2 eggs, well beaten
1¹/₃ cups milk
¹/₃ cup melted butter or
   margarine
1 teaspoon vanilla

Sift the white flour, sugar, baking powder, salt, and cinnamon together. Stir in the whole wheat flour, granola, and raisins. Combine the eggs, milk, butter, and vanilla; pour all at once into the dry ingredients, stirring just until moistened. Turn into a greased loaf pan 9″ x 5″ – or 2 smaller ones – sprinkle granola or grapenuts on top and pat down lightly. Bake in a 350°F oven for 50 to 60 minutes, testing with a toothpick stuck in the middle. Cool on a rack for 10 minutes before removing from the pan. Slice and butter it to serve with a nice cup of tea – or have it with fruit or cheese for dessert.

RUBY'S LEMON LOAF

Tender, moist and finely textured. Everyone says, "This is the best lemon loaf I've ever tasted."

¹/₂ **cup butter or margarine**	**1 teaspoon baking powder**
1 cup white sugar	¹/₂ **teaspoon salt**
2 eggs	
Grated rind of 2 lemons	*Topping:*
¹/₂ **cup milk**	**Juice of 1 lemon**
1¹/₂ cups flour	¹/₂ **cup white sugar**

Cream the butter and sugar together, blend in the eggs and lemon rind then stir in the milk till the mixture is smooth. Sift the flour, baking powder, and salt into the mixture and stir just enough to moisten the dry ingredients. Pour into a buttered loaf pan and bake at 350°F for 45 to 55 minutes.

Meanwhile warm the ¹/₂ cup sugar in the lemon juice to dissolve the sugar. When the loaf comes from the oven dribble the juice over the top and let it soak in. Leave the loaf in the pan for 10 minutes before you remove it to cool on a rack.

VARIATION: If you want to make this into an orange loaf you need only substitute orange rind and juice. You might try a mixture of both.

HONEY RAISIN NUT LOAF

When Mrs. Orval Honsberger brought this to a Lutheran Church Bake Sale it was snapped up immediately. Somebody knew a good thing.

1½ cups raisins
½ cups chopped walnuts
¾ cup boiling water
¼ cup butter
⅓ cup brown sugar
1 egg
½ cup honey

1 teaspoon rum extract, or
   1 tablespoon rum
1¾ cups all-purpose flour
½ teaspoon salt
1 teaspoon baking soda
⅓ cup milk

Add boiling water to the raisins and nuts; let stand until cool. Cream the butter, sugar, egg, honey, and rum until light and fluffy. Sift the flour, salt, and soda into the creamed mixture alternately with the cooled, drained raisins and milk, stirring only until smooth. Pour into a buttered loaf pan and bake at 350°F for 50 to 60 minutes. All quick breads taste better if you eat them soon after they come out of the oven.

APPLE AND CHEESE NUT BREAD

Read the ingredients and see if you can resist trying this. I couldn't and I wasn't disappointed.

½ cup shortening
⅔ cup sugar
2 eggs
1 cup finely chopped apples, unpeeled
½ cup grated old cheddar, or more

½ cup chopped walnuts
2 cups flour
1 teaspoon baking powder
½ teaspoon soda
1 teaspoon salt

Cream the shortening; gradually add the sugar, and beat until fluffy. Add the eggs, one at a time, beating well after each one. Stir in the apples, cheese, and nuts. Sift the flour, baking powder, soda, and salt into the other mixture and stir only until all the flour is dampened. Spoon into a buttered loaf pan, pushing the batter into the corners and sides of the pan. Bake at 350°F for about an hour. Serve slightly warm for the best effect.

VARIATION: You could drop this batter into muffin tins, put them in a 400°F oven and have muffins in 20 minutes.

CATHERINE FROMM'S SOUR CREAM COFFEE CAKE

Catherine used to be head dietitian in Eaton's Georgian Room in Toronto. This glorious creation was baking in Catherine's oven while we sat by her fireplace and made conversation as if we weren't aware of the tantalyzing aromas that wafted around us. Happy moment when we moved to the dining room for tea and demolished the whole cake while it was still hot.

Topping:
1 cup chopped nuts (I think Catherine's were mixed with cashews, if you want to be economical you could use toasted sunflower seeds.)
1/3 cup melted butter
1/3 cup white sugar
1/3 cup brown sugar
1 teaspoon cinnamon

Batter:
1/2 cup shortening
1 cup white sugar
2 eggs
1 teaspoon vanilla
2 cups all-purpose flour
1 teaspoon soda
1 teaspoon baking powder
1/2 teaspoon salt
1 cup sour cream

Mix the topping ingredients first, then the batter: Cream the shortening and sugar, beat in the eggs and vanilla. Sift the flour, soda, baking powder, and salt and stir into the creamed mixture alternately with the sour cream. Spread half the topping mixture in the bottom of a well-buttered tube pan; spoon half the batter over it. Sprinkle the rest of the topping over the batter then spoon in the rest of the batter. Bake at 350°F for about 45 minutes till it is done.

While she was making the tea Catherine let the cake stand for a few minutes before turning it out on a large cake plate to cool slightly before all of us had three generous portions apiece. It's so comforting to eat with fellow gourmands, or need I say gluttons?

MRS. ABNER EBY'S ORANGE GINGERBREAD

This is the best gingerbread I've ever tasted: it has terrific flavour, texture, tenderness and style. With a glaze on top.

1 cup orange juice (fresh, frozen or dissolved crystals)
Rind of 1 orange
1 cup molasses
1 cup butter or margarine
1 cup brown sugar
3 eggs, beaten
2¹/₂ cups flour

1 teaspoon salt
1¹/₂ teaspoons soda
1 teaspoon cinnamon
1 teaspoon allspice
2 teaspoons ginger
Glaze:
1¹/₂ cups icing sugar
Enough orange juice to make it pour

In your blender put the orange juice and rind; blend till the rind is ground up. In a saucepan melt the butter, add the brown sugar and molasses, pour in the orange juice mixture and heat until the sugar is dissolved – don't let it boil. Cool then beat in the eggs. Sift the dry ingredients over the wet ones and stir only until blended. Pour into a large cake pan, about 9″ x 13″, and bake at 325°F for about an hour. While it is baking make a glaze of icing sugar and enough orange juice to make it pour easily, but not too thin. When the gingerbread comes out of the oven pour the glaze over it while it is hot and spread it evenly. Let the gingerbread cool on a rack in the pan. Serve it with whipped cream or ice cream as a dessert or with a cup of tea any time. It's a big cake but it won't last long.

IRISH SODA BREAD

At Rundles in Stratford they always serve fresh soda bread with the first course. Sometimes they shape it into neat, round buns.

1 cup white flour
1 cup whole wheat flour
1 teaspoon baking soda

1 teaspoon salt
¹/₈ cup margarine
1 cup buttermilk or sour milk

Sift the flour into a bowl with soda and salt. Rub in the margarine; make a well in the centre and add the buttermilk. Knead until smooth and free from stickiness. Form into loaves, make a cut across each – a cross for good luck. Bake at 325°F for about 40 minutes.

LORNA'S BONANZA BREAD
2 loaves

Makes 2 loaves or 1 loaf and 18 muffins, supplies protein, calcium, iron and vitamin A. Besides all that it has terrific flavour.

1 cup sifted flour
1 cup whole wheat flour
$^1/_2$ teaspoon salt
$^1/_2$ teaspoon baking soda
2 teaspoons baking powder
$^2/_3$ cup dry milk powder
$^1/_3$ cup wheat germ
$^1/_2$ cup packed brown sugar
$^1/_4$ cup chopped walnuts
$^1/_2$ cup chopped roasted
  peanuts

$^1/_2$ cup raisins
3 eggs
$^1/_2$ cup vegetable oil
$^1/_2$ cup molasses
$^3/_4$ cup orange juice
1 cup mashed bananas (3)
$^1/_3$ cup chopped dried
  apricots or dried apple
  schnitz

Combine the dry ingredients, nuts, and raisins in a large bowl. Blend thoroughly. Whirl eggs in blender until foamy. Add oil, molasses, orange juice, and bananas, whirling after each addition. Add apricots; whirl to chop coarsely. Pour mixture into the bowl of dry ingredients. Stir only until moistened. Pour into 2 greased loaf pans. Bake at 325°F for 1 hour.

VARIATIONS: For a more tangy orange flavour add $^1/_2$ small orange, including peel to the blender ingredients. Use other nuts in place of walnuts if you like but don't substitute for peanuts which are used for nutritional balance. Instead of bananas you might substitute raw chopped apple, or grated carrot, applesauce, peaches, pears, grated zucchini.

Think of all the fun you can have trying all those; and good eating.

CHRISTINA SCLANDERS' MIRACLE BEER BREAD

Ever run out of bread at your house? You can make a loaf with a hard crust, a yeasty texture and taste in exactly 1 hour and 5 minutes. Really good.

3 cups self-raising flour
3 tablespoons sugar

1 bottle of beer at room
  temperature

Mix the flour and sugar, pour the beer in slowly to prevent frothing, stir till the flour is moistened. Plop the dough into a buttered loaf pan and bake it in a 350°F oven for 1 hour. Remove from pan and cool on a rack.

I could hardly wait to try this after Chris gave me her recipe. I had no self-raising flour which is a homogenized combination of cake and pastry flour, baking powder, and salt; I improvised by adding 4 teaspoons of baking powder and a teaspoon of salt to all-purpose flour. The result was not as good as the bread I'd eaten at Chris' house – but not bad. I'm going to keep on experimenting. I've also bought a package of self-raising at the supermarket – to be prepared for emergencies.

12

Cookies
and Squares

There are no statistics to prove it but I think the Region of Waterloo must be the greatest cookie-baking area in Canada, perhaps North America – maybe the world. All of us natives bake cookies for every occasion or non-occasion. The farmers' wives sell cookies at the markets; so do church groups, Girl Guides, city wives, and bearded young men. There are always big fat cookies – and little fancy ones – for sale at the church bazaars and baking sales, at the Elmira Maple Syrup Festival, the Wellesley Cheese and Apple Butter Fest, the New Hamburg Mennonite Sale. Kitchener has two cookie factories – one started in 1892, the other in 1967 – which every day sell millions of cookies to stores throughout Canada, the United States, Japan, the Far East, and the Caribbean.

I think my sister Norm makes the best cookies. She always has boxes of them stashed away in her cupboard or freezer and they are consistently neat and delicious. When a recipe calls for shortening, she uses butter. This is her secret: she melts it long enough to come to a bubble, and that gives all her cookies a superior flavour.

In a corner of my kitchen counter I have an old black cookie jar with red cherries painted on the side; I can't say it is always full, but there are always cookies in it. As soon as I can feel the last layer on the bottom I get busy and make another batch just in case someone should call on me. I must have something on hand at all times: for the lawn mowers, the snow blowers, my nieces and nephews, Kennie and Patti, never fail to lift the lid of my cookie jar to see what is there – my half-mile-away neighbour Bonnie Bennett; Robbie Cosford and Terrylynn Field, who live at the far end of the lake and often walk around; Ray Bryant with his Jehovah's Witness disciples or his wife and nine children. A full cookie jar means one is always prepared.

NORM'S DATE AND NUT DROPS
about 4 to 5 dozen

These are crisp and have a good flavour. You can't stop at one or two.

1 cup butter	$^1/_4$ teaspoon soda
1 cup brown sugar	$^1/_4$ teaspoon salt
2 eggs	$^1/_2$ teaspoon baking powder
2 cups nuts, chopped	1 teaspoon cinnamon
2 cups dates, chopped	$^1/_2$ teaspoon cloves
2 tablespoons orange or lemon juice	$^1/_2$ teaspoon allspice
1$^1/_2$ cups flour (half could be whole wheat)	

Blend butter, sugar, eggs, and beat well. Add nuts, dates, stir in the orange or lemon juice, then the dry ingredients sifted together. Drop teaspoonfuls on a buttered baking sheet. They spread. Bake in a 375°F oven for 12 to 15 minutes.

MAGGIE'S ROLL AND SLICE COOKIES

In Neil's Harbour, Maggie's son copied this recipe for me; he told me, "There ain't none made better than these." Maggie said, "Keith, don't say ain't."

³/₄ cup lard	1 teaspoon soda
1 cup firmly packed brown sugar	1 teaspoon salt
	3 cups oatmeal or rolled oats
¹/₂ cup white sugar	1 cup chopped raisins or dates
2 eggs	
1 teaspoon vanilla	1 cup chocolate or butterscotch chips
1¹/₂ cups flour	

Cream the lard and sugars together until light; add the eggs and vanilla, beating well. Stir in the flour, soda, and salt sifted together, until the mixture is smooth. Mix in the oatmeal and any or all of the other ingredients. Form into a roll, chill for a while then slice as thin as you can. Arrange on buttered cookie sheets – they spread – and bake in a 350°F oven for 8 to 10 minutes. You should have 109: Keith says, "And that ain't never enough."

FRUIT JUMBLES

Mother loved these soft spicy drop cookies; she made them more often than any other – and in big batches.

³/₄ cup butter	1 cup chopped walnuts
1¹/₂ cups brown sugar	3 cups flour
2 or 3 eggs	1 teaspoon soda
1 teaspoon vanilla	1 teaspoon cinnamon
2 tablespoons milk	¹/₂ teaspoon cloves
Pinch of salt	¹/₂ teaspoon nutmeg
2 cups chopped dates	

Mother's recipe gives no directions for mixing except to sift the soda and spices with the flour after mixing the rest in the order given. Drop spoonfuls on buttered cookie sheets and bake at 350°F for about 12 minutes; don't overbake or they'll be too dry.

ICE BOX GINGER SNAPS

Happy day when Mother made these.

½ cup each butter and lard
½ cup each brown sugar and
  molasses
1 teaspoon soda dissolved in
  2 tablespoons vinegar

1 teaspoon salt
1 tablespoon powdered
  ginger
½ teaspoon lemon flavouring
1 teaspoon cinnamon

Mix these ingredients and then add enough sifted flour to make a stiff dough. Roll into a couple of long cylinders, wrap in waxed paper and put into fridge overnight. Slice wafer thin with a very sharp knife and bake at 400°F, watching them like a hawk for they brown very quickly and should not be too dark.

CRACKLE-TOP PEANUT BUTTER COOKIES
rolled balls

Norm declares these are the best.

¾ cup butter
¾ cup brown sugar
¾ cup white sugar
¾ cup peanut butter
1 beaten egg

1 teaspoon vanilla
1¾ cups unsifted flour
½ teaspoon soda
½ teaspoon salt
White sugar

Mix the butter, both sugars, peanut butter, egg, and vanilla; beat until light. Sift the soda and salt with the flour and mix well with the peanut butter mixture. Shape teaspoonfuls of dough into balls, roll them in a dish of white sugar to coat. Place on unbuttered cookie sheets 2 inches apart. Do not flatten. Bake at 375°F for about 12 minutes. Don't let them brown.

KITCHEN SINK COOKIES
drops

"So called because you can add whatever you like and they always seem to be a success," Nancy writes about her recipe. "These are my favourite cookies and I've tried a lot. They are for people who love chocolate but want a combination of healthy ingredients; they keep long because of the honey. I think they are dynamite!"

1 cup whole wheat flour
1/4 cup soy flour
1 1/3 cups rolled oats
1/4 cup milk powder
1/2 teaspoon salt
1 1/2 teaspoons cinnamon
1/2 teaspoon ground nutmeg and cloves
2/3 cup raisins
2/3 cup chocolate chips, or 1 package
2 eggs beaten

1/4 cup oil or melted butter
1/4 cup honey
1/4 cup molasses

Options to be added (just about anything):
Nancy prefers 1/4 cup peanuts and/
or 1/3 cup sunflower seeds
or 3/4 cup coconut
or 1/4 cup sesame seeds

Mix all the dry ingredients, including your choice of options. Beat the eggs, add oil, honey, molasses, and beat. Pour liquid into dry ingredients and stir till moistened. If mixture is too dry, add milk or water. Drop onto unoiled cookie sheet. Bake for 10 to 12 minutes.

BARBIE'S SUPER SIMPLE OATMEAL COOKIES

These are Barbie's standbys. She – or Patti or Kennie – whips them up in no time to keep the cookie jar full. Which means they make them very often.

1/2 cup brown sugar
1/2 cup white sugar or brown
1 cup margarine (or half butter)
1 egg
1 teaspoon salt

1 teaspoon soda
1 cup flour
2 1/2 cups oatmeal (or 1 cup coconut, 1 1/2 cups rolled oats)
1 teaspoon vanilla

Mix everything together, roll pieces in balls and press down with a fork on a buttered cookie sheet. Bake at 350°F till golden, about 12 minutes. Barbie always doubles the recipe or she'd be making more the next day.

CAROL HUDGINS OWN COOKIES
drops or rolls

When I came home from town one summer evening I found a
little plastic packet of cookies fastened to my door knocker.
Who was the cookie fairy? After tasting the cookies I wanted
the recipe. Next day Carol came down the lake in her sailboat
and wrote it for me. She is a home economist; the cookies are
her own invention.

³/₄ cup butter
1 cup brown sugar
1 large egg
1 teaspoon vanilla
1 cup rolled oats
¹/₄ cup soy flour and/or ¹/₄ cup
   wheat germ
¹/₄ cup milk powder
³/₄ cup whole wheat flour

2 teaspoons baking powder
1 teaspoon salt
1¹/₂ cups of any mixture of
   walnuts, chocolate chips,
   sesame and sunflower
   seeds, raisins, dates,
   peanuts, or any chopped
   nuts.

Cream the butter and sugar, beat in the egg and vanilla. Fill a
2-cup measure with the rolled oats, soy flour or wheat germ,
milk powder, whole wheat flour, baking powder and salt. Stir
into the creamed mixture and add as much as you like – about
1¹/₂ cups altogether – of any mixture of the chips, seeds, fruit,
and/or nuts. Either drop by teaspoonfuls on a buttered cookie
sheet or roll into a cylinder, wrap in waxed paper, put in
fridge and slice and bake as needed. Bake at 350°F for about
12 minutes.

NIPPY CHEESE BITS
balls

These are tangy and light.

¹/₂ cup butter or margarine
³/₄ cup all-purpose or whole
   wheat flour
1 cup nippy cheese, grated
   fine

Dash cayenne
¹/₄ teaspoon salt
2 cups rice crispies
Nuts or cheese for topping

Blend the butter with the flour – use your hands – then add the cheese and mix it thoroughly along with the salt and dash of cayenne. Gently combine with the rice crispies. Shape into balls, place them on a buttered cookie sheet and flatten them slightly. Put a nut on top or a very small square of cheese as a trimming. Bake in a 300°F oven for 10 to 12 minutes. Be careful not to let them burn; they should be cheese colour, not brown.

EVA'S CHOCOLATE MINT COOKIES

These are neat and her children love them – so do the grown-ups.

^{2}/₃ cup butter or margarine, or lard	2 cups flour
1 cup white sugar	^{2}/₃ cup cocoa
1 egg	1 teaspoon baking powder
^{1}/₂ teaspoon salt	^{1}/₂ teaspoon soda
	^{1}/₄ cup milk

Thoroughly cream the butter and sugar. Add the egg and beat well. Add the sifted dry ingredients alternately with the milk. Mix and chill. Roll to ^{1}/₈ inch thickness and cut with a fancy cutter. Bake at 350°F till crisp, about 10 minutes. Put together like a sandwich with mint filling:

^{1}/₂ cup icing sugar	3 or 4 teaspoons cream or milk
Few grains salt	
2 drops oil of peppermint or 1 teaspoon peppermint flavouring	

EVA'S CHEWY MOLASSES COOKIES

"We just love these," Eva told me. "They're best made with apple molasses."

1 cup molasses	2 teaspoons soda
1 cup brown sugar	Flour to make a soft dough
2 eggs, beaten	White sugar for dipping

Mix in the order given. Roll in balls and dip the balls in sugar. Bake on buttered cookie sheets at 350°F for about 10 or 12 minutes. When cold put the cookies into a crock, cover it with a cloth till the cookies are soft and chewy, then cover tightly.

GRANDMOTHER BOMBERGER'S MOLASSES COOKIES

Grandmother Bomberger, who is a vigorous eighty-seven, got this recipe from an earlier Grandmother Bomberger. "Make them big," she told me. "Children love them."
Cream together:

2 cups brown sugar	**¹/₂ pound lard**

Add and mix:

1 teaspoon salt	**1 cup sour cream**
2 eggs, beaten	**1 cup molasses**
1 teaspoon soda wet with a	**1 dessertspoon ginger**
little water	**About 7 cups flour**

Use only enough flour to make a soft dough. Put in the fridge overnight. Roll out about ¹/₂ inch thick and cut with a jar ring. For topping: beat up an egg, brush over the top of each cookie and sprinkle it with white sugar. Put the cookies on buttered baking sheets and bake in a 350°F oven about 12 to 15 minutes – but watch them. The newspaper carrier calls regularly for a treat and Grandmother Bomberger always has one ready.

JOE FROGGER'S COOKIES

Long ago, for a jug of rum, an old Marblehead gent would bake and barter a batch of cookies that were plump as the bullfrogs and wide as the lily pads in a pond beside his cottage. His recipe is almost identical to Grandmother Bomberger's, except: instead of a cup of sour cream he used ¹/₄ cup rum and about ¹/₂ cup water. He used no eggs and he added 1 teaspoon cloves, 1 teaspoon nutmeg, and ¹/₂ teaspoon allspice. He cut them with a large tomato can. Ruby's grandchildren, Christine, Peter, and Katie Cuff, call them Water Lily Pads and can never get enough.

CHRISTMAS COOKIES

One year before Christmas I was carried away by so many good cookie recipes that I must have made a thousand. I thought I'd be eating Christmas cookies till Easter – because not many people venture to come to my cottage in winter through the winding, snow-blocked lane.

One morning I woke up inspired: I made out a list of people who had invited me to parties or whom I just wanted to have, I dashed into town, bought cards that looked like our snowy woods and wrote, "Put on your boots and come to Sunfish for cookies and coffee any time from nine in the morning till midnight on Boxing Day or New Year's Day." After I mailed them I counted and found out I'd invited over 200 people! To my little cottage in the country where any day I might be snowed in!

What if they all came at the same time? How would they navigate our single track lane with swamp and a stream on the sides? Backing up half of a third of a mile to let another car pass could mean disaster.

And where would they park their cars? In summer there is room for ten against the rail fence if people are careful. But space for 200? There couldn't be. I kept looking at the flat, frozen, snow-covered lake, thinking what a great parking space that would be – but of course there is no way to drive down to it.

Every day for the rest of the week it kept snowing and blowing. I couldn't get in touch with Noah Sauder, the Old Order Mennonite farmer with no telephone who that year was blowing our snow. Maybe the lane would be blocked and no one could get here. But what if they tried? And got stuck in a drift? My mother worried, my sister worried, and I worried – I really worried.

Christmas came, Boxing Day came, Noah came early and blew out the snow. Twenty-eight people arrived in the afternoon, ate cookies and cheese, drank coffee and wine. On New Year's Day the first guests came right after lunch; all afternoon they kept coming and going with such regularity that one would have thought they were scheduled. Over one hundred people drove through the lane, parked their cars, ate cookies and seemed to enjoy themselves. Only one car got stuck, just when a group was leaving and could give it a shove.

Several enthusiasts suggested that I should have a cookie party every year. "Make it a traditional thing," they said. "It's such fun to come out to this beautiful spot in the country." I agreed. I'd like nothing better than to repeat the performance.

Ten years have passed and I haven't repeated it yet–I remember those awful preliminaries.

But every February when I'm still eating leftover Christmas cookies I think I might try another cookie party next New Year's Day.

LEP COOKIES

I'm repeating the recipe for Lep Cookies that I gave in *Food That Really Schmecks* for two reasons:

First: Because I've found an easier way to make them. I don't know what my mother's grandmother would have thought about the short cut but it certainly suits me, and I think Mother might have welcomed it, too.

Second: One day before Christmas my niece Mary Lou called me from Toronto. She told me she wanted to make Lep Cookies, which are a tradition in our family. "Do you *bake* them, Auntie Ed?" she asked me. "Of course," I told her. "But in *Schmecks* you didn't *say* so."

Mother's grandmother's recipe makes eight cookie jars full; this is only one quarter of that amount.

2 eggs
1 cup brown sugar
1 pint molasses
1 teaspoon ground cloves
1 teaspoon cinnamon
$^1/_2$ teaspoon nutmeg
1 teaspoon aniseed
1 cup sour cream
$^1/_2$ pound almonds, blanched and sliced or sunflower seeds

1 teaspoon soda
1 cup chopped citron peel
1 cup chopped mixed peel
7 cups flour

Topping:
Egg white with a bit of water
Whole or split almonds

Stir everything together but the flour. Heat the mixture to lukewarm in a heavy pot or the top of a double boiler, stirring continuously. When warm – not hot – stir in the flour. Put the mixture into a cool place for a day or two. The dough will then be stiff enough to roll. Divide into four pieces and roll each piece. Wrap the rolls in waxed paper and put them back in the cold till they are stiff. When you are ready to bake them, slice the rolls into cookies about ¼ inch thick. Brush the tops with egg white beaten with a bit of water, press an almond into the centre of each cookie and place them on buttered cookie sheets. Bake at 350°F for about 10 minutes.

The Leps will be crisp at first, later they become chewy. They'll keep fresh-tasting long after all the other Christmas cookies have become stale. And they freeze well.

SPRINGERLE

Another Christmas tradition in our family was the making of springerle (pronounce the *e* on the end). We didn't have the boards that are needed to press down on the dough to emboss the cookies in pretty pictures of birds, animals and flowers; they always had to be borrowed from the Berner family whose grandparents had brought them from Germany when they emigrated to Kitchener – then called Berlin – long, long ago.

Springerle making was an exacting procedure: Mother made the dough, Daddy rolled it out and pressed the wooden forms on it, Mother examined the result to make sure the pictures were clear, then cut the cookies apart.

I haven't seen a springerle board since I was a child. Now you can buy springerle rolling pins in specialty shops. They work quite well but I miss a certain little rabbit and the fat dove with the olive twig that was on those old German boards.

4 eggs	**1 teaspoon baking powder**
2 cups granulated sugar	**2 to 3 tablespoons aniseed**
3¹/₂ to 4 cups sifted all-	
purpose flour	

Beat the eggs until light; add the sugar gradually and beat until creamy. Beat in the flour and baking powder sifted together

¹/₂ cup at a time until the dough is of a consistency to roll. On a well-floured surface roll the dough to ¹/₃ inch thickness. Flour the springerle boards or rolling pin and press hard over the dough to leave clear-cut designs. If the dough is too soft, knead in more flour. If you get a good imprint, cut the cookies apart with a knife. Sprinkle buttered cookie sheets with aniseed and arrange the cookies on the sheets. Let them stand uncovered overnight in a dry place at room temperature. Preheat the oven to 300°F and bake the springerle for 15 minutes or until thoroughly dried. They should not be browned, they are virginal – or do I think so because they belonged to my childhood?

CHOCOLATE CHIP MERINGUES

Whenever you have a couple of egg whites left over you can whip up a batch of these in a few minutes. But guard them, they'll be eaten just as quickly.

2 egg whites at room
 temperature
¹/₂ cup white sugar
¹/₈ teaspoon cream of tartar

1 teaspoon vanilla
1 cup chocolate chips, more
 or less

Whip up the egg whites with the sugar, cream of tartar, and vanilla until stiff but not dry. Stir in the chocolate chips and drop by spoonfuls on a foil-covered cookie sheet. Bake at 200°F for 1 hour until dry but not brown.

DATE AND NUT MERINGUES

Instead of chocolate chips fold into the meringue (above) ¹/₂ cup chopped dates and ¹/₂ cup chopped nuts.

LORNA'S MELTING MOMENTS

They don't need chewing, these don't.

1 cup butter
¹/₂ cup icing sugar
2 cups sifted flour

Pinch soda
Cherries or pecans for
 topping

Cream the butter, add the sugar gradually, beating to a cream. Add the flour with the soda and mix with an electric beater, for fifteen minutes. Spoon onto unbuttered cookie sheets and top each one with a small piece of red or green cherry or a piece of pecan. Don't crowd them, they spread. Bake at 350°F for about 8 minutes. Handle them delicately.

SALOME'S MONSTER COOKIES
drops

Salome enclosed this recipe with her Christmas card. She wrote: "Knowing you like to eat and try recipes that are different, here is one that is flying through our Old Order Mennonite community at a great rate. People make half batches and still have cookies all over the place. Mix them in a very large dishpan and you'll have anywhere from 300 to 600 cookies, depending on the size. Best of all they taste delicious."

1 pound margarine
2 pounds brown sugar
4 cups white sugar
1 dozen eggs
3 pounds peanut butter
8 teaspoons soda

18 cups oatmeal
1 pound chocolate chips
$^1/_2$ cup vanilla
2 cups peanuts or other nuts
1 pound smarties

Combine the margarine, sugar, eggs, and peanut butter, then add the remaining ingredients except the smarties which are more colourful if put on top of each cookie. Drop by teaspoons on buttered cookie sheets and bake at 350°F for 10 minutes.

Salome wrote, "Vera, my son's wife, and we made half a batch together and still have lots. You should try them sometime when you want a lot of cookies."

MARY LIZ HEARN'S ALMOND SHORTBREAD

These are super: more tasty than ordinary shortbread because of the nuts – and more expensive. Try them with sunflower seeds.

1 cup butter	8 ounces of finely chopped
3 tablespoons white sugar	almonds
2 cups flour	Fine sugar for rolling

Blend the sugar with the butter, add the flour and almonds and work to a smooth dough with your fingers. Break off bits and roll them into small log-shaped cookies. Place them on a buttered sheet and bake at 350°F for about 20 minutes. Don't let them brown. Cool slightly and roll in fine sugar then put them in your safest hiding place.

When I was an eager young housewife I used to make fancy cookies that I thought were a work of art: each one was individually decorated and looked too pretty to eat, people said – though they probably didn't taste as good as they looked. Now I make the best tasting cookies I can with the least effort and little or no decoration but a sprinkling of sugar or nuts, a nut pressed into the centre or an icing that I can dribble over very quickly.

There are times though, like receptions, or weddings, Christmas, or parties, when a plate of cookies needs more than just bulk and schmecks appeal. My friend Lorna has given me some of her fancy recipes: she loves to make pretty fussy little morsels to dress up a plate – and they taste good, too.

NOËL REFRIGERATOR COOKIES

These are neat, easy to make, and don't need decorating to look festive.

1/2 cup butter	2 cups all-purpose flour
1/2 cup shortening	1 teaspoon baking powder
1/2 cup brown sugar	1/2 teaspoon soda
1/2 cup white sugar	1/2 teaspoon salt
1/2 teaspoon lemon extract or	1 1/2 cups vari-coloured peel,
juice	chopped fine
1/2 teaspoon vanilla	
1 teaspoon almond extract	
2 eggs	

Cream the butter, shortening, sugar, and flavourings until fluffy. Add the eggs and beat them in. Sift in the flour, baking powder, soda, and salt, and work them and the peel into the creamed mixture till the dough is smooth. Chill for an hour or so then shape into rolls and chill again till firm. Cut in ¹/₂-inch slices. Place slices on a lightly buttered cookie sheet. Bake at 375°F for 7 or 8 minutes. Don't let them become brown; they should be pale with all those lovely coloured bits of peel showing through.

LORNA'S FILBERT FANCIES

¹/₂ pound filberts, put through   **1 cup fruit sugar**
the grinder   **1 teaspoon vanilla**
Whites of 2 eggs, not beaten

Mix all together and mould into whatever shape you think most attractive – bars, circles, crescents – keep fiddling, then bake at 350°F until golden brown.

MACAROON DAINTIES

Lorna says these are a Christmas special – very rich. To serve they should be placed in those little paper bonbon cups.

1 cup brown sugar   **¹/₂ cup chopped mixed peel**
¹/₈ teaspoon salt   **¹/₂ cup sliced dried apricots**
¹/₄ cup butter   **¹/₂ cup candied cherries**
2 tablespoons cold water   **1 cup blanched almonds**
1 teaspoon vanilla   **2 cups shredded coconut**
1 cup chopped candied red   **¹/₂ cup chopped dates**
**   and green pineapple**   **2 stiffly beaten egg whites**

Boil the sugar, salt, butter, and water to soft ball stage (235°F), approximately 5 minutes. Add the remaining ingredients, folding in the beaten egg whites at the last. Drop small teaspoonfuls on a buttered pan and bake at 275°F for about 20 minutes. Ration these or some greedy person will gobble them.

RUM BALLS
not baked

Everyone pops one of these into the mouth at the first passing.

1¼ cups crushed vanilla
  wafers
1 cup icing sugar
1½ cups chopped pecans

2 tablespoons cocoa
2 tablespoons corn syrup
¼ cup rum
½ cup granulated sugar

Combine the finely crushed crumbs, icing sugar, pecans, and cocoa. Add the corn syrup and rum and mix well. Shape into 1-inch balls, roll in the granulated sugar and store in a tightly covered box with a lock on it.

FLORENTINES

I bought my first Florentine at a patisserie in Paris; I thought it the most sublime chocolate-orange confection that I had ever eaten. I had another in Venice. Wherever I went on that first trip to Europe I looked for and found more: in Lugano, Berne, Innsbruck, Munich, Heidelberg and Cologne; I've since found some in Toronto, at the Kitchener market and Rundles Restaurant in Stratford. Undoubtedly they are a universal favourite. This recipe should make about thirty. Imagine having that many! I've never before had more than one at a time. Very expensive to buy.

¾ cup of the heaviest
  whipping cream you can
  get
¼ cup sugar
¼ cup all-purpose flour
½ cup blanched slivered
  almonds
¼ cup dessicated coconut
  (optional)

½ cup finely diced preserved
  orange peel
¼ cup sliced candied
  cherries (optional)
6 ounces semi-sweet
  chocolate

Thoroughly blend the cream and sugar; stir in the flour, almonds, coconut, and fruit. Drop dessertspoonfuls of the mixture well apart on a heavily greased and floured baking sheet.

Flatten them to make them round and about 3 inches wide – they'll spread. Bake in a 350°F oven for about 10 minutes; they burn easily so keep watching and take them out when they are golden and lightly brown around the lacey edges. Leave them on the baking sheet for a few minutes to become firm but remove them before they are cold.

Melt the chocolate over hot water. Turn the cookies upside down and spread the underside with chocolate. Dry on waxed paper, bottoms up. Allow to dry overnight at room temperature, if you can wait that long – I certainly couldn't.

SQUARES

Faster to make than cookies because you don't have any rolling or dropping from a spoon, squares are usually richer and gooier, can often be cut large enough for a dessert. They are a great invention and Eva has told me they are becoming even more popular than pies in her Mennonite community.

JEAN SALTER'S CRUNCHY OAT SQUARES

Crisp, great flavour, and not too sweet.

²/₃ cup brown sugar, packed	3 tablespoons corn syrup
¹/₂ cup butter	1 tablespoon lemon juice
¹/₂ cup margarine	2¹/₃ cups rolled oats
¹/₄ teaspoon salt	2¹/₃ cups wheat flakes

Put sugar, butter, margarine, salt, and syrup into a pan and heat until dissolved. Add lemon juice. Cool slightly and stir in the rolled oats and wheat flakes. (You could use all oats if you haven't wheat flakes.) Pack the mixture on a greased cookie sheet or roasting pan and bake in a 350°F oven for about 20 to 30 minutes. Watch them. When golden, leave to cool then chill before cutting into squares or bars.

You may have a small dishful of crumbs after you've cut them; they make a good topping for ice cream or yogurt.

RICH AND GOOEY NUT SQUARES

Lucky the girl who takes these to a box social; they attract young men like flies.

¹/₃ **cup butter**	**1 teaspoon baking powder**
¹/₂ **cup brown sugar**	¹/₄ **cup finely chopped nuts**
1¹/₃ **cups sifted flour**	

Cream the butter and brown sugar, add the flour and baking powder, sifted together, then stir in the chopped nuts. Pat firmly into a 13″ x 9″ pan and bake at 350°F for 7 minutes only. No longer. Remove from the oven.

Meanwhile you could be stirring up:

2 eggs	**1 teaspoon vanilla**
³/₄ **cup corn syrup**	**3 tablespoons flour**
¹/₄ **cup brown sugar**	³/₄ **cup coarsely chopped nuts**
¹/₂ **teaspoon salt**	

Beat the eggs until foamy, add the corn syrup, sugar, salt, vanilla, and flour. Mix well and pour over the baked part. Sprinkle the chopped nuts on top and bake at 350°F for about 15 minutes. Do not overbake. Cut in squares while warm.

CHOCOLATE CRISPIE CRACKLES
unbaked

You can make these in 5 minutes, and rationalize as you eat half a dozen that they are just breakfast cereal.

¹/₄ **cup cocoa**	¹/₄ **cup white or brown sugar**
3 tablespoons butter	**3 cups Rice Crispies**
¹/₄ **cup corn syrup**	¹/₂ **cup nuts (optional)**

Combine the cocoa, butter, corn syrup, and sugar in a saucepan; cook over low heat, stirring until the mixture comes to a boil. No longer. Remove from the heat, add the crispies and nuts and stir until they are coated. Pour into a buttered 9″ x 9″ pan and pat down. Cut into squares or drop spoonfuls on waxed paper till they're set. The latter is risky, someone might snitch.

GRANOLA BARS

Kae Hobson loves these – and so do her grandchildren.

2 cups dessicated coconut, or less
1½ cups rolled oats
1½ cups raisins
2 cups sunflower seeds
½ cup sesame seeds
¾ cup peanuts or soy nuts

½ cup dried fruit – apricots, prunes, apples, etc. (optional)
½ teaspoon salt
1 cup liquid honey
1 teaspoon vanilla
½ cup peanut butter, or more

Mix all the dry ingredients; thoroughly blend the honey, vanilla, and peanut butter. Grease your hands and mix the whole works really well. If you want thick bars press everything into a 9″ x 12″ pan, pressing down with a heated spoon. If you want thin crisp bars spread the mixture on well-buttered cookie sheets and press down. Bake at 275°F till golden. Cool the pans on a rack and cut with a hot knife. I defy you to stop at eating one bar.

SHOO-FLY SQUARES

When the ladies of the big Anglican church in Galt-Cambridge had a money-raising luncheon, the recipes they used came from *Food That Really Schmecks*: to make the use of dessert plates and forks unnecessary, they baked the Shoo-fly Pie with a wet bottom in large sheets that could be cut in squares and eaten from one's fingers.

Pastry for a 9-inch cake pan
Bottom part:
¾ cup boiling water
½ teaspoon soda
1 cup molasses

Top part:
1½ cups sifted flour
1 cup brown sugar
¾ cup shortening
¼ teaspoon salt

Pour boiling water over soda in a bowl and stir in the molasses. Pour into the pastry-lined cake pan. Mix ingredients for top part and sprinkle over the molasses mixture. Bake in a 350°F oven for 30 to 40 minutes. Let cool and cut in squares.

PECAN FINGERS

Hannah told me all the ladies at her quilting for Magdalene wanted this recipe.

1 cup dark brown sugar
1 cup soft butter
1 egg
1 teaspoon vanilla
2 cups all-purpose
  flour

Topping:
1 egg, beaten
$^1/_2$ cup dark brown sugar
1 cup coarsely chopped
  pecans
$^1/_2$ cup dark brown sugar

Cream 1 cup brown sugar and butter until fluffy. Add 1 egg and vanilla and blend well. Stir the flour into the creamed mixture, working until well blended. Spread in a buttered cake pan. Brush with 1 beaten egg. Sprinkle $^1/_2$ cup brown sugar over it, then sprinkle the nuts over that, then the other $^1/_2$ cup of brown sugar – as evenly as you can. Don't let any part be uncovered. Bake in a 350°F oven for 20 to 25 minutes, until nicely golden. Cool in the pan then cut in fingers to serve. Hannah says dark brown sugar gives the best flavour but any brown sugar will do. Good luck.

CHOCOLATE ORANGE BARS

This is a great combination.

$^1/_3$ cup soft butter
$^1/_2$ cup brown sugar
2 egg yolks
1 tablespoon grated orange
  rind
1$^1/_4$ cup sifted all-purpose
  flour
1 teaspoon baking powder

$^1/_4$ teaspoon salt
$^1/_3$ cup orange juice

Topping:
$^1/_2$ cup chocolate chips
$^1/_4$ cup chopped walnuts
2 egg whites
$^3/_4$ cup brown sugar

Beat the butter, $^1/_2$ cup brown sugar, and egg yolks together until fluffy. Stir in the orange rind. Sift the flour, baking powder, and salt together and add to the first mixture alternately with the orange juice. Turn the batter into buttered pan and spread evenly. Sprinkle with chocolate chips and walnuts. Beat the egg whites until fluffy, add ³/₄ cup brown sugar gradually and keep beating until stiff and glossy. Spread over the other layers in the pan. Bake about 35 minutes in a 325°F oven, or until the meringue is golden and dry to the touch. Cool in the pan and cut in squares or bars. Then eat it; don't let it sit around till the meringue looks stale.

CRANBERRY CHEWS
makes 4 dozen

On her file card with this recipe Lorna has written, "delicious."

1¹/₂ **cups sifted flour**   ¹/₄ **teaspoon salt**
2 **tablespoons sugar**   ¹/₂ **cup butter**

Combine until the mixture is crumbly, then press evenly into a large pyrex pan and bake at 350°F for 10 minutes.

1¹/₂ **to 2 cups cranberry sauce**

Spread evenly over the baked layer.

2 **eggs**   ³/₄ **cup coconut**
1¹/₂ **cups firmly packed**   ¹/₂ **cup coarsely chopped**
    brown sugar   **pecans or filberts**
2 **tablespoons flour**   1 **cup wheat flakes**
1 **teaspoon vanilla**

Beat the eggs with the brown sugar, flour, and vanilla until fluffy. Stir in the coconut and nuts. Spread over the cranberry layer; sprinkle with the wheat flakes. Bake 30 minutes at 350°F, or until the topping is firm. Cool in the pan and cut into bars. These would make any party plate look festive.

OATMEAL CHOCOLATE SQUARES

Sheila Hutton says this is an easy one to make for a party.

1 **cup butter or margarine**   3 **cups rolled oats**
¹/₄ **cup white sugar**   6 **ounces chocolate chips**
²/₃ **cup brown sugar**   . ³/₄ **cup peanut butter**

Melt the butter, add the white and brown sugars, then the rolled oats; press into a large ungreased pan. Bake for 15 minutes at 350°F, and cool in the pan. Melt the chocolate chips and peanut butter together, spread on top of the baked mixture and refrigerate until firm. Cut in squares.

JEAN SALTER'S RAISIN MUMBLES

With a name like that how could they be anything but great?

Filling:
2¹/₂ cups raisins
¹/₂ cup sugar

2 cups water
1 tablespoon lemon juice
2 tablespoons corn starch

Cook all but the corn starch over slow heat for about ¹/₂ an hour then thicken with the corn starch dissolved in very little water.

Top and bottom:
³/₄ cup soft butter
1 cup dark brown sugar
1³/₄ cups flour

¹/₂ teaspoon salt
¹/₂ teaspoon soda
1¹/₂ cups rolled oats

Mix together and divide into two. Press half into a buttered baking tin, pour on the raisin filling then top with the remainder. Bake in a 400°F oven for 20 to 30 minutes. Cool and cut in squares.

BONNIE BENNETT'S SQUARES

Bonnie (age thirteen) lives at the top of the hill on our road and often she brings me her favourite creations.

1 cup butter
1 cup brown sugar
1 teaspoon vanilla
2 cups sifted all-purpose
  flour

1 cup chocolate chips
1 cup walnuts

Mix all the ingredients and press them into a 9" x 9" unbuttered pan. Bake in a 350°F oven for about 25 minutes till they are golden. While they are still warm cut into squares or bars and take some to share with your neighbour.

DATE AND ORANGE SQUARES

These taste even better than old-fashioned date squares and are easier and quicker to make if you have a blender or food processor.

Filling:
1¹/₂ cups pitted dates
³/₄ cup sugar
Grated rind of an orange

1¹/₂ cups boiling water or half orange juice
¹/₂ to 1 cup chopped pecans (optional)

Put the dates, sugar, orange rind, and boiling water into the blender or processor and whirl until it is like soft jam. Stir in the chopped pecans. (If you don't have a blender all is not lost: you must chop the dates, grate the orange rind, and gently cook them with the sugar and water to a jam-like consistency before adding the nuts.)

Top and bottom:
1 cup butter
1¹/₄ cup brown sugar
1¹/₂ cups flour

1 teaspoon baking powder
¹/₂ teaspoon salt
1¹/₂ cups rolled oats

Cream the butter and brown sugar together; add the flour, baking powder, and salt, sifted together, then the oats; mix until crumbly. Pat half the mixture into the bottom of a buttered, 9-inch square pan, spread the date filling over it, then cover with the remaining oats mixture. Bake in a 325°F oven for 45 minutes, but watch it. Serve warm or cold. With or without whipped or ice cream it is a fabulous dessert.

BLONDE BROWNIES

Caroline Haehnel makes these using sunflower seeds instead of nuts – less expensive and no bother chopping. They taste as good or better, she says.

¹/₃ cup liquid shortening
1¹/₂ cups brown sugar
2 eggs, beaten
1 teaspoon vanilla
1 cup flour

1 teaspoon baking powder
¹/₂ teaspoon salt
1 cup toasted sunflower seeds or nuts
¹/₂ cup chocolate chips

Blend the shortening, sugar, beaten eggs, and vanilla. Sift the flour, baking powder, and salt into the shortening mixture and blend well. Stir in the nuts and chips or sprinkle the chocolate bits on top after you have spread the batter in a buttered 9-inch square pan. Bake at 350°F for about 30 minutes, or until the top springs back when touched lightly. Cool and cut into bars. These may be iced if you want to guild the lily.

CHEERY CHERRY BARS

A great thing to do with the cherries you froze last summer – or fresh ones. Romance blossoms when these appear at an Old Order Mennonite Singing.

Mix and pat into a buttered 9″ x 9″ cake pan:

1 cup flour   **¹/₂ cup butter**
¹/₄ cup white or brown sugar

Bake for 10 minutes at 350°F while you mix together:

1 cup brown sugar   **¹/₄ cup flour**
¹/₄ teaspoon salt   **2 eggs, slightly beaten**
¹/₂ teaspoon baking powder

Fold in:

¹/₃ cup coconut   **¹/₂ cup walnuts**
1 cup cherries, or more

Spread the mixture over the half-baked dough in the pan and bake at 325°F for about half an hour, till golden. If you want to be fancy you may ice them by blending:

1 cup brown sugar   **¹/₄ cup table cream**
1 tablespoon milk or cherry
  juice

Boil 2 minutes, let cool and add enough icing sugar to thicken.

These will be a hit when you serve them. Don't try to keep them; they should be eaten fresh.

PLATZ

When Rudy Wiebe came to the Provident Bookstore in Kitchener to autograph his latest novel, they served coffee and Platz, a Russian Mennonite fruit coffee cake. It was so popular that I asked Gloria Dirks for her recipe.

1½ **cups flour**
1 **tablespoon baking powder**
1 **teaspoon sugar**
½ **teaspoon salt**
½ **cup butter or margarine**
½ **cup table cream or whole milk**

Topping:
Fruit, in sections: plums, or apples, apricots, or peaches
1 **cup sugar**
½ **cup flour**
3 **tablespoons butter**

Sift together the 1½ cups flour, baking powder, 1 teaspoon sugar, and salt. Cut in the butter as you would for pastry; blend in the cream. Pat out the dough into the greased 9″ x 13″ pan. Place fruit sections side by side on the dough and sprinkle with the crumbs made by blending together the topping sugar, flour and butter. Bake at 350°F till golden. Cut in squares. (At the bookstore the Platz had a single piece of fruit placed neatly in the centre of each square.)

13

Cake is a Miracle Thing

My first encounter with cake came when I was barely tall enough to reach the hanging corner of the tablecloth on our big square kitchen table. Mother had run across the street to borrow an egg from Mrs. Hessenhauer and I was left playing alone on the kitchen floor. With the bright blue enamel mixing bowl on the edge of the table where Mother had been stirring up a cake. It didn't take me long to give the tablecloth a tug that brought the bowl down on my lap. Mother found me blissfully licking the creamy batter that slathered me from head to toes. I've liked licking cake batter ever since.

Whenever people told Mother she was a fabulous cook – and everyone who ate at our house said that – Mother would say with a show of modesty that she hadn't baked a cake till after she was married. We never knew whether that meant she was proud of not having been taught by her grandmother who brought her up to be a lady, or whether her pride was in having taught herself how to successfully follow a recipe.

Mother didn't teach us how to bake either. When she stirred up a cake she gave us jobs to do that kept us out of her way in the kitchen. "Norma and Ruby, you can straighten up the living room; Edna, you can dust the stairway," and I'd be banished to those shapely cherry-wood spindles – three on each step – up that long curving staircase from the hall to the high ceiling and along the balustrade on the second floor, the farthest place in the house from the good kitchen smells. Maybe that's why I still avoid dusting and enjoy baking.

There's something magical about putting things together that are inedible by themselves: like flour, baking powder, soda, cocoa, cinnamon, sour milk, or whatever, and blending them to make something completely different and delectable like a CAKE. A layer cake, a square or a round one, a big oblong cake, a rich fruity loaf cake to be cut in thin slices, a cake to be served with coffee or tea, with fruit or ice cream, as a dessert by itself, slathered with icing or a glaze, a cake is a creative accomplishment that can be enjoyed from the batter to the last crumb.

People have said to me, "I never make cakes, they're too chancey." Of course they are, part of the adventure and fun is the uncertainty. One day I'll make a cake that is moist, tender, and delicious; next time it might be coarse and soggy, or high, dry, and tasteless as a sponge. I don't know why. Maybe I forgot something vital or baked it too long, maybe I didn't follow the recipe exactly, maybe the recipe was faulty, maybe I substituted an ingredient that didn't work, maybe all the ingredients weren't at room temperature when I started, maybe my oven temperature was wrong. Once I forgot to put in the flour and soda. If I were a food chemist I'd probably have all the answers; all I know about baking I've found out by trial and error after error after error. But I keep on baking cakes, dry, soggy, or perfect.

A multitude of errors can be smothered by a sticky or fluffy icing; sprinkled with toasted nuts, who cares what's underneath? If you reheat a cake and serve it with a custard or a fudge sauce who's to know you hadn't intended it to be a pudding in the first place? Or a sherry-laden trifle? And like cake batter, icing is good licking, too.

DATE OATMEAL CAKE
8" x 8"

This cake from *Food That Really Schmecks* was the Grand Prize Winner of the 10th Anniversary Competition of *Homemaker's Magazine*. People sent in the recipe they liked best of all those published in the magazine in ten years. This was the favourite. Surely 1,232,000 homemakers couldn't be wrong.

Pour **1 cup boiling water** over **2 cups rolled oats**, mix well, cool slightly, then blend in:

³/₄ cup butter or margarine
2 cups brown sugar
2 eggs
1¹/₂ cups finely chopped dates

1 cup coarsely chopped
  walnuts

Sift together:
¹/₂ cup flour
1 teaspoon soda
¹/₂ teaspoon salt

1 teaspoon cinnamon
1 teaspoon cloves

Pour the oatmeal mixture into the dry ingredients and mix well. Bake in an 8-inch square greased pan at 350°F for 45 minutes, or until done. It is so moist and rich it hardly needs icing – but, if you insist, use one made with brown sugar.

CHOCOLATE CHIP DATE CAKE
8- or 9-inch square

Whenever Norm serves this cake I hear someone say, "Gee, this is good cake."

1¹/₂ cups boiling water
1 cup chopped dates
1 teaspoon soda
¹/₂ cup shortening
1 cup sugar
2 eggs, beaten
1 teaspoon vanilla
1¹/₂ cups flour

¹/₂ teaspoon salt

Topping:
¹/₂ cup brown sugar
¹/₄ cup walnuts
1 cup (6 oz.) chocolate
  chips

Pour boiling water over the dates, add soda and let cool. Cream the shortening and sugar, add the beaten eggs, vanilla and the cooled dates. Sift the dry ingredients together and stir into the date mixture. Beat well and pour into an 8- or 9-inch greased square pan. Combine the brown sugar, chocolate chips, and walnuts; sprinkle them over the batter. Bake at 350°F for 45 to 50 minutes. The topping will be crisp, the cake light as a feather.

JEAN SALTER'S RICH SEED CAKE
6-inch loaf pan

Jean got this recipe from her English grandmother. Because it was simple and easy she baked it in the trim little galley of the vessel that she and her husband Don sailed from England to Barbados. It has a fine, firm texture the colour of daffodils.

2 cups flour	³/₄ cup butter or margarine
¹/₂ teaspoon salt	³/₄ cup sugar
¹/₂ teaspoon baking powder	2 or 3 eggs
2 teaspoons caraway seeds	A little milk

Sift the dry ingredients and add the seeds. Cream the shortening and sugar and beat in the eggs gradually. Add the dry ingredients, and if necessary, enough milk to give a dropping consistency. If you like you could add a teaspoon of vanilla or a tablespoon of brandy. Put the rather thick batter in a 6-inch loaf pan and bake at 350°F for about an hour. Cut it in thin slices and serve it with tea. It doesn't need icing.

CARROT CRUMB CAKE
(from a Croatian lady in Saskatchewan)
9" x 9"

People keep thanking me for the wonderful carrot cake recipe in *Food That Really Schmecks*; they say there couldn't be a better one. I agree. But this carrot cake with the crumb topping is moist, light, delicious, and easier to prepare, especially if you have a blender.

After picking dandelion blossoms in my lawn to make wine, Pamela and Gerry Noonan and I ate the whole slightly warm cake at a sitting. No regrets.

¹/₂ cup soft margarine
1 cup sugar
1 egg
1¹/₂ teaspoons vanilla
1 cup sour milk or buttermilk
1 to 1¹/₂ cups raw grated carrots
2 cups pastry flour

2 teaspoons baking powder
¹/₂ teaspoon soda
¹/₄ teaspoon nutmeg
1 teaspoon salt
Topping:
¹/₂ cup brown sugar
4 tablespoons flour
3 tablespoons melted butter

If you have a blender: put the margarine, sugar, egg, vanilla, buttermilk, and raw carrots cut in slices, into the blender and keep whirling till the carrots are finely chopped. Pour the mixture over the flour, baking powder, soda, nutmeg, and salt sifted together. Stir till blended, then pour into a 9″ x 9″ cake pan. Sprinkle with the crumbled topping mixture and bake at 350°F for 45 minutes.

If you don't have a blender you'll have to grate the carrots first. Cream the margarine and sugar, beat in the egg and vanilla, stir in the carrots and alternately add the buttermilk and sifted dry ingredients.

SCHOKOLADEN SCHICHTKUCHEN
2 layers

A Grade 7 boy made this fudge layer cake for the Kinderkochfest. I made it for Patti's 14th birthday dinner and everyone ate two big pieces.

2 cups flour
1 teaspoon soda
1 teaspoon salt
¹/₂ cup cocoa
2 cups brown sugar, packed

¹/₂ cup shortening, butter, or margarine
1 cup buttermilk or sour milk
1 teaspoon vanilla
3 unbeaten eggs

Sift the flour, soda, salt, and cocoa into a mixing bowl; add the sugar, shortening, buttermilk, and vanilla and beat for 2 minutes. Add the eggs one at a time and beat another 2 minutes. Pour the batter into 2 layer pans and bake for 30 minutes in a 350°F oven. (If you want a big oblong cake, 13 ″ x 9 ″, bake for 40 to 45 minutes.) Invert layers on a rack to cool.

I used Lorna's Super Chocolate Chip Icing (**page 249**) to cover both layers, lit the candles on top and we sang, "Happy birthday, dear Patti."

APPLE SAUCE FRUIT CAKE
13 ″ x 8 ″ or thereabout

Mary Garwood is a decorator but she knows how to make the lightest fruity cake that any of her winter friends in Arizona ever tasted.

2 cups sifted flour	1 1/2 cups granulated sugar
1 teaspoon soda	2 eggs
1/2 teaspoon salt	3/4 cup snipped pitted dates
1/2 teaspoon cinnamon	3/4 cup chopped walnuts
1/2 teaspoon ground cloves	3/4 cup seedless raisins
1/2 teaspoon nutmeg	1 1/2 cups applesauce
1/2 teaspoon allspice	
2 tablespoons cocoa	
1/2 cup soft shortening	

Sift together the flour, soda, salt, spices, and cocoa. In another bowl blend the shortening and sugar, beating in the eggs one at a time till fluffy; stir the cut-up dates, walnuts, and raisins into the flour mixture and blend into the egg mixture alternately with the applesauce until the batter is smooth. Pour into a greased pan about 13 ″ x 8 ″ and bake at 350°F for 55 to 60 minutes. Let cool and ice with a mocha icing.

DRIED APPLE SCHNITZ

Every autumn Eva spends days peeling, coring, and schnitzing apples: she spreads the apple segments on pans in the oven and on top of her big black wood-stove; and when they are thoroughly dry and crisp she stores them in sacks in an upstairs room where they'll keep for months, becoming spongey and chewy.

"And how do you use them?" I asked her.

"We used to cook them with prunes – schnitz and gwetcha – and have them on the table every day for breakfast." She smiled. "Now I pack them in plastic bags and sell them at the Waterloo market to the university students. They're crazy for them as snacks." Eva brought me her handwritten cookbook. "Lovina sometimes makes dried schnitz into a really good cake." I copied the recipe.

SCHNITZ or FARMERS' FRUIT CAKE
9" x 13"

I could hardly wait to try it – with some of Eva's dried schnitz. The cake was divine – big, rich, moist and with that elusive old-fashioned flavour.

2 cups dried apple schnitz	4 cups flour
2 cups molasses	1 teaspoon cinnamon
1 cup butter or lard	1 teaspoon allspice
2 cups brown sugar	$1/2$ teaspoon nutmeg
2 eggs, well beaten	2 teaspoons soda
1 cup buttermilk or sour milk	

Soak the apples overnight in water. In the morning drain them and put them through a food chopper (or processor). Simmer the apples in the molasses with the butter for an hour. "If you don't put the butter in, the apples will form into a hard taffy ball," Eva told me. When the apples have cooled add the brown sugar, well-beaten eggs, buttermilk, flour, spices, and soda. Pour into a 9" x 13"pan and bake at 350°F for an hour. Test it with a toothpick. The top is crusty and chewy and doesn't need icing which might detract from the fantastic flavour.

ZUCCHINI CAKE
13" x 9" or thereabout

Norm said this was the best-tasting cake she'd ever eaten at my house: moist and heavy, in the East European tradition, it would probably keep well but never lasts long enough to be tested.

1 cup white sugar
1 cup brown sugar
2¹/₂ cups flour
2 teaspoons soda
1 teaspoon baking powder
1 tablespoon cinnamon
1 teaspoon ginger
¹/₂ teaspoon cloves
1 teaspoon salt

1 cup oil
1 tablespoon vanilla
3 eggs
2 cups grated, unpeeled zucchini
1 cup raisins
1 cup chopped walnuts
2 tablespoons grated orange rind

Into a fairly large bowl measure the sugars, flour, soda, baking powder, spices, and salt, sifted together. Pour in the oil, add the vanilla and break in the eggs; beat all together till well blended. Stir in the zucchini, raisins, nuts, and orange rind. Pour into a 13" x 9" pan and bake in a 350°F oven for 45 to 50 minutes. Cool in the pan on a rack.

RAISIN SPICE CAKE
9" x 9"

An unpretentious little cake that tastes good and stays moist.

¹/₂ cup shortening
1 cup sugar
1 well beaten egg
1 cup buttermilk or sour milk
1 teaspoon vanilla
1¹/₂ cups raisins
2¹/₂ cups flour
¹/₂ teaspoon soda

1 teaspoon salt
¹/₂ teaspoon cinnamon
¹/₂ teaspoon cloves
³/₄ cup chopped nuts

Topping:
¹/₄ cup chopped nuts
¹/₄ cup sugar

Cream the shortening and sugar, add the beaten egg, the buttermilk, vanilla and raisins. Sift the flour, soda, salt and spices together, stir into the egg mixture. Blend well, but don't overdo it. Stir in the ³/₄ cup nuts. Pour the batter into a 9″ x 9″cake pan, sprinkle the ¹/₄ cup chopped nuts on top, then the ¹/₄ cup sugar, and bake in a 350°F oven for about 40 to 50 minutes. If you serve this with a scoop of maple-walnut ice cream be prepared to serve seconds and hand out the recipe.

MATTIE BEARINGER'S MAPLE SYRUP CAKE

Two layers or a big one, sweet and light, you can stir it up in a hurry.

¹/₂ **cup butter or margarine**	1 **tablespoon baking powder**
¹/₄ **cup sugar**	³/₄ **teaspoon soda**
2 **eggs**	¹/₄ **teaspoon ginger**
1 **cup maple syrup**	¹/₂ **teaspoon salt**
2¹/₄ **cups all-purpose flour**	¹/₂ **cup hot water**

Beat the butter and sugar until light and creamy; add the eggs one at a time, beating well after each one. Blend in the maple syrup gradually. Add the sifted dry ingredients alternately with the hot water: 3 additions of dry, 2 of water. Blend well, then spread batter evenly into a 13″ x 8″ pan or 2 8-inch layer pans. Bake at 350°F for 45 minutes for the large pan, 25 to 30 for the layers. Cool on a wire rack. Fill and frost with a butter icing, using maple syrup as a moistener.

NORM'S YUMMY HONEY CAKE
8″ x 8″

A tasty, tender little cake that you can stir up in no time – and eat as quickly.

1 **cup dates, finely chopped**	1 **teaspoon baking powder**
1 **cup boiling water**	¹/₂ **teaspoon salt**
¹/₄ **cup soft shortening**	³/₄ **teaspoon soda**
¹/₂ **cup honey**	*Topping:*
1 **teaspoon vanilla**	¹/₂ **cup brown sugar**
¹/₂ **cup brown sugar**	¹/₄ **cup butter**
1 **egg**	¹/₄ **cup fruit juice or milk**
1¹/₂ **cups all-purpose flour**	¹/₂ **cup shredded coconut**

Pour the boiling water over the dates and let them cool. Beat the shortening, honey, vanilla, brown sugar, and egg till well blended. Sift the dry ingredients into the creamed mixture, adding the cooled date mixture as you stir until well combined. Pour into an 8" x 8" pan and bake in a 350°F oven for about half an hour. Let the cake cool in the pan on a rack. Combine the topping ingredients and boil gently for 10 minutes. Pour and spread over the cooled cake and call your neighbours over.

CIDER CAKE
2 8-inch layers

Here's a cake that was perfect: it looked just like a picture and had great flavour as well. I was really proud of it.

¹/₂ cup margarine or butter	**¹/₄ teaspoon baking soda**
1¹/₂ cups lightly packed	**¹/₂ teaspoon nutmeg**
brown sugar	**1 teaspoon cinnamon**
2 eggs	**¹/₂ cup milk**
2 cups cake and pastry flour	**¹/₂ cup cider**
2 teaspoons baking powder	**1 cup chopped walnuts**
³/₄ teaspoon salt	

Cream the margarine and blend in the brown sugar. Beat in the eggs until the mixture is fluffy. Stir the sifted dry ingredients into the creamed mixture alternately with the milk and cider, making 3 dry and 2 liquid additions, combining lightly after each. Fold in the chopped nuts. Pour into 2 buttered 8-inch round layer cake pans lightly dusted with flour. Bake at 350°F for about 30 to 35 minutes.

Frost with a butter icing moistened with cider, using apple butter or icing as a filling between the layers.

Five days after I baked this cake my guests exclaimed how tasty and moist it was. Why did half of it last so long? Because I hid it, that's why.

Don't be discouraged if whatever you make doesn't look like the glamorous pictures in magazines or gourmet cookbooks: the photographers need to use all sorts of tricks to get their effects – whipped cream would melt under hot lights so they use shaving cream. A plump roasted chicken is usually raw or it would appear shrunken; and sometimes photographers use dye to make things look good.

HURRY UP CHOCOLATE CAKE
9" x 9"

You probably have this recipe but I want to make sure everyone else has it, too. It's always so moist, coarse and chocolate that I often wonder why I ever try any other. Your little helpers will love making it.

1¹/₂ **cups flour**	**1 teaspoon vanilla**
1 cup white sugar	**1 teaspoon vinegar**
3 rounded tablespoons cocoa	¹/₂ **cup margarine or butter**
1 teaspoon baking powder	**1 cup lukewarm buttermilk or**
1 teaspoon soda	**sour milk**
¹/₂ **teaspoon salt**	

Sift all the dry ingredients into a 9" x 9" cake pan. Stir them well to blend. Bump the pan up and down on your counter to level off. Make 3 hollows in the mixture with a spoon. Put 1 teaspoon vanilla in one hole, 1 teaspoon vinegar in another and ¹/₂ cup melted margarine or butter in the third. Over all this pour the lukewarm buttermilk. Stir and blend until it is smooth with no flour showing. Thump it on the counter again. Bake in a 350°F oven for about half an hour. Leave in the pan to cool; ice with chocolate mocha icing and try to stop tasting before you've gone too far.

NUTTY PEACH CAKE
from Mrs. Omer Horst
tube pan

Baked in a tube pan, this great, moist, flavourful cake can be cut in thin slices. But don't let that fool you, they'll all want several pieces as on one night when fifteen people came to my cottage and this cake and another disappeared completely. Success!

2 cups all-purpose flour
1 teaspoon salt
$^{1}/_{2}$ teaspoon baking powder
$^{1}/_{2}$ teaspoon soda
$^{1}/_{2}$ teaspoon cinnamon
1 cup sugar
$^{3}/_{4}$ cup vegetable oil

3 eggs
$1^{1}/_{2}$ cups mashed peaches (unpeeled)
1 teaspoon lemon juice blended with the peaches
1 cup pecans or walnuts

Sift the dry ingredients into a bowl, add the oil, eggs, and mashed peaches with the lemon juice over them. Beat until it's all thoroughly combined; the batter is lovely to taste. Stir in the nuts. Pour into a buttered and floured tube pan and bake in a 300°F oven for about 1 hour and 15 minutes, or until a toothpick comes out clean when you prick it.

Invert the cake on a rack and let it slide out of the pan to cool. Drizzle over the top of the cake a thin icing made with butter, icing sugar, and almond flavouring, moistened with milk, syrup, or honey.

I had trouble the first time I made this: when I turned it out of the pan the bottom stayed in. I manoeuvred it out but the patched result was bumpy, so I served thick slices on individual plates with whipped cream hiding the defects and there wasn't a crumb left – only praise for the flavour.

HONEY WALNUT CAKE
from Ella Sittler
2 layers

This high layer cake is a real show-off, with great flavour and texture, and tanny-gold icing.

$^{1}/_{4}$ cup butter
$1^{1}/_{2}$ cups chopped walnuts
$^{1}/_{4}$ cup honey

1 teaspoon soda
1 teaspoon salt
1 cup buttermilk

Batter:
$^{3}/_{4}$ cup butter
$1^{1}/_{4}$ cups granulated sugar
2 eggs
$2^{1}/_{2}$ cups flour

Honey Nut Frosting:
$^{1}/_{4}$ cup butter
$2^{1}/_{2}$ cups brown sugar
$^{1}/_{4}$ cup cream or whole milk
$^{1}/_{2}$ cup honey-nut mixture

Melt ¹/₄ cup butter in a cake pan in the oven; spread the walnuts over the butter and drizzle the honey over the nuts. Put the pan in a 350°F oven for 10 minutes, not longer; it will be bubbly. Take it out of the oven and let it cool while you stir up the batter.

Cream ³/₄ cups butter and 1¹/₄ cups sugar until light. Add the eggs and beat till well blended. Sift the flour, salt and soda together and blend it with the egg mixture alternately with the buttermilk.

Remove half a cup of the nut mixture from the cake pan to be used in the icing. Scrape the rest of the nut mixture into the cake batter and fold it in. Pour the batter into 2 buttered and lightly floured layer pans. (If you don't want a layer cake you could put it in the pan you used for the honey-nut mixture.) Bake in a 350°F oven for about 30 minutes for the layers (slightly longer for the deeper pan). Cool in the pans for 10 minutes then turn out on a wire rack to finish cooling.

Frost each layer with Honey Nut Frosting: put all the ingredients – including the reserved honey-nut mixture – into a pan and bring to a gentle boil for about 2 minutes. Set aside to cool, beat it till it is the right consistency to spread on the cake. You'll get your reward.

MILDRED'S ORANGE WALNUT CAKE
tube pan

Whenever a cake is baked in a tube pan I think it should be for a party; this is so easy to make that it needn't be. It has a super flavour and texture.

¹/₃ cup margarine or butter	2 cups flour
1 cup sugar	¹/₂ teaspoon soda
1 teaspoon salt	1 teaspoon baking powder
3 egg yolks	1 cup finely chopped walnuts
Rind of 1 orange, grated	3 egg whites, beaten stiff
1 cup buttermilk or sour milk	³/₄ cup orange juice

Cream the margarine and sugar till light, add the salt and egg yolks, mix well. If you have a blender put the orange peel into it with the buttermilk and whirl it till the rind is very fine; stir it into the sugar mixture. Sift the flour, soda, and baking powder together and blend into the batter. Fold in the walnuts, then the stiffly beaten egg whites. Pour into a buttered tube pan. Bake in a 350°F oven for 50 minutes or slightly longer.

While you're waiting for the crucial moment, heat in a saucepan ³/₄ cup sweetened orange juice – the real thing or whatever you use instead – and when the cake comes safely out of the oven drizzle the hot juice over it with a spoon. Let the cake stay in the pan till it cools slightly then turn it out carefully on a pretty serving plate.

Make a butter icing with icing sugar, enough orange juice to moisten it, and a teaspoon almond flavouring or Cointreau. Slather the icing on the top of the cake and let it run down the sides. It doesn't have to cover it, the cake has enough flavour without embellishment.

LAURIE BENNETT'S PUMPKIN RING
tube pan

Pumpkin cakes are often rather heavy, but Laurie's was light and delicious as the Irish Mist she served with it at a dessert party on St. Patrick's Day.

¹/₃ cup shortening	1 teaspoon soda
1¹/₃ cups sugar	³/₄ teaspoon salt
1 egg	¹/₂ teaspoon cinnamon
1 cup pumpkin, cooked and mashed	¹/₄ teaspoon ground cloves
	¹/₃ cup water
1²/₃ cups cake flour	¹/₃ cup chopped nuts
¹/₄ teaspoon baking powder	²/₃ cup raisins

Cream the shortening and sugar, beat in the egg and pumpkin. Sift together the flour, baking powder, soda, salt, and spices. Beat the flour mixture alternately with the water into the pumpkin mixture. Stir in by hand the chopped nuts and raisins. Pour into a greased and floured tube pan and bake 50 minutes. Invert and cool on a rack. Laurie iced hers with a white icing that covered the inverted bottom of the cake and ran down the sides. Very neat. Oven temp. 350°F.

NEVER FAIL SPONGE CAKE
tube pan

This is a cake for times of celebration and making money for good causes. Barbie and thirteen-year-old Patti often bake this one: it's big and light as an angel food cake but less trouble and fewer eggs. Only one drawback – it's torn apart and eaten in a few minutes.

6 egg whites, at room
   temperature
³/₄ teaspoon cream of tartar
³/₄ cup sugar
6 egg yolks
³/₄ cup sugar
1¹/₂ cups flour
1 teaspoon baking powder

¹/₂ teaspoon salt
¹/₂ cup fruit juice or water
1 tablespoon grated orange
   peel
1 teaspoon vanilla or rum
   flavouring

Add cream of tartar to the egg whites and beat at high speed until foamy; gradually add ³/₄ cup sugar, continuing to beat until stiff peaks form. To the egg yolks add ³/₄ cup sugar; sift together the flour, baking powder, and salt, add to the yolk mixture alternately with the fruit juice, orange peel, and flavouring; blend at low speed until moistened; beat 1 minute at medium speed. Pour in the egg whites and, by hand, carefully fold them in until just blended. Pour the batter into an ungreased tube pan. Bake 40 to 45 minutes in a 350°F oven. Invert and cool thoroughly before removing from the pan. Serve with fruit, whipped or ice cream. It really doesn't need any icing. Icing would weigh it down. But if you need icing for an occasion you could use Heavenly Fluff Frosting (page 246).

SPICY MARBLE CAKE
loaf or tube pan

I've spent a long time looking for a good marble cake recipe. The one in *Food That Really Schmecks* is terrible: high, dry, and tasteless. Sorry about that. At last I've found one: Joan Picard, who lives in Chesley, sent me this one, moist and tasty.

¹/₂ **cup shortening**	¹/₂ **teaspoon salt**
1 cup sugar	²/₃ **cup milk**
2 eggs	**1¹/₂ teaspoons cinnamon**
2 cups sifted all-purpose	³/₄ **teaspoon cloves**
flour	³/₄ **teaspoon nutmeg**
2 teaspoons baking powder	¹/₄ **cup molasses**

Cream together the shortening and sugar; add the eggs, one at a time, beating after each. Sift together the flour, baking powder, and salt; add them alternately with the milk to the creamed mixture. Divide the batter into two parts. To one part add the spices and molasses. Drop spoonfuls, alternating light and dark batters, into a greased loaf or tube pan. Draw a knife through the batter to get the marbled effect. Bake in a 350°F oven for about 50 to 60 minutes. Test it. Cool 10 minutes then remove from the pan to a rack.

CHOCOLATE MARBLE CAKE

Sometimes I want a chocolate marble cake with a chocolate icing. I tried this several times before I was satisfied with it.

Follow Joan's recipe (above) to the place where you divide the batter. Then, instead of spices and molasses, to half the batter add a blend of ¹/₃ cup cocoa, ¹/₄ cup corn syrup, and 1 or 2 tablespoons hot water. The result delighted my soul. The guests I made it for each ate two thick slices and I sent them home with the cake that was left – to prevent eating it all myself.

JEAN SALTER'S BOILED FRUIT CAKE

Jeannie got this recipe from her auntie in England who made a specialty of it because everyone liked it so well.

2 cups mixed dried fruit	**1 teaspoon baking soda**
1 cup butter	**1 egg, beaten**
1¹/₄ cups water	**2 cups flour**
1 cup sugar	**1¹/₂ teaspoons baking powder**
¹/₂ **teaspoon vanilla**	
Spices according to taste:	
cinnamon, ginger, nutmeg, etc.	

Combine the first four ingredients in a large saucepan and
bring to the boil. Remove from the stove and stir in the vanilla
and 1 teaspoon baking soda. Leave to cool, then add the beaten
egg, then the combined flour and spices and baking powder.
Mix well, put in a buttered cake tin and bake in a 325°F oven
for about 1¼ hours.

PINEAPPLE COCONUT FRUITCAKE
3 small loaves

Marg Phelan had this recipe photostated because so many
people who ate it at her house wanted to make it.

1½ cups diced candied pineapple	1 cup sugar (Marg says she uses less)
1½ cups light raisins	4 eggs
½ cup diced orange peel	1 cup pineapple juice
1 cup chopped walnuts	2 cups all-purpose flour
2 cups (7 oz.) flaked coconut	1 teaspoon baking powder
1 cup butter	1 teaspoon salt

Combine the fruits, nuts, and coconut. Cream the butter and
sugar until fluffy. Add the eggs, beating well after each one.
Stir in the pineapple juice. Sift together the flour, baking
powder, and salt; add to the sugar mixture. Fold in the fruit.
Spoon into three 8″ x 4″ buttered and floured loaf pans. Bake
in a 300°F oven for 1½ hours, but look before that. Cool,
remove from the pans. Wrap separately and store in a cool
place for 2 weeks before you cut it. No cheating.

RHUBARB UPSIDE DOWN CAKE

This is an easy dessert.

¼ cup butter	4 to 5 cups rhubarb
1 cup brown sugar	

Turn on your oven to 350°F. Melt the butter in a 9″ x 9″ baking
pan, add the diced rhubarb and sugar mixed together and
spread over the butter, covering the bottom of the pan. If you
are using frozen rhubarb put it in the oven to thaw while you
mix up the batter.

Batter:

1 cup sugar	**¹/₄ cup shortening**
1¹/₂ cups flour	**1 egg**
2 teaspoons baking powder	**1 teaspoon vanilla**
¹/₂ teaspoon salt	**About ²/₃ cup milk**

Sift the sugar, flour, baking powder, and salt, add the soft shortening and cut it into the flour mixture. Beat up the egg in a cup, stir in the vanilla and fill the cup with milk, beating all together; pour the liquid over the flour mixture and blend till smooth. Spread the batter over the rhubarb evenly. Bake at 350°F for about 30 to 40 minutes until the cake tests done. It will be light as a feather, delicious; serve warm with a scoop of vanilla ice cream. Don't turn it upside down on a plate – simply cut it in squares and lift out each square with a pancake turner and plop it rhubarb-side-up on a serving plate.

If you want a Rhubarb Upside-Down Gingerbread Cake simply add ¹/₂ teaspoon each of cinnamon, nutmeg, ginger and ¹/₂ cup of molasses instead of half the sugar.

CHRISTMAS CAKE AT RUNDLES

John Walker, the *chef de cuisine*, made this a month before Christmas. He covered it with his own almond paste, let it rest for a couple of weeks before icing it glamorously with scrolls and rosettes, applied with a pastry tube. As he wrote Merry Christmas on the top he said, "Never abbreviate the word 'Christmas', it's vulgar."

2¹/₄ cups raisins (large ones)	**Rind of 1 lemon and 1 orange**
2¹/₄ cups currants	**1 glass whisky**
2¹/₄ cups sultanas (small raisins)	**¹/₂ pound butter or margarine**
³/₄ cup cherries	**1 cup brown sugar, packed**
¹/₂ cup ground almonds	**6 eggs**
¹/₂ cup whole almonds	**2¹/₂ cups flour**
³/₄ cup chopped peel	**1 teaspoon spice**

Line a large round or square tin with greaseproof paper. Clean the fruit; cut the cherries into 2 or 4. Blanch the whole almonds and chop them. Mix the fruit, nuts, ground almonds and grated rind. Add ¹/₃ of the whisky and leave for about 1 hour. (The size of the glass of whisky was never disclosed, but Leslie, the *sous-chef* said, "We put in lots of booze.") Beat the butter and sugar, add the beaten eggs, mix the sifted flour and spice. Fold in the fruit. Spoon into the prepared tin. Put into the oven at 325°F for 1 hour, then reduce to 300° and bake about 2 hours more. Pour remainder of whisky over the cake and leave to cool. When cold remove from the tin and wrap in foil until Christmas, unless you want to put on almond paste and icing.

SCHWARZWAELDER KIRSCHTORTE
(Black Forest Cherry Torte)

The recipe for the winning Black Forest torte in the Kinderkochfest Competition was very long and complicated and not nearly as delicious as the version my smart little niece Barbie has concocted.

1 sponge cake + ¹/₃ cup cocoa
  (page 241)
¹/₂ cup Kirsch or rum or liqueur
Filling:
¹/₂ cup butter
3¹/₂ cups icing sugar
2 teaspoons very strong
  coffee
3 or 4 cups pitted cherries

Icing:
2 cups whipping cream
¹/₄ cup sugar
1 teaspoon vanilla
Chocolate curls

Barbie bakes her favourite Never Fail Sponge Cake (page 241), adding ¹/₃ cup cocoa to be sifted with the flour. When the cake has cooled she carefully slices it into 4 layers. She sprinkles each layer with Kirsch or rum or liqueur (¹/₂ cup all together). To make the filling she blends together the butter, icing sugar and coffee till creamy like icing, and spreads ¹/₃ of it over the bottom layer of the cake. Into it she presses ¹/₃ of the cherries. Barbie uses sour frozen ones. (If they have thawed, or if canned cherries are used, they should be well drained.) She repeats this operation on the next two layers, putting each layer of cake on top of the one below before she fills it. She puts the fourth layer on top. Finally she whips the cream, adds the ¼ cup sugar (less if sweet cherries are used) and the vanilla. She slathers it on top and round the sides of the cake then decorates it with chocolate curls. The result is a triumph and should be eaten as soon as possible. No problem.

GUGELHUPF BIERKUCHEN (Beer Cake)
in a gugelhupf, bundt or tube pan

No sugar, no eggs, an elusive flavour: this cake is a winner. It is moist, heavy, and keeps well if you let it.

1 cup molasses
½ cup butter or margarine
1 bottle of beer
1 cup raisins
2⅔ cups sifted flour
½ teaspoon salt
1 tablespoon baking powder

¼ teaspoon baking soda
½ teaspoon cinnamon
½ teaspoon nutmeg
½ teaspoon ginger
1 cup coarsely chopped
 filberts or pecans

Combine the molasses, butter, and beer in a saucepan and heat only until the butter melts; stir in the raisins and let the mixture cool for 15 minutes. Sift together the dry ingredients. Stir in the nuts. When the beer mixture has cooled pour it over the dry ingredients and stir until smooth. Pour the batter into a greased and floured tube pan and bake in a 350°F oven for about 1 hour. Test it. Turn it over on a cake rack and let it cool a bit before dribbling a glaze over it.

GLAZE: Mix 1 cup icing sugar and enough liquid honey to moisten the icing sugar to the dribbly stage. Pour it over the top of the cake and let it run down the sides. If you don't have honey try maple or corn syrup.

HEAVENLY FLUFF FROSTING

This luscious, foolproof icing is for an angel cake, birthday cake, sponge cake, or any cake that needs to be glamorous for an occasion. It stays fluffy for several days, won't get crusty or runny. For me it has never failed.

2 egg whites

³/₄ cup sugar

¹/₃ cup corn syrup

2 tablespoons water

¹/₄ teaspoon cream of tartar

¹/₄ teaspoon salt

1 teaspoon vanilla or other

    flavouring

Put everything but the flavouring into the top of a double boiler over fast-boiling water. Start beating immediately with a rotary beater – preferably an electric one – and don't stop beating until the mixture stands in stiff peaks; it won't take very long. Remove from the heat, add the flavouring and keep on beating until it is thick enough to spread easily.

MAPLE WALNUT ICING
for a 9" x 9" cake

¹/₂ cup butter

1 cup brown sugar

¹/₄ cup milk

1³/₄ cups icing sugar, more or

    less

1 teaspoon maple flavouring

¹/₂ cup broken nuts

Melt the butter in a saucepan over moderate heat until lightly browned. Stir in the brown sugar and keep stirring until the mixture is bubbling (it will separate). Remove from the heat and stir in the milk. Return to moderate heat and bring back to just boiling, stirring constantly. Off the heat stir in icing sugar gradually. Add a little cream if necessary to make right consistency to spread. Stir in the nuts.

BUTTERSCOTCH FROSTING
for two 8 or 9-inch layers

Rather like penuche, and you know how good that is.
Into a blender put:

¹/₄ cup soft butter

1 teaspoon vanilla

1 tablespoon corn syrup

2 tablespoons hot water

Cover and blend on high speed for 5 seconds.
Add **1 cup firmly packed dark brown sugar** and blend again for 10 seconds.

Add **1 tablespoon hot water** and blend until smooth.

Add **1¹/₂ cups icing sugar** and blend until smooth, stopping to stir down.

RAISIN ORANGE ICING
for 2 layers

Smooth, moist, tart, and especially good on cakes that have spices or fruit.

¹/₂ cup raisins
Outer rind of half an orange
Juice of an orange (¹/₃ cup)
2 tablespoons butter

2 tablespoons cream or whole milk
2¹/₂ to 3 cups icing sugar

Put everything but the sugar into your blender and blend until the raisins are fine. Gradually add the sugar, while blending, until you have added 1 cupful. Scrape it out into a bowl and keep adding enough sugar to make smooth, spreadable icing.

EVA'S WHIPPED ICING
to fill and ice a large torte

Eva says it whips up real nice and can be stored in the fridge for future use. It's smooth, delicious, and makes a cake look like a dream.

2 tablespoons corn starch
¹/₂ cup milk
¹/₂ cup double-strength coffee
1 cup granulated sugar

1 cup butter at room temperature, don't use a substitute
1 teaspoon vanilla or preferred flavouring

Stir together until smooth the corn starch and milk, then stir in the hot coffee and cook over moderate heat, stirring until thick. Remove from the heat and cool. Into a beater bowl measure the sugar, butter, vanilla, and beat until snowy white, about 10 minutes, scraping down the sides of the bowl several times. Add the cool corn starch mixture and beat at high speed for 10 to 15 minutes more, or until it is like whipped cream. Eva says you can get almost the same effect by using 1 cup of milk – omitting the coffee – and only ¹/₂ cup of butter.

COCOA FUDGE ICING
for a 9" x 9" cake

Really fudgy, easy to make and almost foolproof.

1 cup sugar, brown or white
¹/₄ cup cocoa
¹/₄ cup milk

¹/₄ cup butter
¹/₂ teaspoon vanilla

Combine the sugar and cocoa, stir in the milk till it's smooth, drop in the butter and stir over moderate heat. Boil for one minute only. Remove from heat and cool as quickly as you can (put in cold water in the sink). Stir in the vanilla and beat until it's creamy and thick. It stays soft – but firm – on the cake.

LORNA'S SUPER CHOCOLATE CHIP ICING
for 2 layers

This has that real chocolate flavour and it stays soft.

6 ounces semi-sweet
chocolate pieces
¹/₂ cup light cream

1 cup margarine or butter
2¹/₂ cups icing sugar

In a saucepan combine the chocolate, cream, and margarine; stir till smooth, remove from heat and whisk in the icing sugar – it will be thin. Beat it over ice till it holds shape (put ice cubes and water in a bowl with the saucepan on top).

Of course, I hadn't time to do that so I used only ¹/₄ cup cream and after I'd whisked in the icing sugar I set the saucepan in my fridge till the icing had set and then iced the cake. If you hadn't eaten Lorna's icing and known it was better you'd have thought mine was pretty good, too.

MARSHMALLOW CHOCOLATE CHIP ICING
for a 9" x 9" cake

This would make any cake look good and taste even better.

1¹/₂ cups miniature
marshmallows, or large
ones cut up

1 cup chocolate chips
4 tablespoons milk or cream

Put everything into the top of a double boiler and heat over boiling water, stirring until the chocolate and marshmallows are melted. Spread quickly over the cake.

GLAZE
about 1 cup

An ideal icing for buns, coffee cakes, or tube cakes that need a thin icing on top that will run down the sides.

1¼ cups sifted icing sugar
1¼ tablespoons butter, softened

1 teaspoon vanilla or other flavouring
1½ tablespoons boiling water

Sift the sugar into a bowl; blend in the butter, vanilla, and boiling water, beating until it is smooth, adding more boiling water drop by drop if necessary. Beat several minutes until it is creamy then spread it on lukewarm buns, cake, etc.

ICING TO KEEP A FRUIT CAKE MOIST

Mrs. Moore, who came from the U.S. to live in Bamburg with her grandson, sent me this recipe. She wrote: "I sent this in to a St. Petersburg, Florida, paper and got $5.00 for it."

1 large sweet potato, baked
1 teaspoon butter

1 teaspoon vanilla
Icing sugar

Scoop out the baked sweet potato from the skin, mix with the butter and vanilla and work in enough powdered sugar to make it right for spreading.

CREAM CHEESE ICING

Especially good on a carrot cake or one with apples, raisins, spices.

½ cup soft cream cheese
¼ cup butter

1 cup icing sugar
½ teaspoon vanilla

Beat the cream cheese and butter until fluffy, then beat in the icing sugar and vanilla until it is smooth and spreadable.

14
Pies and Tarts

Because there are seventy-four pie recipes in *Food That Really Schmecks* I didn't think I'd have enough different ones for a chapter in this book. But I've been running into so many fantastic pies lately that they can't be ignored or merely included with the desserts. Thirty-four pie recipes must have a chapter of their own.

I think every one is a winner. Some are Old Order Mennonite specials that you won't find in any other cookbook, a few are for company only – too rich or fancy for everyday fare – the rest are just great schmecksy favourites of my family and friends.

Could you resist Mrs. Addison Eby's Sour Cream Elderberry Pie, Eva's Backwoods Pie, Lemon Apple, Pear Streusel, Five Star Peach, Thanksgiving Pumpkin, Peanut Molasses (from Guyana), Glazed Fresh Strawberry, Kentucky Derby Pie, Southern Pecan (fom a New Orleans friend), Crème de Menthe, Satan's Choice, and Raspberry Angel?

SPEEDY PAT-IN PASTRY
1 shell without a top

Ever since Norma Morrison gave her this recipe Norm hasn't made pastry any other way – nor have I. It's so easy: crisp, tender, tasty, and needs no rolling.

1½ cups sifted flour,	**¾ teaspoon salt**
all-purpose or whole wheat	**½ cup corn oil**
1½ teaspoons sugar	**3 tablespoons cold milk**

Sift the flour, sugar, and salt directly into a 9-inch pie plate. Combine the oil and milk in a measuring cup and beat with a fork until it is creamy. Pour all at once over the flour in the pie plate. Mix with a fork until the flour is completely dampened. Push the dough with your fingers to line the bottom and sides of the plate. If you're fussy press it down with another pie plate to get it even. Flute the edges and fill with whatever filling you've chosen. If you are making a baked shell to be filled later, prick the entire surface of the pastry with a fork and bake at 425°F for 15 minutes, but watch it.

BARBIE'S PERFECT PASTRY
4 shells

Barbie bakes lots of pies. She keeps 3 or 4 shells in her freezer and fills one in a jiffy when she wants a pie for dinner.

1 pound lard	**1 teaspoon baking powder**
6 cups flour, half pastry,	**1 egg**
half all-purpose	**1 tablespoon vinegar**
2 teaspoons salt	**Water to fill up the cup**

Blend the lard, flour, salt, and baking powder with a pastry blender until the mix is fairly fine. In a measuring cup beat 1 egg and 1 tablespoon of vinegar; add enough water to fill up the cup. Add this to the flour mixture, mix gently with a fork. Don't work with it any more than you have to.

Bake filled pies at 450°F for 15 minutes then reduce to 350°F.

MERINGUE PIE SHELL

When Norm entertains she loves to make glamorous desserts that would send her guests round the bend to obesity if they weren't a one-time treat. Her favourite is a meringue crust into which she pours various irresistible fillings: chocolate or rum with almonds, ice cream with fresh peaches or strawberries, lemon filling, or pineapple and nuts in whipped cream. Her meringue is light, crisp, and never embarrassing to chew or cut with a fork.

$^2/_3$ cup egg whites *at room temperature* (about 4 large eggs)	$1^1/_3$ teaspoons vinegar
	$1^1/_3$ teaspoons water
	1 cup white sugar
$^1/_8$ teaspoon salt	$^1/_2$ teaspoon almond flavouring

Beat all the ingredients together till they are really stiff and glossy – better overdo it than under. Spread evenly in a well-buttered large pie plate, raising the meringue around the sides of the pan. Preheat the oven to 400°F and *turn it off*. Put the pie into the oven and forget about it till the oven is cold – overnight is a good time. The shell will be pale beige. If it has cracked, the oven was too hot, if it is tough it was too cool. But that never happens to Norm's. All she has to do on the day of the party is put the filling into the shell. The meringue will keep for days in a dry storage place.

CRUMB CRUST FOR UNBAKED PIE
for a 9-inch pie

Try this with graham wafers, gingersnaps, vanilla wafers, or chocolate wafers – very finely crumbled. It's quick, easy and has more flavour than pastry.

1$^1/_2$ cups wafer crumbs	$^1/_3$ or $^1/_2$ cup melted butter
$^1/_3$ or $^1/_2$ cup sugar	

Combine the crumbs with the sugar and melted butter. Press the mixture firmly against the bottom and sides of the pie plate, using the back of a spoon. Bake for 10 to 15 minutes in a 300°F oven.

FRUIT PIES

Fresh or unsweetened frozen raspberries, blueberries, cherries, peaches, apples, apricots, plums, strawberry-rhubarb, Concord grapes, elderberries, gooseberries, red and black currants, and raisins. Self-respecting cooks in Waterloo County don't bother with recipes to make regular fruit pies: their experienced guesses give them delicious results.

The amount of fruit depends on the size of the pie plate: about 3 cups of berries for an 8-incher, 4 cups for a 9-inch shell, 5 cups for a 10-inch. Sliced fruits – like apples, peaches and pears – require 1 more cup for each size. Some fruits are sweeter than others and require less sugar; some are more juicy and require more flour to thicken them. For 9-inch pies $3/4$ to 1 cup sugar combined with 2 tablespoons to $1/4$ cup flour and 2 tablespoons of soft butter mixed with the fruit should give you a very good pie. Topped with a full vented pastry crust, lattice strips or crumbs made by blending $1/2$ cup sugar, $1/2$ cup flour and $1/4$ cup butter, your pie will be a winner.

RASPBERRY ANGEL PIE

This glamorous summer dessert was designed for celestial beings: Ruby's lady friends love it.

Meringue shell (page 253)
3 oz. package of raspberry
   jello
$1^1/4$ cups boiling water

1 cup fresh raspberries, or
   more
1 cup whipping cream

Add boiling water to the jello powder and stir until the powder is dissolved. Chill until the mixture is the consistency of egg whites. Mash the fresh raspberries slightly, whip the cream until stiff and fold both into the jello. Chill until the mixture holds its shape when dropped from a spoon. Pile into the prepared meringue shell, chill several hours. Garnish with sweetened whipped cream and whole raspberries at serving time.

This could be just as angelic if you made it with strawberries.

FRUIT CUSTARD PIES

My favourite. A small box of berries will go a long way if you dot the fruit over the custard in an unbaked shell. More delicate than pies made with masses of fruit.

¹/₂ **cup sugar**	**3 eggs, beaten**
1 teaspoon flour	**2¹/₂ cups milk**
¹/₂ **teaspoon salt**	¹/₂ **to** ³/₄ **cup fruit**

Combine the sugar, flour, salt, and beaten eggs. Scald the milk and add it gradually. Pour into the pie shell, dot the berries over the custard. Bake at 350°F for about 45 minutes, or until a silver knife stuck into the middle comes out clean.

Try it with cherries, blueberries, strawberries, raspberries, red or black currants, raisins or dried currants, soaked first.

SOUR CREAM ELDERBERRY PIE

Mrs. Addison Eby says this tastes best if made with real cow cream. If you are poor city folk you'll just have to make do with what you can buy.

Pastry for a 9-inch crust	**1 cup sour cream**
1 cup sugar	**2 cups elderberries**
2 tablespoons flour	

Mix the sugar and flour; blend in the sour cream then gently fold in the elderberries so they won't break while you're doing it. Pour into the pie shell and bake at 425°F for 15 minutes, then at 350°F for another half hour. Put a lattice top on if you like.

I wonder how this would be using blueberries? Why not give it a try?

GLAZED FRESH STRAWBERRY PIE

At seven o'clock in the morning people start lining up to buy pieces of glazed strawberry pie at the New Hamburg Mennonite Sale on the last Saturday in May every year. Fifteen hundred pie shells are baked in advance, strawberries are flown in from California, women from various congregations sit hulling them in the bleachers of the New Hamburg Arena, while other women put the berries into the shells, pour a glaze over them and cover them with whipped cream. I don't have their secret formula for the glaze but I think this one is just as good.

1 baked pastry shell, or
  crumb crust
1 quart, or more, fresh
  strawberries
3 tablespoons corn
  starch
1 cup sugar

$^1/_2$ cup water
1 tablespoon butter
1 tablespoon lemon juice
Sweetened whipped cream

Sort the berries, saving the perfect ones and crushing the others. Combine corn starch and sugar, stir in the crushed berries and water; cook gently until thick and clear, stirring constantly. Remove from heat, add butter and lemon juice, let cool. When the glaze is cold put the whole berries in the bottom of the baked pie shell, pour the glaze over them and chill till set. Serve with sweetened whipped cream over all. This won't keep long – obviously.

SUPER RHUBARB PIE

Spring is here! Spring is here! (Even if you use frozen rhubarb.)

Pastry for a 9- or 10-inch pie
  (with a lattice top – if you
  like)
2 or 3 cups rhubarb

3 tablespoons flour
1 cup sugar
1 or 2 eggs, beaten

Cut the rhubarb in 1-inch pieces and distribute it evenly in the unbaked pie shell. Mix the flour and sugar, beat in the eggs and pour evenly over the rhubarb. Cover the top with lattice or crumbs made of $^1/_2$ cup flour, $^1/_2$ cup brown sugar, $^1/_4$ cup soft butter. Bake the pie for 10 minutes at 450°F, lower the heat to 350°F and bake 35 minutes, till it is set.

SOUR CREAM RHUBARB PIE

This should serve six or eight people but three of us kept saying, "Just a little bit more," until there was none.

Pastry for a large pie
3 or 4 cups cubed rhubarb
1 cup strawberries (optional)
1½ cups white sugar
⅓ cup flour
1 cup sour cream

Topping:
½ cup flour
½ cup brown sugar
¼ cup soft butter

Arrange the rhubarb and strawberries in the unbaked pie shell. Mix the sugar and flour; blend in the sour cream; pour the mixture evenly over the rhubarb. Blend the topping ingredients until crumbly; sprinkle the crumbs over the rhubarb and bake at 450°F for 15 minutes, then at 350°F for an additional 30 minutes till the fruit is tender, the filling set, and the crumbs golden. This is really special.

PEAR STREUSEL PIE

Norm has made dozens of pear pies since Jean Goodwin gave her this wonderful recipe.

Pastry for an unbaked pie
**   shell**
½ cup all-purpose flour
¾ cup lightly packed brown
**   sugar**
¾ cup dessicated coconut

⅓ cup melted butter
Enough fresh pears to fill the
**   pie shell, or canned pears,**
**   drained**

Combine the flour, sugar, coconut, and butter. Sprinkle a little in the bottom of the unbaked pie shell. Arrange the pears, cut in half, face down, over the crumbs in the pie shell. Cover with the remaining crumbs. Bake at 425°F for 10 minutes with foil over the pie so the coconut won't burn. Turn the heat to 350°F for 20 minutes till the pears are soft and the topping is golden, taking the foil off to give it a chance to brown slightly. Serve with whipped cream on top if you need to hide a burnt spot, but the pie is good enough without any fancying.

FIVE-STAR PEACH PIE

This is super, one of the best desserts ever made, not difficult and quite foolproof. You can make it in 2 small pie plates or in a 9" x 13" pan to serve squares on individual plates.

Crust:
2 cups flour
²/₃ cup fine white sugar

¹/₂ teaspoon salt
³/₄ cup butter or half
　margarine

Blend the crust ingredients, in the order given, with a pastry blender. Pat into a buttered pan or 2 pie plates. Bake 15 minutes at 350°F, but watch it. While this is happening, make the filling:

2 beaten eggs
¹/₂ teaspoon almond or
　vanilla flavouring
1 cup fine white sugar
¹/₄ cup flour

³/₄ teaspoon baking powder
¹/₄ teaspoon salt
4 to 5 cups sliced peaches
³/₄ cup chopped nuts
Whipped cream (optional)

Beat the eggs, add the flavouring, sugar, flour sifted with the baking powder and salt. Blend, then add the sliced peaches and nuts. Pour this mixture over the half-baked crust and bake 30 to 45 minutes at 350°F. Keep watching it. When it has cooled slather the top with whipped cream, but you really don't need to. When the peach season comes round again grasp the opportunity to make this, though I suppose you could try it with canned or frozen peaches.

APPLE CREAM CUSTARD SCHNITZ PIE

Menno Frey's wife served this to her quilting circle and the ladies all wanted the recipe.

Pastry for a 9-inch pie
4 or 5 baking apples
1 tablespoon lemon juice
¹/₂ cup sugar
3 eggs

³/₄ cup heavy cream
¹/₄ cup apple cider
¹/₄ teaspoon nutmeg
2 tablespoons sugar for
　topping

Core and cut the apples in eighths (schnitz); toss them with the lemon juice and sugar. Arrange the apple schnitz, round side down, in the pie shell, starting with a circle round the outer edge and another circle inside that, filling in the centre. Bake in a 400°F oven for 20 minutes. Beat the eggs slightly, stir in the cream, apple cider, and nutmeg. Pour over the apples, continue baking another 10 minutes. Sprinkle the top with 2 tablespoons sugar and bake 10 minutes longer, or until the top is golden and the centre firm. Cool on a rack before cutting.

LUSCIOUS APPLE PIE

All the girls in Ruby's bridge club have gone home with this recipe.

Baked pastry shell or a crumb crust	**1 teaspoon almond flavouring**
6 to 8 medium cooking apples	*Topping:*
1 cup sugar	**1 cup flour**
¹/₂ cup water, or less	**¹/₂ cup brown sugar**
2 tablespoons butter	**¹/₃ cup shortening**

Core and slice the apples; add the sugar, water, and butter. Cook until tender, cool and add the almond flavouring. Mix into crumbles the flour, sugar, and shortening. Spoon the apple sauce into the pie shell, cover with the crumbles and bake in a 400°F oven for about 15 minutes, until the topping is golden. Keep your eye on it. Serve hot or cold with whipped cream, ice cream, or slices of cheese. No wonder those girls never lose weight.

MAPLE SYRUP PIES

Ammon Martin has a large maple bush and for many springs has sold syrup at the Kitchener and Waterloo markets. His tall, slim, beautiful, friendly daughters used to go with him, until Hannah married Sylvanus and Eva married Melvin. Now Eva and Melvin have a sugar bush of their own and Eva makes delicious pies that use maple syrup.

BACKWOODS PIE

Eva says she uses the late-run maple syrup for this pie: it has a stronger flavour and is not so sweet.

Pastry for a 9-inch pie 1 cup milk
1 cup brown sugar 1 tablespoon butter
1½ tablespoons flour 3 egg yolks
1 cup dark maple syrup 3 egg whites

Beat all together but the egg whites; beat them until stiff and fold them in last. Pour into pie shell. Bake in a 325°F oven until set, about 40 to 50 minutes.

MRS. ELAM WIDEMAN'S COCONUT PIE

Eva says this makes a wonderful winter pie.

Pastry for a 9-inch pie 1 cup milk
³/₄ **cup sugar** 1 cup maple syrup
2 tablespoons flour ³/₄ cup sour cream
¹/₂ **teaspoon soda** 1 teaspoon vanilla
2 eggs, slightly beaten 1 cup coconut

Stir the sugar, flour, and soda together then add the rest of the ingredients, blending well. Pour into the unbaked pie shell and bake at 325°F until set, about 40 to 50 minutes.

GRANDMOTHER'S LEMON APPLE PIE

Aunt Janie Roth says they loved this pie when she was a little girl because it was just a little bit different.

Pastry for a 9-inch pie, with a 1 egg yolk
    lattice or full covering 2 tablespoons lemon juice
1 tablespoon butter ¹/₄ cup hot water
1 cup sugar 2 or 3 large apples, grated
2 tablespoons flour 1 egg white, beaten stiff

Stir everything together, folding in the egg white last. Pour into an unbaked pie shell, put on a lattice or full covering. Bake in a 350°F oven till the crust is baked a pale gold.

MARDI'S THANKSGIVING PUMPKIN PIE

This really is one to be thankful for: more bother and more glamorous than the old-fashioned kind that grandma makes, it has a wonderful flavour.

Baked pie shell, or ginger-
snap or graham wafer
crust
3 egg yolks
$^1/_2$ cup white or brown sugar
$1^1/_4$ cups cooked, mashed
pumpkin
$^1/_2$ cup milk
$^1/_2$ teaspoon salt

$^1/_2$ teaspoon ginger, or less
$^1/_2$ teaspoon cinnamon, or less
$^1/_2$ teaspoon nutmeg, or less
1 tablespoon gelatine
$^1/_4$ cup cold water
3 egg whites
$^1/_4$ teaspoon cream of tartar
$^1/_2$ cup white sugar

Beat the egg yolks, add the $^1/_2$ cup sugar, pumpkin, milk, salt, spices; thicken in a double boiler, stirring fairly often. Soften the gelatine in the $^1/_4$ cup of cold water. Stir the moistened gelatine into the thickened pumpkin mixture and cool. Beat the egg whites, at room temperature, with cream of tartar and $^1/_2$ cup sugar until stiff and glossy; fold into the pumpkin mixture when it is cold. Spoon into the baked pie shell and let it set. I had this pie at Mardi's one Thanksgiving day years ago and I've never forgotten it.

VANILLA PIE
Eva's recipe makes 4 pies (you could divide it)

Wherever there's a gathering of Old Order Mennonites you'll find Vanilla Pies – "and they're all a little bit different yet," Eva told me.

4 pie shells
6 heaping tablespoons flour
2 cups brown sugar
2 cups dark maple syrup
6 cups water
$2^1/_2$ teaspoons vanilla

Crumb topping:
$1^1/_2$ cups flour
$1^1/_2$ cups oatmeal
1 cup brown sugar
1 teaspoon baking powder
1 teaspoon cream of tartar
1 cup butter

Mix the flour with the sugar and it won't lump. Stir in the maple syrup and water; boil until the mixture is syrupy. Let cool and add the vanilla. Blend the ingredients for the crumb topping, cutting in the butter till it is crumbly. Divide the syrup evenly among the 4 pie shells, sprinkle the crumbs over each and bake at 425°F for 10 minutes, then at 325°F for about 25 more. (Wouldn't it be a mess if they all boiled over?)

SOUR CREAM RAISIN WALNUT PIE

You won't get thinner on this one – but you'll certainly enjoy it.

Pastry for a 9-inch pie	**2 egg yolks, slightly beaten**
1 cup sour cream	**1 teaspoon vanilla**
1 cup white sugar	**2 egg whites at room**
¹/₂ cup raisins, chopped	**temperature**
Pinch of salt	**2 tablespoons sugar**
³/₄ cup walnuts, chopped	

Mix all the ingredients but the last two; fill the unbaked pie shell. Bake at 425°F for 10 minutes, then at 325°F until done, about 30 minutes more. Make a meringue of the egg whites and 2 tablespoons sugar; when the pie has partially cooled, spread the meringue and return to the oven until the meringue is golden. Watch it – it won't take long.

To prevent pie crusts from becoming soggy put the shell in the oven for 5 minutes before putting in the filling.

PEANUT MOLASSES PIE

Lynette Heath, a girl in Guyana who works in the Canadian High Commissioner's office, read my little book *Sauerkraut and Enterprise*, then gratefully sent me this recipe. She wrote: "Yesterday our police band played the Canadian and Guyana national anthems with the instruments that were given to them on Canada Day last year by the Canadian government." She also told me that John Erb, an Anglican priest with Waterloo County pioneer Mennonite forebears, had taken Guyana by storm.

Pastry for a 9-inch pie
¹/₂ **cup molasses**
¹/₂ **tablespoon butter**
1 or 2 eggs
¹/₂ **cup sugar**

1 tablespoon flour
¹/₄ **teaspoon salt**
¹/₂ **cup milk**
¹/₂ **teaspoon vanilla**
³/₄ **cup chopped peanuts**

Line a large enamelled plate or pie dish with pastry. Heat the molasses and butter to boiling point and leave to cool. Whisk the eggs, gradually beat in the combined sugar, flour, and salt. Stir in the milk and vanilla, then the cooled molasses. Add the chopped nuts and pour into the pastry shell. Put it in a hot oven, 425°F, for 10 minutes, then decrease the heat to 350°F and bake until the filling is set and the pastry is crisp and golden, about 20 to 30 minutes. Wouldn't the police band love that? And John Erb, too.

SHOO-FLY PIE

Lorna got this recipe for me from her Mennonite neighbour, Mrs. Jesse Shantz, who made the best shoo-fly pie Lorna had ever tasted.

Pastry for a 9-inch pie

Crumbs:
1 cup flour
²/₃ **cup brown sugar**
**1 tablespoon lard or
   shortening**
¹/₂ **teaspoon cinnamon**
Dash allspice and nutmeg

Liquid:
²/₃ **cup corn syrup**
¹/₃ **cup molasses**
1 egg, slightly beaten
³/₄ **cup cold water**
¹/₄ **cup hot water**
¹/₂ **teaspoon soda**

Mix the crumb ingredients till they are crumbly. Blend the liquid ingredients, adding the soda to the hot water before stirring it in with the rest. Mix the liquid and half the crumb mixture together in a few stirs, not really blending. Pour into the pie shell and sprinkle the reserved crumbs over the top. Bake in a 350°F oven for 45 minutes or longer.

If you have space, keep pie or tart shells in your freezer, then all you need do when you want a pie is make up a filling.

AUNTIE MARY'S LEMON MOLASSES PIE

Besides the great flavour of this unusual pie we loved the topping because Auntie Mary always made cookies for us kids out of the part that was left over.

Pastry for a fairly large pie, or 2 small ones

Filling:
¹/₂ cup brown sugar
2 tablespoons corn starch
¹/₂ cup molasses
1 egg, slightly beaten
Juice and rind of one lemon
1 cup boiling water

Topping (and cookie dough):
¹/₂ cup sugar
¹/₂ cup sour cream
1¹/₄ cups flour
¹/₂ teaspoon soda

For the filling blend the sugar, corn starch, molasses and egg. Gradually stir in the rind and juice of 1 lemon and the boiling water. Cook over low heat or a double boiler until thickened. Make the topping by blending all the ingredients to make a tender dough to be rolled out ¹/₄ inch thick. Pour the filling into the pie shell, cut the topping dough into strips and lay them over the filling in a lattice pattern. (Place any remaining strips on a cookie sheet and bake them along with the pie, but don't forget them.) The pie will take about 40 minutes in a 350°F oven, the cookies about 20 minutes.

GRAHAM WAFER PIE

This was Mother's most special company pie, high and so different from the fruit pies we usually had. This was the glamour pie of its day.

20 graham crackers, rolled fine, about 2 cupfuls of crumbs

¹/₂ cup white sugar
1 cup melted butter (or ³/₄ cup)

Blend these together, take a little more than ²/₃ of the mixture to line a large pie plate and press it in firmly. Bake at 300°F for about 15 minutes, then cool.

Filling:
3 egg yolks
¹/₂ cup white sugar
2 tablespoons corn starch
2 cups milk
¹/₂ teaspoon vanilla

Meringue topping:
3 egg whites, beaten stiff
at room temperature
3 tablespoons sugar

Beat the egg yolks, blend in the sugar mixed with the corn starch, then the milk and vanilla. Heat over water in a double boiler, stirring until thick. Cool before pouring into the wafer shell. Beat the egg whites with the 3 tablespoons of sugar, spoon over the cold custard in the pie shell; sprinkle the rest of the wafer crumbs over the meringue. Bake in a 300°F oven until the meringue is set, about 8 minutes. But watch it – what a shame if it was more than just tinged with gold.

CRÈME DE MENTHE PIE

Whatever Jill makes is strictly gourmet – and greatly appreciated by my nephew John's medical associates, despite the massive calorie count. They ski a lot.

Make a crumb crust with cream-filled chocolate wafers **(page 253)**.

Filling:
24 large marshmallows
²/₃ cup milk

¹/₄ cup crème de menthe
¹/₂ cup whipping cream

In the top of a double boiler heat the marshmallows and milk, stirring until the mixture is melted and blended. Cool and add the liqueur. Chill until completely cold but still syrupy before you fold in the whipped cream. Pour into the pie shell and chill overnight – the flavour is better the next day. Sprinkle with a few reserved chocolate wafer crumbs or shavings of bitter chocolate. Very small servings should make it stretch.

Fancy rich desserts are fine to serve at a dessert coffee party because your guests probably didn't eat much before they came. After a good big dinner serve something light and refreshing.

MERINGUE TARTS
12 or more meringue shells

One of Norm's favourite and most impressive desserts is one of her easiest, and most versatile.

6 egg whites, at room temperature
$^1/_4$ teaspoon salt
$1^1/_2$ teaspoons water
2 teaspoons vinegar or lemon juice

$1^1/_3$ cups white sugar
$^3/_4$ teaspoon almond flavouring

Beat the egg whites with the salt, water and vinegar until soft peaks form. Add the sugar gradually, beating all the while, and continue beating until the meringue is glossy and very firm. You can't overdo it. On greased foil or brown paper on a baking sheet, with a pastry bag or with a spoon and knife shape the meringue into 3- to 4-inch rounds, building up the sides to a depth of $1^1/_2$ inches. Bake in a 275°F oven for about an hour or preheat your oven to 375°F, turn it off, put the shells in and let them stay there till the oven cools.

Norm stashes the cooled, baked shells away in tightly covered tin boxes and when she needs them she fills them with chocolate or lemon butter or with strawberries or peaches alone or over ice cream. There are all sorts of things you can use in meringue shells. All of them glamorous and delicious.

SATAN'S CHOICE

This pie really is sinful: I shouldn't even give it to you, but it is a way to use those almond chocolate bars the little school kids keep selling to make money for their hockey uniforms or a trip to Paris. If you make the servings small you could serve 10. It's very easy to make and better than eating those chocolate bars pure.

Crumb crust (page 253)
15 marshmallows
4 almond chocolate bars

$^1/_2$ cup milk
1 cup whipping cream
Reserved crumbs

Melt the marshmallows and chocolate bars with the milk in a double boiler, then cool. When the chocolate mixture is cold, whip the cup of cream, fold it in and pour it into the crumb crust. Sprinkle with the reserved crumbs. Chill for some time till it is set but serve it at room temperature. Your conscience may bother you but you'll love every mouthful.

FRUIT COCKTAIL PIE

This is one of Norm's party standbys beautiful to look at, refreshing, easy to make, and foolproof. It can be made a day before the event.

Graham Cracker Crust or Meringue Shell for a big pie (page 253)
25 marshmallows
¹/₂ cup milk

28 oz. tin of fruit cocktail
1 cup whipping cream, whipped
Maraschino cherries (optional)

Melt the marshmallows in the milk in a double boiler then let them cool. Add the fruit cocktail – juice and fruit – stirring it to blend well. Fold in the whipped cream. Spoon the mixture into the pie shell, decorate it with cherries, if you like, and let it stand in a cool place until set.

OLD-FASHIONED SOUTHERN PECAN PIE

Delicious the way Beverley Nye makes it. She comes from New Orleans, is now living in Stratford, Ontario, where she and her husband Tait Baynard have the Sage and Sagittarius Gallery and work at their painting.

Pastry for a fairly large pie
1 cup dark brown sugar
2 tablespoons flour
³/₄ teaspoon salt
2 tablespoons melted butter
4 eggs, beaten

1 teaspoon vanilla
1 cup light corn syrup
1 cup pecan nuts – the fresher and fatter the better

Mix all together with the pecans floating on top. Pour into the pie shell and bake at 350°F for 45 to 50 minutes. Beverly made several of these for our Stylish Entertainment class at Rundle's Restaurant and we all asked for her recipe.

KENTUCKY DERBY PIE

This is always a winner on Derby Day in Louisville, Kentucky, even if the favourite horse loses.

Pastry for a 9-inch crust	**1 teaspoon vanilla**
1 cup sugar	**2 tablespoons Bourbon, or**
¹/₄ cup butter	**dark rum or rye**
3 beaten eggs	**¹/₂ cup chocolate chips**
³/₄ cup corn syrup	**¹/₂ cup pecan pieces**
¹/₄ teaspoon salt	**Whipped or ice cream**

Cream the sugar with the butter, add the beaten eggs, corn syrup, salt, vanilla and liquor. Sprinkle the bottom of an un-baked pie crust with the chocolate chips and broken pecan pieces. Pour the filling over them carefully and bake at 375°F for about 45 minutes. Serve with ice cream or whipped cream slathered on top. A friend in Louisville sent this fabulous recipe to Sheila Hutton.

JEAN SALTER'S BUTTER TARTS

I've eaten these at Jean's and can well recommend them.

Pastry to line the cups of	**¹/₂ cup brown sugar**
muffin tins	**¹/₂ cup corn syrup**
Boiling water	**1 egg, slightly beaten**
¹/₂ cup raisins	**¹/₄ teaspoon salt**
¹/₄ cup butter	**¹/₂ teaspoon vanilla**

Pour boiling water over the raisins; soak until the edges begin to turn white, then drain. Cream the butter and sugar, add corn syrup and slightly beaten egg, salt and vanilla. Combine with the raisins. Half fill the pastry-lined muffin tins. Place in a 375°F oven and immediately turn down to 250°F. Bake for about 20 minutes and do *not* allow filling to bubble.

COFFEE ALMOND TARTS

I liked these so well at Caroline Haehnel's I asked her for the recipe. I think she made it up.

16 three-inch tart shells	**¹/₄ teaspoon salt**
2 eggs, beaten	**¹/₄ cup melted butter**
1¹/₂ cups dark brown sugar	**1 teaspoon vanilla**
2 teaspoons instant coffee powder	**1 cup chopped almonds, or sunflower seeds**
2 tablespoons water	

To the eggs, add the sugar, instant coffee, water, and salt, beating well. Add the melted butter, vanilla, and nuts. Spoon into tart shells and bake at 425°F for 12 to 15 minutes, but watch the rim of the pastry. Caroline put hers in muffin tins.

Quite a few pie fillings could be put into tart shells if you prefer them that way – but don't bake them as long.

15

Desserts and Dessert Sauces

One day in December, Eva invited me to have dinner with Bevvy and David and half a dozen of her relatives. The men in their Sunday black suits sat on one side and one end of the long table, the women, their heads covered with dainty white prayer caps, sat on the other side. Eva and the hired girl hovered over us, refilling dishes with meats, vegetables, salads, bread and butter, pickles and relishes. Besides a bowl of fruit with cookies and cake, there were four desserts: butterscotch pudding, backwoods pie, jelly roll, and homemade ice cream. All of us had some of each. Eva said, "I've got so much cream and maple syrup yet, I have to think up ways for using them; I just daresn't let them waste."

An hour later, when the dishes were done and we sat in her front living room, she passed red shiny apples, buttered popcorn, a fruit drink, homemade candies and squares.

I love luscious desserts and revel in excuses to make them, but I avoid temptation by never making any except when my family and friends come for a meal and on rare occasions when I have a dessert and coffee party for about thirty people. Then I can splurge.

Last time I was planning what I would have, Norm said, "Make only one thing or everyone will want to taste everything and you won't have enough." But how could I enjoy making the same thing five times? One taste and I'd have had it all.

I followed my own inclination and came up with Baba au Rhum, Plum Crumble, Grand Marnier Café, Sour Cream Peach Pie, mixed fruit in a bowl, and Seed Cake.

Norma was right: every one tried everything. Nothing was left except a feeling of satisfaction that my party had been a culinary success.

FRUIT ROLL
8 to 10 servings

Fruit rolled in a fluffy biscuit blanket baked in syrup. Try it with rhubarb, or strawberries, raspberries, peaches, apples, raisins, any other fruit you fancy.

Syrup:
2 cups water
1¹/₂ cups brown sugar
Butter the size of an egg

Biscuit dough:
2 cups flour
2 tablespoons sugar
1 teaspoon salt
1 tablespoon baking powder
¹/₃ cup shortening
²/₃ cup milk, or more

Filling:
3 tablespoons softened butter
¹/₂ cup brown sugar
3 cups cubed fruit (fresh or frozen)
¹/₂ teaspoon cinnamon (optional)

Blend the syrup ingredients in a 13″ x 9″ baking pan and put it in the oven while it is heating to 400°F. Meantime sift the dry ingredients for the biscuit dough; cut in the shortening till fine, stir in the milk to make a soft dough. Roll the dough ⅓ inch thick into an oblong about 6″ x 12″ and spread with the filling. Roll like a jelly roll, pinch the edges to seal. Slice 1½ inches thick and place the slices cut-side-down in the pan of boiling syrup, or lay the entire roll in the hot syrup in the baking pan. Bake the cut rolls in a 400°F oven for about 20 minutes, 30 to 40 for the uncut version. Serve warm.

EVA'S MINCE MEAT ROLLS

Instead of the fruit filling Eva spreads the dough with 1½ cups prepared mince meat, makes the syrup in a saucepan, and pours the hot syrup over the rolls at the table.

APPLE BETTY

Another version. You just can't beat an Apple Betty. At the bottom of this recipe someone named George wrote, "Undoubtedly delicious."

**1 quart sliced apples,
   not peeled**
¾ cup sugar
1 tablespoon flour
1 teaspoon cinnamon

Topping:
**1 cup rolled oats or wheat
   flakes**
½ cup brown sugar
½ cup flour
¼ teaspoon soda
¼ teaspoon baking powder
¼ cup melted butter

Core and slice the apples. Blend the next three ingredients then stir the mixture into the apples in a buttered baking dish. Combine the rolled oats, brown sugar, flour, soda and baking powder with the melted butter to make crumbs. Pour the crumbs over the apple mixture in the casserole and bake at 375°F for 35 to 40 minutes. Serve hot or cold with whipped or vanilla ice cream. You'll find out George wasn't wrong.

AUNTIE'S APPLE DUMPLINGS
10 servings

When Mother made apple dumplings we didn't want anything else for supper.

2 cups flour
2 teaspoons baking powder
1 teaspoon salt
²/₃ cup shortening
¹/₂ cup milk
5 apples peeled, cored and
   cut in half
3 tablespoons sugar

¹/₂ teaspoon cinnamon

Sauce:
2 cups brown sugar
2 cups water
¹/₄ cup butter
¹/₄ teaspoon cinnamon or
   nutmeg

Sift together the flour, baking powder and salt; cut in the shortening until the mixture is crumbly. Add the milk and mix just enough to hold the dough together. Pat the dough into a ball, put it on a floured surface and roll it till it is about ¹/₄ inch thick. Cut the rolled dough into squares – more or less – large enough to cover half an apple placed on each square. Fill the cavity in the apple with the sugar and cinnamon mixed together. Bring the corners of the square of dough to the centre top and pinch them and the sides together to cover the apple completely. Put the apples an inch apart in a buttered baking pan and pour the sauce over them. To make the sauce: simply combine all the ingredients and pour over the dumplings in the pan. Bake at 375°F for about 40 minutes. Have a look before that. Serve the dumplings hot with whole milk or cream poured over them if you think it necessary.

EVA'S FRUIT BATTER PUDDING

Made with fresh or frozen or soaked dried fruit, whatever you happen to have.

3 tablespoons butter
¹/₃ cup sugar
1 egg
1 cup flour
1¹/₂ teaspoons baking powder

³/₄ cup milk
¹/₄ teaspoon salt
¹/₂ teaspoon almond
   flavouring

In a buttered baking dish Eva puts at least 2 cupfuls of fruit, usually more, with sugar to taste. Over it she pours the batter, mixed in the order given. She bakes it at 350°F for about half an hour. Serves it with whipped or ice cream, or just so.

DRIED FRUIT PUDDING

Lorna has been experimenting with the dried mixed fruit she buys at the health food store. She soaks it in cider, apple juice, or white wine overnight, or for several hours, adds sugar to taste blended with 1 tablespoon of corn starch, or 2 of flour; she puts it in a buttered baking dish and covers it with a batter similar to Eva's Fruit Batter Pudding, and bakes it at 350°F for about half an hour. She said it was a great success.

SPEEDY APPLE NUT PUDDING

It didn't take longer than twelve minutes to get this dessert into the oven on the day my publisher, Jack McClelland, called to say he'd be coming from Toronto in time for lunch. The pudding turned out well and Jack had two helpings.

1 egg	**1 teaspoon baking powder**
³/₄ cup white or brown sugar	**1¹/₂ cups chopped apples,**
¹/₂ teaspoon salt	**not peeled**
¹/₂ cup flour	**³/₄ cup finely chopped nuts**

Beat the egg, pour in the sugar and salt and beat together. By hand, stir in the flour and baking powder sifted together. Stir in the apples and nuts. Spread in a buttered 9-inch pie plate or a square cake pan, if you'd rather serve squares than wedges. Bake in a 325°F oven for about 35 to 40 minutes. Serve hot or cold with whipped cream or ice cream.

One day in August I had dinner with a friend who served imported California green seedless grapes for dessert. Can you imagine that? When the Kitchener and Waterloo markets were teeming with homegrown peaches, plums, apricots, apples, pears, cantaloupes and grapes in all their glorious splendour.

FRUIT FRITTERS
for 6 people

This recipe was in a great grandmother's cookbook. Almost any kind of fruit may be used in fritters: apples, bananas, pears, peaches, plums, etc., are all suitable. Apples should be pared, cored and cut into round slices about half an inch thick. They may be seasoned with a little lemon juice and nutmeg. Bananas should be cut into slices about an inch thick. Pears may be cut in quarters. Plums may be pitted with a lump of sugar replacing the pit.

2 egg yolks	2 tablespoons melted butter
¹/₂ cup milk	2 egg whites
1 cup flour	Lard or shortening for
¹/₂ teaspoon salt	deep frying
2 teaspoons sugar	Powdered sugar

Beat the egg yolks till light and add the milk. Pour this on the flour and beat until smooth. Now add the salt, sugar and butter; beat vigorously for 5 minutes. Set the mixture away in a cool place until it is time to use it. Prepare 6 large tart apples, or as many pears, peaches, bananas, or plums. Have lard about 3 inches deep in the kettle and very hot. Beat the whites of the eggs to a stiff froth and stir into the batter. Dip the slices of fruit into the batter, coating them thoroughly. Lift the fruit by passing a fork under it, and drop into the hot fat. Cook for 3 minutes till golden all round; drain on brown paper for half a minute. Arrange on a hot dish, sprinkle with powdered sugar and serve immediately with a fork and dessert spoon.

GLOWING CHERRY BETTY

Loaded with nourishment, you won't have to force anyone to eat this. Try it with various fruits. Stir together in a bowl:

2 cups pitted cherries, frozen or fresh, with their juice	3 tablespoons flour
¹/₂ cup white or brown sugar mixed with	¹/₂ teaspoon almond flavouring

Turn the mixture into a buttered 9″ x 9″ cake pan.

Topping:

½ cup rolled oats
½ cup whole wheat flour
½ cup wheat germ
1 cup shelled, toasted
   sunflower seeds

¼ cup brown sugar or honey
4 tablespoons butter or
   margarine

Mix topping ingredients well and sprinkle over the cherry mixture. Bake at 350°F for 45 to 50 minutes. Serve hot or cold with liquid cream, whipped cream or ice cream.

NEW ORLEANS BREAD PUDDING

Norm and Ralph ordered Bread Pudding at a restaurant in New Orleans; they liked it so well that they went back next day to have it again and get the recipe from the chef. I've never been fond of bread pudding but must admit this has redeeming features.

1½ cups milk
¼ cup butter
2 cups bread cubes
1 cup sugar
3 eggs, beaten

1 cup raisins
Sprinkle of cinnamon
1 teaspoon rum flavouring,
   or more of the real thing

Warm the milk, add the butter, and when it has melted pour the hot liquid over the bread cubes. Soak for about 5 minutes, then add the sugar, eggs, raisins, cinnamon, and rum. Pour the mixture into a buttered 8″ x 8″ baking dish, set it in a pan of hot water in a 300°F oven and bake about 40 to 50 minutes until the pudding is puffed up and brown and a knife inserted in the centre comes out clean.

Serve with this super sauce:

1½ cups white sugar
2 cups water
4 thin slices orange

4 thin slices lemon
½ to 1 cup rum

Simmer the sugar, water, and fruit slices. Cool and add the rum. Pour a little over the pudding and garnish it with whipped cream.

CLARA MAY'S STEAMED BREAD PUDDING

The Ingraham family was always glad when there was enough bread left from last week's baking to make this great pudding.

2 cups dried bread
Water
¹/₄ cup sugar, white or
   brown
1 egg
3 tablespoons shortening
¹/₂ teaspoon soda

1 cup molasses
1 cup raisins
Lemon or vanilla or
   rum flavouring
1 teaspoon cinnamon
¹/₂ teaspoon ginger
About 1 cup flour

Moisten the bread with water then squeeze it out till it's almost dry, rub it together with your hands till there are no lumps, Clara May told me. Add all the other ingredients and finally about 1 cup of flour till the mixture is like a cake batter. Put it in the top of a double boiler or in a steamer and steam for about 1¹/₂ hours. Serve with a brown sugar sauce flavoured with rum. No wonder this was Henry's favourite puddin'.

EVA'S STEAMED SUET PUDDING

Humidify your house while you enjoy the old-fashioned aroma of molasses and raisins.

¹/₂ cup finely ground suet
   or shortening
³/₄ cup molasses
1 cup buttermilk
¹/₄ cup brown sugar
   (optional)

1 cup raisins
2 teaspoons soda
Add spices if you like
Enough flour to make a firm
   batter

Mix in the order given, pour into a buttered bowl, cover, and steam for an hour. Serve with a sauce:

1 cup brown sugar
2 tablespoons flour
2 cups boiling water

1 teaspoon vanilla or rum
2 tablespoons butter

Blend the sugar and flour, add the boiling water gradually until the sauce thickens. Stir in the flavouring and butter. Eva says, "I don't always measure, I just put things in."

LORNA'S CHOCOLATE RICE PUDDING

The cooking smells were tantalizing one day while my family and I were playing Parcheesi. We could hardly wait to eat.

2 cups cooked rice
2 cups milk
1/2 cup white sugar
3 tablespoons cocoa
1/2 teaspoon salt

1 teaspoon vanilla
Piece of butter (the size
  depends on your waistline)

Put the cooked rice and milk in the top of a double boiler, mix the sugar, cocoa, and salt and stir into the rice. Cook over gently boiling water for 45 minutes. Keep looking at it and give it a stir now and then. It should be creamy, not stiff. Add the vanilla and butter before serving.

HOT FUDGE PUDDING
6 servings

This is a dandy little pudding to make on a cold winter day. Ruby says she always made this when her family was mad at her. Then they weren't.

1 cup sifted flour
2 teaspoons baking powder
1/2 teaspoon salt
3/4 cup sugar
6 tablespoons cocoa
1/2 cup milk
1 teaspoon vanilla

3 tablespoons melted
  shortening
3/4 cup chopped walnuts
3/4 cup brown sugar
2 tablespoons butter, melted
1 3/4 cups hot water

Sift the dry ingredients and 2 tablespoons of cocoa. Stir together the milk, vanilla and melted shortening; add to the dry ingredients, mix well, then stir in the nuts. Pour into a 9″ square pan. Now mix the brown sugar and 4 remaining tablespoons cocoa; sprinkle the mixture over the batter in the pan. Pour on the melted butter then carefully pour on the hot water. Bake at 350°F for about 40 minutes. Serve hot. They'll love you for this.

GRANDMOTHER'S CROWNEST

An upside-down apple pudding. Martina Schneiker says this is her husband's favourite dessert.

12 medium apples
1 cup white sugar

Batter:
1 cup flour
3 tablespoons sugar
1 teaspoon baking powder
¹/₂ teaspoon salt
3 heaping tablespoons
shortening
¹/₄ cup milk

Topping:
1 pint whipping cream
1 teaspoon white sugar
Cinnamon

Core and slice the apples, stir in the 1 cup sugar and pour into a buttered 9″ x 13″ pan. Sift the flour with 3 tablespoons sugar, baking powder, and salt; blend in the shortening. Pour in the milk and mix until the right consistency for rolling. Roll out the dough to cover the apples in the pan, venting the top. Bake at 350°F for 35 minutes. Cool completely. When ready to serve invert on a platter, giving it a quick flip. Cover with sweetened whipped cream and a sprinkle of cinnamon.

MRS. FABING'S PLUM CAKE

In the fall when prune plums are ripe, people drive miles and miles to Fabing's Restaurant beside the Sunoco station in St. Jacobs to get a piece of the best plum cake that has ever been produced. But the recipe is a well-guarded secret.

PLUM FOOL

This is a favourite British way of dealing with plums.
Put any number of whole plums and a very small amount of water into a large saucepan, cover and cook slowly over low heat till the plums are soft. Put them through a sieve, discarding the pits and skin that remain. The result should be a

smooth and fairly thick purée. Sweeten to taste – some plums will need more sugar than others.

Set the plums aside until they are completely cold, then stir in fresh thick cream, in an amount equal to the amount of plums. Refrigerate to chill thoroughly, but do not freeze. The result is smooth, rich and light. My Devon friend Kath says that actually many British cooks stir in thick cornstarch-custard sauce in place of the cream, it's more economical. You know how the British are always putting custard on their desserts – even an apple pie or gooseberry tart.

PARTY PLUM CAKE
9 servings

This glazed dessert has a professional look but is easy to make.

¹/₄ cup butter	¹/₂ cup milk
1 cup sugar	2 egg whites, stiffly beaten
2 egg yolks, slightly beaten	2 cups pitted plums; blue or
1¹/₂ cups flour	green – but the blue are
1 teaspoon baking powder	prettier
¹/₂ teaspoon salt	

Cream together the butter, sugar and egg yolks. Sift together the flour, baking powder, and salt; add to the creamed mixture alternately with the milk. Fold in the beaten egg whites. Pour the batter into a greased 9″ x 9″ cake pan, place the plums neatly on top. Sprinkle over the plums crumbs made of:

¹/₂ cup brown sugar	1 teaspoon cinnamon
2 tablespoons flour	¹/₄ cup butter

Bake in a 350°F oven for about 45 minutes. While the cake is baking blend the glaze:

³/₄ cup icing sugar	¹/₂ teaspoon vanilla or almond
1 tablespoon cream or milk	extract

When the cake comes out of the oven, dribble the glaze generously over it. When it cools it will be shiny and handsome. Serve it warm or cold, with or without ice cream.

MOCHA NUT TORTONI

Lorna gave us this super dessert one night at dinner; she served it in the little glass dishes in which it was frozen, eliminating the temptation to have second helpings – which we certainly didn't need, but longed to have.

2 egg whites
¼ cup granulated sugar
2 cups whipping cream
Another ¼ cup granulated sugar
2 tablespoons instant coffee powder

2 egg yolks, slightly beaten
1 teaspoon vanilla
½ cup semi-sweet chocolate pieces, or 2 squares
½ cup minced, toasted almonds

Beat the egg whites until quite stiff; then gradually add ¼ cup sugar while beating. Whip the cream with other ¼ cup sugar and coffee. Add the egg yolks and vanilla. Fold into the beaten egg whites. Melt the chocolate over hot, but not boiling, water, then cool slightly; quickly fold the chocolate and almonds into the egg-white mixture. Turn into 12 custard cups or 16 two-ounce paper soufflé cups. Freeze until firm then freezer-wrap and freeze longer. To serve garnish with almonds and whipped cream. It was so gooooood.

MOCHA RUM MOUSSE
6 servings

Lorna says this is a quick and easy one to prepare in your blender.

6 ounces semi-sweet chocolate pieces
5 tablespoons hot strong coffee

4 egg yolks
2 tablespoons light rum
4 egg whites

Put the chocolate, coffee, egg yolks, and rum in your blender; cover and blend at high speed for 1 minute. Beat the egg whites until stiff but not dry. Slowly pour in the chocolate mixture, and with a spatula fold until no egg white shows. Spoon into sherbet glasses and refrigerate for 1 hour at least. Top with whipped cream – if you think you must.

EVA'S ICE CREAM

Ice cream is so handy to have in the freezer to serve with other desserts or with fruit or a sauce. Joanna and Julia and little Florence love it pure.

2¹/₂ cups whipping cream **Pinch of salt**
6 eggs, separated **1 teaspoon flavouring**
1 cup sugar

Whip the cream. Beat the egg whites stiff, fold in the beaten yolks and the sugar. Fold in the whipped cream, the salt, and flavouring. Pour into freezer trays and freeze for several hours, then fold it over to prevent liquid from forming on the bottom. After another hour fold it over again.

GINGER ICE CREAM
6 to 8 servings

¹/₃ cup preserved ginger **¹/₂ teaspoon gelatine**
¹/₃ cup sugar **1 tablespoon cold water**
¹/₃ cup water **1 pint whipping cream**
3 egg yolks, beaten

Cook the ginger, sugar, and water to 230°F then a bit at a time blend it with the beaten egg yolks and cook in a double boiler until it thickens. Soak the gelatine for 5 minutes in the spoonful of water and add it to the ginger mixture while it is hot. Cool it and when it is really cold, but not stiff, fold it into the stiffly whipped cream. Pour into a refrigerator tray and freeze without stirring further. Good.

COFFEE CARAMEL ICE CREAM

Another of Lorna's: for a hot day in July after a long, long swim.

1 cup sugar **¹/₄ cup strong coffee**
1¹/₂ cups scalded milk **Pinch salt**
3 egg yolks **1 pint whipping cream**
3 tablespoons flour or **1 teaspoon vanilla**
    2 tablespoons corn starch

Melt the sugar over low heat until caramel colour; add it to the scalded milk, stirring continuously. Beat the egg yolks, add the flour, coffee and salt. Stir into the hot milk and cook on *low* heat until thickened. Cool in fridge. Whip the cream, add vanilla and the chilled mixture; mix well but not overly. Freeze 2 hours before devouring. Needs no stirring during the process, thus avoiding temptation.

CRANBERRY ICE CREAM

Lorna's recipes are always different, delicious, and lovely to look at.

2 teaspoons gelatine
1/4 cup cold water
2 cups cranberry sauce
1/2 cup orange juice
A few grains of salt

1 tablespoon lemon juice
2 tablespoons corn syrup
1 1/4 cups whipping cream
1 cup cut-up marshmallows

Soften the gelatine in the cold water. Put cranberry sauce into a pan and mush it until the berries are well broken. Add the orange juice and bring to the scalding point. Stir in the softened gelatine. Add salt, lemon juice, corn syrup. Cool completely. Beat the whipping cream until stiff. Fold in the marshmallows and the cold cranberry mixture. Freeze until firm, stirring once or twice.

BANANA PRUNE WHIP
4 servings

This is a tart little dessert to whip up in your blender.

10 pitted prunes
1/2 cup water
2 tablespoons lemon juice
2 ripe bananas

2 or 3 tablespoons dark
brown sugar or honey
1/3 cup light cream

Put the prunes in a saucepan with the water and lemon juice. Simmer them for 5 minutes then let them cool in the liquid. Pour the whole bit into your blender with the bananas broken into chunks, the sugar and cream. Spin until the mixture is thick and light. Divide it among 4 serving dishes; it deserves stemmed glasses. Chill for at least an hour, garnish with chopped pecans and watch the happy faces.

PATSY BEAN'S QUICK, EASY AND DELICIOUS DESSERT

Patsy says this is the best dessert she knows. You can make it in 5 minutes, keep it indefinitely, serve it any time, and everyone loves it.

5 cups rice crispies
1 cup melted butter
1 cup coconut

¹/₂ cup white or brown sugar, or half of each

"Slosh it all together till it's well mixed," Patsy says. "Use your hands, it's messy but easier." Put half of it into a buttered pyrex cake pan – a big one. Cover it with ice cream, as thick as you like, then put the other half of the rice crispies mixture on top. Put it in your freezer where it will turn hard and keep as long as you let it. You need a sharp knife to cut it, that's all. Patsy says you can double or triple it if you need it for a crowd.

WATERMELON BOAT

The day Dorothy Cressman came to our Book Group's annual pot-luck supper carrying a scooped-out half watermelon filled with balls of cantaloupe, honey dew melon, watermelon, pineapple pieces, strawberries, and green seedless grapes, with mint sprigs, we all cheered at the sight. And the refreshing taste was as good as the look.

GRAND MARNIER CAFÉ
4 to 6 servings

A few tablespoons of brandy, wine, or liqueur can give a bland, easy-to-make dessert both flavour and flair. Watch the reaction of your guests when you tell them your secret ingredient.

1 envelope unflavoured
  gelatine
2 cups milk or cream
1 rounded tablespoon
  instant coffee powder

¹/₂ teaspoon salt
¹/₄ cup sugar
1 or 2 tablespoons Grand
  Marnier, or whatever
2 egg whites, beaten stiff

Soften the gelatine in the cold milk in a saucepan, add the coffee powder and heat, stirring until the gelatine and coffee are dissolved, no longer. Add salt and sugar, then chill until it is slightly thickened. Stir in the Grand Marnier, Cointreau, or whatever you prefer or have. Fold in the stiffly beaten egg whites. Pour the lovely stuff into a glass bowl that will show it off, or into individual frosted sherbets. Let it set – a day ahead of your party if you like. A piece of fruit cake goes well with it.

QUIVERING EGGNOG
8 servings

Easy and soothing at Christmas time.

3 eggs
¹/₂ cup sugar
Dash of salt
1 teaspoon vanilla

2 cups milk
1 cup cream
¹/₂ cup rum or sherry
Sprinkle of nutmeg

Put all this in your blender and give it a good whirl – then don't drink it. Give it a chance to quiver.

2 envelopes gelatine
  moistened in ¹/₄ cup water

³/₄ cup hot milk

Dissolve the moistened gelatine in the hot milk, pour it into the blender with the eggnog, whirl for a second then pour it into a pretty glass bowl and keep it in a cool place till it is set. Sprinkle nutmeg on top and serve it with Christmas cake and cookies.

COFFEE JELLY

You wouldn't waste leftover coffee, would you? All you need is 1 tablespoon gelatine for every 2 cups coffee.

Moisten the gelatine in ¼ cup cold coffee. Heat ½ cup coffee to almost boiling and stir it into the gelatine till it is dissolved. Add the remaining 1¼ cups cold coffee, stir it well and chill till the jelly sets. Serve it with plain or sweetened whipped cream and pass some crisp fresh cookies.

LEMON SYLLABUB

This is the favourite dessert at Rundles Restaurant in Stratford. The *chef de cuisine* whips it up in a few minutes, the guests linger lovingly over every sip.

³⁄₄ **cup fine granulated sugar** **2 large lemons**
¹⁄₂ **cup dry white wine** **2 cups whipping cream**

Whisk the sugar and white wine. Take the zest off the lemons and squeeze out the juice; add both zest and juice to the sugar-wine mixture and blend well. Add the cream and whisk until thick and light. (You can do this with your electric mixer.) Pour into individual wine glasses, chill for 2 hours, garnish with a twist of lemon and a sprig of mint. At Rundles they serve it with a couple of lady fingers and listen to the exclamations of delight.

STRAWBERRY DELIGHT
8″ x 13″ pan

Light, refreshing and delicious, this was my favourite of the seven desserts Laurie Bennett served at a dessert party on St. Patrick's Day. She made it five days in advance.

Bottom: *Top:*
¹⁄₂ **cup butter** **2 cups frozen strawberries**
¹⁄₄ **cup brown sugar** ²⁄₃ **cup white sugar**
1 cup flour **2 egg whites, beaten**
¹⁄₂ **cup chopped pecans** **1 cup cold evaporated milk**
 1 tablespoon lemon juice

Blend the butter, sugar, and flour, add the chopped pecans; pat into an 8″ x 13″ pan and bake at 350°F for 10 minutes. Then cool. Beat the frozen strawberries, add the sugar. Beat the egg whites till stiff and fold them into the strawberry and sugar mixture. Beat the cold evaporated milk and lemon juice, then add to the strawberry mixture. Pour over the cold crust and freeze till you're ready to use it – if you can avoid its discovery that long.

CHOCOLATE MINT MOUSSE
4 to 6 servings

My downfall.

9 chocolate covered mint
   patties
1 teaspoon water
2 egg yolks

2 egg whites, beaten stiff
1/2 cup whipping cream,
   plus more for topping

Heat the patties and water in a double boiler, stirring until the patties are melted and the mixture is smooth but not really hot. Beat in the 2 egg yolks one at a time, stir for 1 minute over the heat of the double boiler. Cool. Fold the cooled chocolate mixture into the stiffly beaten egg whites, then gently fold in the stiffly whipped cream. Spoon into individual stemmed glasses. You don't need much. Chill until serving time. Garnish with green tinted whipped cream and a green cherry or sprig of mint.

BABA AU RHUM
12 large, 24 small babas

This favourite dessert of France is always greeted with exclamations, "You made babas! I thought they had to be imported." I tasted my first baba at a little café in the shadow of Sacré Coeur in Paris, and it wasn't as good as this recipe, which is not at all tricky, and the babas freeze perfectly.

1 tablespoon yeast
1/4 cup lukewarm water
1/4 cup milk
1/2 cup butter
1/2 teaspoon salt
1/4 cup sugar

1 cup flour, sifted
3 eggs at room temperature
1 tablespoon rum
1/2 cup chopped citron,
   mixed peel or currants
Another 1/2 cup flour

Dissolve the yeast in water. Heat the milk and butter, pour into a large bowl, stir in the salt and sugar; let cool to lukewarm then add the yeast. Stir in 1 cup flour and beat in the eggs, one at a time. Stir in the rum and fruit, then the ¹/₂ cup flour. Cover and let rise in a warm place until doubled. Spoon the bubbly batter into greased muffin tins or custard cups and let rise again until double. Bake in a 400°F oven for 10 minutes. Remove them from the pans and pour over them the following Rum Sauce. Or cool them, wrap them in foil and freeze them. (Reheat and soak in the sauce.)

Rum Sauce:
1 cup brown sugar
1 cup corn syrup
¹/₂ **cup water**
1 tablespoon butter
¹/₂ **cup rum**

Heat all but the rum to boiling point, stirring occasionally. Add the rum. Pour over the warm babas and let them soak up enough sauce to make them moist and spongy. They should be served warm. For a party I put mine in a wide dish that holds all of them and alongside have a glass bowl filled with whipped cream to blob over each serving. There's never a baba left.

MOCHA TORTE
(John's Birthday Party Cake)

John would have no other. Ruby says it will serve 12 generously but has been known to be eaten by eight.

Buy or make a 9¹/₂-inch angel cake. Slice it carefully into 5 horizontal layers. Put together with filling the day before the party and chill in fridge over night.

Mocha filling – cream well:
1 cup butter or margarine
1¹/₂ cups icing sugar
Add pinch of salt
1 teaspoon vanilla
2 egg yolks

Beat thoroughly and add:
2 squares bitter chocolate, melted
6 tablespoons double-strength coffee
2 egg whites beaten stiff and folded in

In the early afternoon of the party ice the torte with whipped cream sweetened and flavoured with vanilla. Garnish with curls of semi-sweet chocolate, or however you like. Chill until needed.

ENGLISH CHRISTMAS PUDDING
2 medium-sized puddings

An old favourite of Jean Salter's family. Jean's father (now retired) was a pilot who brought the big ships into port at Southampton.

2 cups raisins	¹/₂ pound beef suet,
1 cup currants	finely shredded
¹/₂ cup chopped candied peel	2 cups dry white bread-
¹/₂ cup blanched almonds	crumbs
1 cup flour	Grated rind of 1 lemon
¹/₄ teaspoon salt	6 eggs, beaten
1 teaspoon baking powder	1¹/₂ cups brown sugar
1 teaspoon mixed spice	¹/₄ cup brandy or rum
1 teaspoon nutmeg	Stout or heavy ale to mix

Clean the fruit and chop the peel and almonds. Sift the flour, salt, baking powder, and spices together; add the finely shredded suet and rub it into the flour. Add the fruit, breadcrumbs and grated rind of lemon. Beat the eggs, brown sugar and rum together then mix well with the fruit mixture, adding enough stout or ale to give the batter a stiff dropping consistency. It is best if you can leave it to stand overnight before putting into greased bowls. Cover and steam for several hours. Jean says she doubles this recipe because the puddings keep so well from one Christmas to the next, even out of the freezer.

CONNIE'S CRISPY CRUNCH ANGEL CAKE TORTE

Here is an expensive company dessert that violates my economic principles. But it is so easy to assemble and so scrummy to eat that you might like to try it. You have to go out and shop for everything that goes into it, but if you're entertaining you'll have to shop anyway.

1 angel cake (you can make it   2 cups whipping cream
  or buy one ready made)
8 Crispy Crunch candy bars
  (I hope the price doesn't
  go up again before you
  read this.)

Cut the cake in 3 layers. Whip the cream and break the candy
bars into it, reserving some to sprinkle on top. Slather the mixture on each layer, sides and top. Then savour every delicious,
extravagant mouthful – or maybe you'd better just imagine it.

DESSERT SAUCES

BUTTERSCOTCH SAUCE
about 1¹/₂ cups

1 cup brown sugar   1 cup cold water
2 tablespoons corn starch   1 teaspoon vanilla or rum
¹/₈ teaspoon salt   flavouring or 3 to 4
2 tablespoons butter   tablespoons rum or brandy
2 dessertspoons water

Combine the sugar, corn starch, salt, butter, and 2 dessertspoons water in a saucepan over heat; stir until it melts and
turns brown. Add 1 cup cold water, cook till it thickens.
Remove from heat, add flavouring. It's even very good without
rum.

RUM OR BRANDY HARD SAUCE

Take equal quantities of softened butter and icing sugar and
beat thoroughly together. Slowly beat in brandy or rum, a few
drops at a time. When you can mix in no more without it
separating, put it in the refrigerator to harden and serve with
hot Christmas pudding.

FUDGE SAUCE – HOT OR COLD
about 2¹/₂ cups

Is there anything better than hot fudge sauce on ice cream? We used to go to the Busy Bee every night after school for a Hot Fudge Sundae with toasted almonds – until they raised the price to 15 cents. Miserable day!

¹/₂ **cup cocoa**
1 cup sugar
¹/₄ **teaspoon salt**
1 cup corn syrup

¹/₂ **cup milk**
2 to 4 tablespoons butter
1 teaspoon vanilla

Put everything but the vanilla in a saucepan and cook over medium heat, stirring all the time; bring to a full rolling boil and let it go for 3 minutes. Take from the heat and add the vanilla. Serve hot for a more fudgy flavour.

Store it in the fridge with a lid that's hard to get off. It will thicken but can be thinned for pouring by placing in a pan of hot water. It won't last long.

RUBY'S SHERRY SAUCE

1¹/₂ tablespoons corn starch
¹/₂ **cup sugar**
¹/₄ **teaspoon salt**
1 cup hot water

1 lemon, rind and juice
1 tablespoon butter
¹/₂ **cup sherry (or**
      whiskey or brandy)

Combine corn starch, sugar and salt, add water, grated lemon rind and juice; cook gently, stirring constantly until thick and clear. Add butter and sherry. Serve hot.

16

Odds and Ends and Uncategoricals

GRANOLA
about 4 quarts

Ever since Greg Kozack gave me a sample jar of his granola I have been a granola freak. I eat some every day, thinking up new ways to use it without actually gobbling it up in spoonfuls. It's super for breakfast on yogurt with black currant juice or maple syrup. I love it on ice cream or bananas, in muffins and bars, and sprinkled on desserts – anything that needs a bit of crunch. Belle has some every morning with milk as a cereal.

5 cups rolled oats
  (not quick cooking)
4 cups wheat flakes
2 cups wheat germ
2 cups bran
2 cups sunflower seeds
2 cups chopped orange or
  grapefruit peel

1 or 2 cups coconut (optional)
2 cups raisins
2 cups nuts
2 cups soya nuts (optional)
1 cup honey
1 cup molasses
¹/₂ cup vegetable oil

Mix all the dry ingredients but the coconut, raisins, and nuts in a big roasting pan. Heat the honey, molasses, and vegetable oil until well blended then pour over the dry ingredients and mix thoroughly. Put the pan in a 300°F oven and set your timer for 20 minutes. Stir the mixture well, reset your timer and keep repeating until the granola is golden and dry. Stir in the raisins and coconut halfway along. If your nuts are not roasted put them in from the beginning; if you use salted peanuts – as I do – put them in after you turn off your oven.

The granola must be well toasted and crisp or it won't keep well. When mine seems just about right I turn off the oven and leave the granola in it until it cools, stirring a couple of times at first. When it's cold, put it into tightly covered jars and keep in a cool cupboard.

My friend Laurence McNaught gave me a bottle of his granola last summer. It was fantastic. I think he used clarified butter instead of oil and lots of almonds.

EVA'S BREAKFAST CEREAL

While Eva was telling me about this her three little girls said they wanted some – at four in the afternoon. They ate it with milk poured over it and then wanted more.

12 cups oatmeal	**1¹/₂ teaspoons salt**
6 cups wheat germ	**6 cups coconut**
3 cups brown sugar	
1 cup vegetable oil or melted butter	

Mix and toast in the oven until the coconut is browned. Eva's was golden. I tasted a bit of it and wished I could have breakfast at her house occasionally.

YOGURT

"I don't like yogurt," I used to say – though the only yogurt I'd tasted was gucked-up with synthetic fruit flavouring and some that had been on a supermarket shelf too long.

My nutrition-conscious friends kept telling me yogurt was an essential of a healthy diet. They said it was an ancient bacterial culture carried in goatskin bellies wherever people went on their camels or asses or galloping Arabian steeds; that it preserved them from dysentery and stomach aches; it nourished them and they loved it.

All my yogurt friends are proselytizers. For years I resisted them. Until a few springs ago when I visited Kath Reeves in Devon: every morning for breakfast she ate yogurt with such enjoyment that I envied her. Finally I yielded to her pleas to just *try* some, well sprinkled with dark brown sugar and crispy squiggles of bran. I liked it. So well that every morning after that I helped demolish her supply.

When I returned to Canada I immediately bought a quart of plain yogurt at the store and ate it with maple syrup. Wow! It was good too with apple sauce. My favourite is with Ribena – bottled black currant juice – liberally sprinkled with granola. That is a perfect, lasting breakfast, one I look forward to so eagerly that I get up before dawn to enjoy it. (Actually my cats waken me; they like yogurt, too.)

I kept running out of yogurt. "Why not make your own," my friends said. Each one told me a different way of doing it. A few had yogurt-makers they had bought and found foolproof; one put hers in the oven at a very low temperature; in a book about yogurt I read other ways. From the various methods I devised my own. And it works. I've had only two failures in four years – and they were redeemable.

To make yogurt you need a starter culture which you can get from a friend, a health food place, or by buying plain yogurt, eating most of it and keeping some to start your batch. Two tablespoons is enough for 1 jar. I always make 3 quarts at a time, distributed in 4 instant coffee jars; when I'm alone that much lasts 2 weeks.

1. I put 2 tablespoons starter in the bottom of each jar.
2. I blend 1½ cups skim milk powder with 1 quart water; I do that 3 times, pouring each quart into the jars and stirring up the yogurt from the bottom. (If you prefer you can make yogurt with skim, 2%, or whole milk: you must scald it and

let it stand to room temperature before adding it to the starter which also should be at room temperature.)

3. I put my jars on a low rack in my big preserving kettle and fill the kettle with water from the hot water tap. I put my candy thermometer in it and add cold water if necessary till the temperature is about 100°F (37°C). I fill the kettle level with the milk in the jars. Then I put it on the small burner of my stove and set it at simmer. I set my timer to go off every hour to make sure the water temperature has not exceeded 110°F (43°C). It usually takes about 3½ to 5 hours for the yogurt to form. Don't despair. Look at it occasionally to be sure the temperature is constant; turn off the burner and start it again if necessary. Don't stir or jiggle the yogurt; it doesn't like to be agitated. Gently lift up a jar and you can tell if it has begun to thicken like custard.

4. When you are satisfied that it's done remove the jars from the kettle and put them in a cold place, cover them and eat some every day.

5. If – if – by some strange mischance the yogurt doesn't thicken, all is not lost. You still have milk. Try warming it again the next day. I did that once and it took. Or use it in baking in place of buttermilk, or – and I deplore this – dissolve enough gelatine in it to thicken but not stiffen it. With lots of granola it's tolerable.

When Kath visited me last summer and I proudly served her my yogurt, she said, "That's not proper yogurt; it should be made fresh every day with goat's milk."

EASTER CHEESE

The day after Easter, David invited me for supper because Bevvy had just made some Easter Cheese – a great thing to eat when the sap is flowing. Deliciously mild and tender, we put inch-thick pieces in fruit nappies and smothered them in fresh-run maple syrup.

Next day I called on Eva, not knowing that she was having a quilting. "Come in," she said happily, "you're just in time for the lunch." Fourteen ladies, most of them relatives, had been at her house since nine in the morning; she had given them dinner at noon and was giving them a bite before they went home for supper. She, too, had made Easter Cheese, firmer than Bevvy's and cut in thinner slices.

"We all have our own way to make it," she told me. I asked her if it could be kept very long. "Not at our house," she said. "It goes pretty quick." All the ladies, and I, went back for second helpings, covered with maple syrup, before we ate an iced white jelly roll with lemon filling and a chocolate jelly roll with chocolate filling and icing. This is Bevvy's recipe:

2 quarts sweet milk, skim or whole
6 or 7 eggs, beaten a little

1 pint buttermilk or sour milk
1 teaspoon salt
¹/₂ teaspoon sugar

Scald the sweet milk over moderate heat. Mix the beaten eggs and buttermilk, salt, and sugar, and stir slowly into the steaming milk. Stir it in well then cover and let stand for several minutes, about 10 or 20. Stir now and then till it separates, then reduce the heat. When fully separated, a few minutes more, pour it all through a colander with a white cloth inside it. Let it drain a couple of hours till it's dry, then turn out on a plate and it's ready to eat. Too bad Easter comes only once a year.

RICOTTA CHEESE

Jean Johnstone, author of *Wilderness Women*, sent me her recipe for ricotta cheese which Nancy could use in her lasagna.

1 quart milk

Juice of one lemon (2 tablespoons)

Put the milk over low heat and bring to the scalding point (150°F). Remove from heat. Stir in the lemon juice and the milk will curdle. Let the mix sit (without refrigeration) for 2 to 12 hours. This is the mellowing process, and it seems that the more patient you are, the mellower the cheese.

Place 2 thicknesses of cheesecloth in your strainer, place this draining device over a bowl. Pour the mix into the drainer and allow the whey to drain several hours until the curd is dry.

Flavour as you choose: mix with blue cheese, roquefort, peanut butter, honey, nuts, spices, or eat plain.

Get a candy thermometer – they're not just for candy – you need them to make cheese, yogurt and for deep-fat frying.

MOCK HONEY
2 quarts

This recipe came from Melvin Baumann's grandmother. Eva says she's never tried it because she's always had plenty of honey, but if you have a lawnful of clover and a couple of roses it might be fun to experiment. I guarantee nothing.

5 pints of sugar	**Petals of 2 roses**
¹/₂ teaspoon ground alum	**18 red clover flowers**
3 cups hot water	**30 white clover flowers**

Put sugar, alum, and water in a saucepan on the stove and boil 4 minutes – no longer or it will get too thick. Pour this over the separated petals of 2 roses, 18 red clover flowers and 30 white ones. Let stand 15 minutes then strain and put in sterilized jars. That's beating the bees.

PRESERVED GINGER

Belle loves ginger and uses it in baking and candies; she preserves her own. She scrubs the ginger root she buys at the store, boils it for hours till it is tender. Then she peels it, keeping the water that the ginger was boiled in. Harold Horwood preserves ginger too, but he peels his first because it takes less time to boil it before it is tender – but the peeling is tougher.

They both cut the boiled ginger in pieces, measure the water it was boiled in, add an equal amount of sugar and simmer it 5 minutes to make a syrup. They boil the ginger pieces in the syrup for 5 minutes, then put it and the syrup in sterilized little jars for special occasions.

EVER-READY PEEL – ORANGE, LEMON OR GRAPEFRUIT

How often do you come across a recipe that requires a tablespoon or so of grated peel? Do you always have it? I do. Whenever I buy oranges with thin soft peel – navel, temple, or tangerines – I peel them, put the peel in a plastic bag in the freezer of my kitchen fridge and I always have orange peel whenever I need it.

When a recipe calls for a bit of orange rind – or a lot of it – I take what I want out of the bag, pop some into my blender, give it a whirl till the peel is finely chopped; sometimes I add the liquid that is part of the recipe to get better results. It's all so easy, the orange tastes fresh and is always available when oranges aren't.

BELLE'S GINGER CREAMS

These are divine.

2 cups white sugar	2 tablespoons butter
1 cup brown sugar	1 teaspoon vanilla
¾ cup milk	½ cup finely chopped
2 tablespoons corn syrup	preserved ginger

Stirring until the sugar is dissolved, Belle brings the sugar, milk, and corn syrup to a boil over medium heat, letting it reach 238°F on her candy thermometer. She drops in the butter, letting it melt on top. When the mixture has cooled to lukewarm, she beats it until it thickens then adds the vanilla and ginger. She pours it out on a buttered pie plate, cuts it in squares before it hardens and doesn't resist temptation.

MAPLE FUDGE

Eva told me Velina Weber's maple fudge is the best she's ever tasted.

1 quart fresh cream	1 cup maple syrup
9 cups brown sugar	1 cup corn syrup
3 cups white sugar	¼ pound butter or margarine

Mix all together; cook over medium heat until the soft-ball stage (238°F); remove from the stove and beat and beat until it is creamy and thick. Eva says you could easily make half or one-third of the recipe if you don't have that much cream. She milks twenty-one cows every day and has lots of it.

ALMOND CHOCOLATE CRUNCH

Lorna gave me some of this at Christmas, crisp, crunchy, professional; as good or better than the kind I used to buy in an expensive candy shop that shall be nameless.

1 cup butter
2 cups light brown sugar
¹/₃ cup water
¹/₂ cup chopped unblanched
    almonds, toasted

4 ounces unsweetened
    chocolate, melted

Cook the butter, sugar, and water together to the hard crack stage (290° to 300°F). Remove from the heat and stir in the almonds. Pour into buttered 9″ x 14″ pan. When cool spread with the melted chocolate. When crisp break in pieces. Makes 1¹/₂ pounds. Use salted mixed nuts if you'd rather, whole or coarsely chopped. You can also spread the chocolate on both sides; if you do, double the amount of chocolate. These are super.

THE HONEY CURE

If you are run down, irritable and always tired, try taking 3 or 4 teaspoons of honey a day for several months. (That should sweeten and fatten you.)

Do you believe that honey is good for insomnia, constipation, and poor blood? (Mother's little old book says it is.)

Twitching of the eyelids or the corners of the mouth can be cured by taking 2 teaspoons of honey at each meal.

Muscle cramps can be cured by taking 2 teaspoons of honey at each meal. (What a friend we have in bees.)

A SAFE WEIGHT-REDUCING DIET

In case you've been over-indulging in some of the fancy pies, cakes and desserts I've warned you about, I'll spoil all your fun by suggesting that you might like to try this safe diet. It was given to me by a gynecologist who was always furious if a patient came to him weighing half a pound more than she did the last time he saw her. He was always slim and trim himself and he died of diabetes in his early fifties.

This diet is carefully planned to give you everything you need to keep physically and mentally strong and healthy while your body calls upon its excess fat for its fuel supply. The diet gives you a wide choice of foods but you must eat only those recommended and in the amounts specified. NOTHING ELSE! Candy, ice cream, nuts, snacks, soft drinks – or hard ones – may add more calories than an entire meal.

Don't expect to lose much weight the first week; during this time the body tends to store up water in the tissue as it removes the fat. After this initial period, the water itself is eliminated and you will begin to lose a noticeable amount of weight every day. (Isn't that encouraging, fellow sufferers?)

VEGETABLES PERMITTED

asparagus	celery
string beans	cucumbers
beets	lima beans
broccoli	onions
Brussels sprouts	peas
cabbage	radishes
carrots	squash
cauliflower	tomatoes

Beet greens, chard, lettuce, spinach, and other leafy vegetables can be taken in any amounts you like but no butter should be added to any of the vegetables. (Sounds bleak? We must suffer for our sins.)

FRUITS PERMITTED
¹/₂ to 1 cup only

apples
apricots
blackberries
cantaloupe
cherries
grapefruit
honeydew melons

oranges
peaches
pears
pineapple
plums
raspberries
strawberries

Canned fruit should have all the syrup drained from it before it is eaten.

BREAKFAST

A 4-ounce glass of fruit or tomato juice or fresh fruit
¹/₂ cup hot cereal; 1 cup unsugared cold cereal; *or* 1 slice dry toast

1 glass skimmed milk (use part of this on your cereal, drink the rest)
Tea or coffee, without cream or sugar

LUNCH

Consommé or clear broth
Vegetable platter or salad without oil or mayonnaise dressing, use 4 tablespoons of any vegetables on list
Fresh fruit, ¹/₂ to 1 cup

1 slice bread, ¹/₂ teaspoon butter
1 glass skimmed milk or buttermilk
Tea or coffee without cream or sugar

DINNER

1 average serving (4 ounces) of lean meat, fish, or poultry, broiled or roasted: no fried foods allowed ever
2 portions (¹/₂ to 1 cup) of any of the vegetables listed

Fruit (¹/₂ to 1 cup) any on list
1 slice bread with ¹/₂ teaspoon butter
1 glass skimmed milk
Tea or coffee without cream or sugar

Having gained weight while trying out recipes for this book I'm going to be dieting myself – or try to write a neurotic novel that will keep me wan, worried, and sylphlike. (Who am I kidding?)

At Last

More Food That Really Schmecks must go to the printer. I can't change or add any more recipes. I've been working on this book so long that I've often wondered if I'd ever finish it: collecting, selecting, testing, eating, writing, re-writing, eliminating, adding, rejecting, exchanging, abbreviating, checking. I have a cat-food carton full of pages that I've typed and re-typed, thousands and thousands of pages, weighing twenty-eight pounds on my bathroom scales – which also show me that I've gained seven pounds since I started this blissful and frustrating chore.

Food That Really Schmecks was collected and written in two years: I've been working on *More Schmecks* for at least six. Why so long? I think I've been more fussy, more conscientious, more inventive, wanting every recipe to be special and foolproof. Yet I'm sure if I checked through the book fifty more times I'd still find recipes that could be improved or eliminated and replaced.

Anyone who has this book and doesn't have my first cookbook might say "No meat loaf recipe? No lemon meringue pie? No doughnuts?" They are in *Schmecks* and I don't know any better ones. This book is a sequel, not a duplication.

All the time I've been working I've been thinking about the people who have written or talked to me about *Schmecks*, people who will be using this book in little or big kitchens all over Canada, and the world. I hope the recipes will nourish and delight as they have me and the friends, relations, and *Schmecks* users who gave them to me. If they don't work, if you discover any mistakes, please let me know so corrections can be made in the next printing. (R.R. 3, Waterloo, Ontario, N2J 3Z4)

Meanwhile have fun, experiment, improvise, be inventive and a little bit reckless.

Good luck!

Index

METRIC SYMBOLS TO REMEMBER

Quantity	Name of Unit	Symbol
Temperature	degree Celsius	°C
Volume	litre	
	millilitre	ml
Mass	gram	g
	kilogram	kg
Length	metre	m
	centimetre	cm
Energy	joule	J

Liquid Measure

A metric liquid measure cup contains 250 ml which is graduated in 25 ml divisions.

1 quart = 1.14   .1 cup = approximately 285 ml.

Dry Measure

These measures are available in units of three: 250 ml, 125 ml, 50 ml. Conversion to metric usually involves a 5 per cent increase in amounts. All ingredients should be rounded up or down to the nearest unit. Small liquid and dry measures are available in sets of five: 1 ml, 2 ml, 5 ml, 15 ml, 25 ml. The 25 ml is similar to a typical coffee measure. All ingredients should be rounded to the nearest measure.

Mass (Weight)

You will need to know these units when shopping for meats, fruits, and vegetables.

1 kilogram (kg) = 1000 grams = a little more than 2 pounds.

Length

The centimetre (cm) slightly less than ¹/₂ inch is the common unit for measure.

Temperature – Celsius Scale

Freezing point of water 0°C = 32°F.

Boiling point of water 100°C = 212°F.

A Guide to new temperature:

250°F. = 121°C	375°F. = 190°C
300°F. = 149°C	425°F. = 220°C
325°F. = 160°C	450°F. = 230°C
350°F. = 175°C	

Refrigerator Temperature = 4°C

Freezer Temperature = − 18°C